DANCING BAREFOOT
THE PATTI SMITH STORY

DAVE THOMPSON

CHICAGO
REVIEW
PRESS

An A Cappella Book

Library of Congress Cataloging-in-Publication Data

Thompson, Dave, 1960 Jan. 3–

 Dancing barefoot : the Patti Smith story / Dave Thompson.

   p. cm.

 Includes bibliographical references and index.

 ISBN 978-1-56976-325-4

 1. Smith, Patti. 2. Rock musicians—United States—Biography. I. Title.

ML420.S672T46 2011

782.42166092—dc23

[B]

                                    2011018859

Interior design: Jonathan Hahn

Portions of this book appeared previously in *Goldmine* magazine and the author's memoir *London's Burning: True Adventures on the Front Lines of Punk, 1976–1977*.

Published by Chicago Review Press, Incorporated
814 North Franklin Street
Chicago, Illinois 60610
ISBN 978-1-56976-325-4
Printed in the United States of America
5 4 3 2 1

For Cherry, who not only showed me what could be done
but also gave me the resolve to do it.

You want me to dance more? I'm like eighty years old.
—Patti Smith, onstage in Oxford, England, October 2007

CONTENTS

Preface   *vii*

1. The Sheep Lady from Algiers   1
2. Anna of the Harbor   17
3. Ballad of a Bad Boy   27
4. Death by Water   39
5. The Amazing Tale of Skunkdog   55
6. Picasso Laughing   71
7. Ha! Ha! Houdini   83
8. Neo Boy   101
9. Christ! The Colors of Your Energies   117
10. Babelfield   135
11. High on Rebellion   149
12. The Salvation of Rock   159
13. Burning Roses   179
14. Thread   191
15. Scream of the Butterfly   205
16. A Fire of Unknown Origin   221
17. Sandayu the Separate   235
18. Babelogue   245

Appendix: Patti Smith on Record   *255*
Bibliography   *273*
Index   *283*

PREFACE

I N 1979, PATTI Smith was on top of the world. Four albums and ten years into her career, she may not yet have been a household name, but she was at least named in all the households that mattered, and the previous year's "Because the Night" (which she had cowritten with Bruce Springsteen) was already an FM immortal.

But no matter how well the world thought it knew her, she remained an enigma. Like Bob Dylan before her, she represented that precious moment when popular acclaim meshes with artistic precociousness until the two are utterly indivisible. Where, fans and critics alike would ponder, did the private Patti end and the public persona begin? Was there even a dividing line between the two? Or was her entire existence an ongoing art project whose true nature would only be revealed when it was complete?

That was the question I intended to ask her when, with the studious enthusiasm of a nineteen-year-old fanzine editor, I made my way into the sound check for what turned out to be the original Patti Smith Group's final London performance, in the hope of scoring an interview with her.

Unfortunately, Patti wasn't there.

I introduced myself to someone; it turned out to be her brother, Todd, who passed me on to somebody else; it was roadie Andi Ostrowe, and she allowed me to sit unobtrusively in a corner while she went to see if anyone could talk to me. A short while later, guitarist Lenny Kaye ambled over for an interview, which completely threw me, because he wasn't Patti. Neither was pianist Richard Sohl, who also sat in on the conversation, but I was too polite, or shy, to ask if she was around. It was obvious to me that she wasn't. The band sound-checked without her, and left the venue without her.

So did I, and although I wrote up my story and was pleased with the results, I don't believe I ever published it. Instead, it became the first pages in a scrapbook of impressions and memories that I collected over the years, fragments of which appear here for the first time.

This book is not intended to be an analytical biography of Patti Smith. Neither is it a straightforward summation of her life. Rather, it is something in between, a biography that places events in the cultural context of the time, as opposed to the sometimes trendier option of viewing everything through the prism of hindsight.

I have no intention of denigrating or ignoring Patti Smith's accomplishments over the past thirty years, for it is by those accomplishments that her continued influence and importance can best be measured. But as with so many other artists who served as forces for cultural change, Patti Smith's greatest influence emanates from the years during which she was still shaping herself and her career. As a result, the book might well feel chronologically top heavy: it is largely the story of a performer growing up in the New York City of the early-to-mid 1970s, while a large part of the city was growing up around her.

Emphasis on the term "performer"—this is not a tell-all biography. I have steered clear of Patti's private life: her friends away from her music, her lovers away from the spotlight, her family life. While the conscientious may read between a few of the lines and draw conclusions that do not always place Patti's actions in the kindest light, there are few scandals unearthed here, and no secret peeps behind closed doors. Such things are of interest to the personal biographer, but my goal is to document a career, because it is the career that defines the artist, not the "Did she?" / "Would she?" / "Is she?" tattle that almost every public figure contends with at some point in his or her career. Plus, I believe that Patti's audience have too much respect for her, as both a performer and a person, to care about such things.

Hence my decision to allow Patti's own words to guide the book, as opposed those of a multitude of onlookers, hangers-on, and casual acquaintances. (Some quotes, from her and others, have been lightly edited for clarity.) I don't especially care what scandal-hungry groupies or envious peers have to say about Patti, and I don't believe you would, either. These people knew *of* Patti, but they did not know her, and there is a profound difference between the two.

Patti was—and is—both smart and fortunate. She lives her private life in private and has constantly surrounded herself with people who help ensure that it remains there. Nevertheless, I was guided by some remarkable people. I met Ivan Kral, guitarist with the original Patti Smith Group, in 1991, as he worked to help birth the infant Seattle music scene: he was a member of a band called Sky Cries Mary then and was preparing a solo album called *Native*. I interviewed him for the *Seattle Times*, alerting the city to the presence of the genius in its midst, and again for *Alternative Press*. Along with Kaye's thoughts and Sohl's interjections from our 1979 interview, Kral's words helped shape what this book would become.

So did those of many other interviewees, encountered over a number of years for a variety of publications and purposes: Stiv Bators, John Cale, Jim Carroll, Leee Black Childers, Jayne County (formerly Wayne County), Mick Farren, Richard Hell, Iggy Pop, Wayne Kramer, Hilly Kristal, Richard Lloyd, Ray Manzarek, Hilly Michaels, Elliott Murphy, Bobby Neuwirth, Nico, Johnny and Joey Ramone, Lou Reed, Mick Ronson, Rob Tyner, Cherry Vanilla, Tom Verlaine, and Tony Zanetta.

Other friends and associates played their own part in this book: my editors Yuval Taylor and Devon Freeny, Amy Hanson, Jo-Ann Greene, Theresa K., Geoff Monmouth, Tobias Wilcox, Trevor and Oliver, and many more.

Yet when it came to writing this book, I discovered that the only words that could really tell Patti Smith's stories were Patti's own. The people around her at different times in her life convey context and meaning, of course. But only Patti knew what she was saying, thinking, reacting to, and causing to happen as her career unfolded, and it was the unfolding of that career that I was most intrigued by.

Sometimes she exaggerates; sometimes she deceives. Discussing some of her earliest musical memories, for example, she once shaved five years off her actual age in order to press home a particular point. I addressed these discrepancies when I came across them, but I also endeavored never to lose sight of the point that she was making, particularly since the biographical details as she related them were often immaterial to begin with.

Besides, Patti's career is a biography in itself, one that begins with the most implausible outset, continues on through a series of unimaginable events, survives any number of insurmountable crashes, and remains as vibrant today as it was ever in the past. And only she knows how she accomplished that.

So while I thank everybody who spoke to me, including a number who did so off the record, I do not apologize for using their words so sparingly. This is Patti's story, and I have chosen to tell it as Patti might have seen it, had she been on the outside looking in. Because this time, she *was* there.

I

THE SHEEP LADY
FROM ALGIERS

S HE WAS BORN Patricia Lee Smith, Tricia to her friends and
family, in Chicago on December 30, 1946. World War II had
been over for eighteen months, and Christmas for five days, but the
remnants of both were still visible everywhere. The very air, it seemed,
crackled with optimism and hope, a tangible sense that after so many
years of hardship—the Great Depression preceded World War II; the
Great War preceded that—the United States was finally poised to
embrace its long-postponed destiny. The American Dream was coming, and from the upper echelons of society to the lowest rung of the
economic ladder, the mantra that suddenly anything was possible was
coming true.

Grant and Beverly Smith, a skilled pattern- and model-maker and
his homemaker wife, certainly believed in the dream. Born in Delaware
County, Pennsylvania, on July 29, 1916, Grant H. Smith was thirty and
newly discharged from the military when his daughter arrived; his wife,
Beverly Williams, was twenty-six. The Irish American couple had married following the war's end and moved to Illinois because they knew
they'd find work there. They were not wealthy, by any stretch of the
imagination; sometimes, it felt as though they were barely getting by.
Their tiny house was already cramped before the arrival of Patti's sister
Linda in 1948.

One of Patti's earliest memories is of sitting on a stoop in Chicago singing "Jesus Loves Me" while she waited for the organ grinder to come up the street with the pet monkey that made her laugh so hard. But when Beverly became pregnant again, with Patti's brother, Todd, in late 1949, it was time to move on. Patti's Grandpa Williams had a farm in Tennessee, so they lived there for a short while. Then they returned north, to a housing block on Newell Street in Philadelphia. The homes were originally constructed as a GI housing project, but in later years Patti would prefer a more figurative description: army barracks.

It was a grim environment, but Grant Smith continued to struggle to build a better life for his family. Patti rarely saw her father after he took a night job at the Honeywell corporation, making thermostats and regulators for the modern heating products that a lot of her neighbors and friends' families couldn't even afford. To bring extra money into the household, he would offer to do peoples' tax returns for them.

Even at the age of six, Patti was no stranger to music. She grew up listening to her mother's collection of June Christy and Chris Connor jazz records. Later in life, Patti's biographers would describe her mother as a former jazz singer; in fact, she was simply a woman who loved jazz and would sing it around the house. She also sang opera, and Patti would join in. When her school presented a version of Verdi's *Aïda*, Patti played a young Gypsy boy.

Maria Callas was another favorite, and Puccini as well. It didn't matter that Patti couldn't understand what was being sung. The emotion, alive within the voice of the singer, was enough, and Patti would laugh, cry, or rage as the opera's stories unfolded, as if she were Italian born and bred.

"I dreamed when I was a kid about being an opera singer," she told Terry Gross in an interview on NPR's *Fresh Air*. "But I never thought about singing [professionally]. I think I sang in this school choir or something, but I didn't really excel or have any real gift. But what I did have was, I've always, for some reason, been comfortable talking in front of people, or performing in front of people."

Patti was indeed an adventurous child. "I don't want to get too hung up on biochemical warfare," she told a California audience in 1976.

"When I was a kid I ate dirt." Marshalling a bunch of neighborhood boys, she formed a gang called the Cool Cats, built their base out of empty refrigerator boxes, and laid down one law: no girls were allowed. Only sister Linda was ever admitted, in her capacity as the gang's nurse, patching up the wounds that would arise whenever the Cool Cats went out to fight the kids down the block. Even Patti was not immune from this single regulation, which is why her fellow warriors all believed she was a boy.

And then one day her cover was blown. She never did find out how; it was probably one of her gangmates' mothers. But that was it for her life as a Cool Cat. She was kicked out of her own gang.

The rejection did not blunt Patti's intrepid spirit. One day, when she was seven or eight, she found herself walking through an area that the locals called Jericho, an accumulation of truly makeshift homes constructed from shopping trolleys, planks of wood and strips of tarpaulin, and old refrigerator boxes. Just like her old club house. She stopped to look, mindless of the cries of "white cracker" that the predominantly black residents were hurling her way, or the stones and handfuls of dirt that followed the oaths. She just dodged out of the way and continued looking, returning day after day until finally people started to acknowledge her with a wave or a smile. Soon, she laughed years later, she was happily hanging out with them.

Not all of Patti's adventures were so courageous, and many more took place in her mind alone. She was a vivid dreamer, with imaginings that bordered on the hallucinatory, and as time passed, she trained her mind to recall them when she woke, to be written down in one of the pads she was constantly scribbling in. She once boasted that she'd never had a dream that she didn't remember, and she shared many of them with her two siblings, entertaining them with stories of her nocturnal activities. Later, the same training would become a part of her creative process: "Most of my writing and a lot of my songs, or sometimes a melody, comes from a dream," Patti revealed to British journalist Sandy Robertson in 1978.

She credited her mother with teaching her that. "[Mother] was always great in weaving a fantasy world, telling us fairy stories, or getting us involved in stories," Patti told *Mademoiselle's* Amy Gross in 1975. Her mother's fantasies would even inspire her future writing. Destined for Patti's debut album, the poem "Free Money" was rooted in Beverly's weekly dream of striking it rich. Her mom "always dreamed about winning the lottery," she laughed during an interview with Simon Reynolds of the *Observer* in 2005. "But she never bought a lottery ticket! She would just imagine if she won, make lists of things she would do with the money—a house by the sea for us kids, then all kinds of charitable things."

I'll buy you a jet plane, baby . . . And take you through the stratosphere.

Other times, Patti would draw Linda and Todd into the worlds that unfolded from her reading. Both of their parents were very well read—later Patti described them as liberal-minded and sophisticated readers—and she grew up with the same voracious appetite for books. Louisa May Alcott's *Little Women* was a particular favorite, and as soon as Patti was old enough to formulate the notion of hero worship, Jo—the so-capable elder sister who binds the March family together—became her first role model. It was Jo whose example first led her to write; it was Jo who showed her the magic of performance.

Patti began writing her own stage plays, which she would later disparage as the childish constructs that they surely were. But she acted them out with and for her family all the same. Not because she actually enjoyed doing it, but because it was what Jo did. She told writer Scott Cohen in a 1976 interview in *Oui*, "I studied her to see what it takes to be a girl who keeps her family together—who writes, creates, inspires people, likes to teach and to entertain."

"I wasn't a disturbed child. I actually had a happy childhood. I loved my brother and sister. We were inseparable. They thought the world of me," Patti told Terry Gross. She recalled going through some of Todd's possessions following his death in 1994 and discovering some of the childhood memories that he'd written down, "about how I was like King Arthur, and they were like the knights in my court, and they always believed in me, and I invented endless games and plays and stories for us to be involved in."

Jo March was not her sole literary influence. Onstage in Oxford, England, in 2007, she told the audience how, as a child, "I cherish[ed] my

Alice in Wonderland and *Through the Looking-Glass* books, and I learned about the dodo bird in these books, and I couldn't wait till I got older and got to meet one." She also combed the parental bookshelves for copies of Plato and Aristotle, and devoured the Bible as vociferously as she plowed through her father's books and magazines on the UFO phenomenon.

The possibility that our skies were filled with flying saucers was common currency after the end of World War II. Hollywood studios were already churning out their B-movie sci-fi epics; pulp paperbacks and magazines were expounding theory and thoughts. Little green men were everywhere, even if nobody reliable had actually seen one, and it would be decades before the scientific community finally announced its own belief that the whole UFO business was an illusion, a manifestation of the Cold War paranoia that likewise gripped the land.

For it was the age, too, of "reds beneath the bed" and Wisconsin Republican Joseph McCarthy's Communist witch hunts, of irregular classroom rehearsals for the day the bomb was dropped and nifty public information films that told you what to do when it did. "Duck and cover!" That way, you'd be lying down when you were blown into smoldering atoms. Reality, Patti decided very early on, could be as unbelievable as fantasy.

She grew up to be grateful, then, that her parents were firmly aware of that fact. To writer Dave Marsh in *Rolling Stone* in 1976, she described her mother as "a real hip Scheherazade," and she told Jeff Baker of Ore-gonLive.com, "My mother was creative and my father was a very compassionate man. . . . There were people who were anti-Semitic and, of course, if you were homosexual, that was a taboo subject. My mother opened the door to anybody it was closed to elsewhere. I lived in a very poor but energetic household that was filled with religious dialogue and civil rights, all kinds of things."

"Just like I say I'm equal parts Balenciaga and Brando," she told Dave Marsh, "well, my dad was equal parts God and Hagar the Spaceman for Mega City." *I recognize him as the true outcast*, she wrote in a prose piece titled "Grant"; *he is lucifer the unguided light, judas the translator and barabbas the misused. . . . there is no one closer to God than my father.*

Young Patti never did meet a gay Jewish alien, but she would not have been shocked if she had—just as she believed that she would one day meet a dodo. Because it was belief that sustained her, even as a child. Belief that she would wake up every morning, belief that she would grow up and marry, have children and grandchildren, and live a long life. And, because there has to be a negative emotion for every positive one, the belief that she was going to drop dead right now, before she had even reached double figures.

Patti was seven when she had her first encounter with mortality, and it was her own. Scarlet fever did more than turn your tongue red and your skin harsh and bumpy, while you roasted in the arms of virulent fever. In those days, it was a killer.

There were plenty of cures available. The first vaccine for scarlet fever had been created back in 1924. But vaccines came from doctors, and doctors charged money. Money that the Smith family could ill afford to spend. There were occasions, Patti recalled, when things were so tight that even their mother's creativity was stretched to the limit. Patti told NPR's *Fresh Air*, "If my dad was on strike, and we had no food or very little food, [our mother would] make this, like, Wonder Bread with butter and sugar and she'd tell a story and this would become a great delicacy. We'd pretend we were all hiding out from, like, the Nazis or something, and we hadn't eaten in three days and this was our food, and it was so wonderful. She made everything into a game." Even hunger.

Brother Todd and sister Linda had their own medical crises to weather; both of them wound up in the hospital once, struggling with mild malnutrition. But when Patti contracted scarlet fever, by the time the medics finally got a good look at her, any number of complications were on the verge of setting in. Pneumonia, meningitis, sepsis—all can develop from a simple case of scarlet fever, and whether Patti had one, none, or all of them was really immaterial at the time. For a short while there were genuine doubts as to whether she would even survive.

She rallied, but she remained a sickly kid. Reminiscing about her childhood ailments with Jeff Baker in 2010, she catalogued her calamitous health record: "I had TB as a kid and scarlet fever and mononucleosis and the Asiatic flu and the mumps and the measles and the chicken pox. . . . I personally had all those things before I was sixteen, and I was just one child." She also had a wandering eye that rolled upward in its socket. To correct it, she was given "a creepy-looking eyepatch and glasses," Victor Bockris and Roberta Bayley's *Patti Smith: An Unauthorized Biography* quoted her as saying, and the other kids would run from her because they thought she had the Evil Eye.

Illness kept her out of full-time education and kept her from developing the so-called social skills that public school deems so important. "I was very unattractive when I was younger," she mourned to *Mademoiselle*. "I had bad skin and I was very skinny and totally awkward. And that is when I was *six*. But I was never depressed about it because I had a real ugly duckling sense. The tragedy about the ugly duckling was that no one ever took him aside and said, 'Look. You're ugly now, but it's going to pay off later.' And that was my view of myself. I figured I'd just bide my time. I'm a real optimistic person." When she was a child, she recalled in *Crawdaddy* magazine in 1975, "I always had this absolute swagger about the future. . . . I wasn't born to be a spectator."

She made friends, she said, by doing Tex Ritter imitations. She would do anything to make people laugh.

In 1955, shortly before Patti's ninth birthday, the family moved house again, across the state line to Woodbury Gardens, New Jersey. Later, she would call it the biggest turning point in her life, relocating to a single-story ranch house whose closest neighbor was a pig farm. Her father still worked at Honeywell, while her mother found work as a counter waitress at a nearby drugstore.

Around that same time came another great turning point: a neighbor boy asked Patti back to his house to hear a new record, Little Richard's "Tutti Frutti." The way Patti remembered the story, her mouth fell open and she was instantly enthralled. She would also remember being six years old at the time, sitting in her Newell Street clubhouse when the boy stopped by with his invitation. In fact, she would have been at least nine years old and living in New Jersey when that record became a hit, but her point was clear: she discovered rock 'n' roll when it was still young, and she never let go of it.

Little Richard changed everything, first as he assaulted her ears, and then as she read everything she could about him. And before she truly understood what she was discovering, her mind filled in the gaps around the facts that 1950s America could not bring itself to mention, the secret life and times of the flamboyant black man who valued jewelry and fine clothing so highly that his every song shrieked defiance at the mores of normalcy that she was beginning to decipher around her.

"In another decade," she explained to Steve Simels in *Stereo Review* magazine in 1978, "rock 'n' roll would be Art. But when I say a decade, I mean for *other* people. For me, since 1954 or something, it *has* been Art. Since Little Richard, Elvis Presley, Jimi Hendrix. I mean, these guys are masters. . . .

"Being great is no accident," she continued. "Little Richard wasn't an accidental phenomenon; he knew what he was after. He might not define it with intellectual terminology, but he was defined by what he did. I don't think Jackson Pollock wrote a manifesto first and then did all his painting according to it."

She started building a record collection of her own. The drugstore where her mother worked stocked a bargain bin full of used and ex-jukebox records. Over the years, she recalled to Thurston Moore in *Bomb* magazine, she received a copy of Harry Belafonte's 1956 "Banana Boat Song" (which Patti confused with Jo Stafford's 1951 song "Shrimp Boats"), Patience and Prudence's 1957 classic "The Money Tree," and, "embarrassingly enough," Neil Sedaka's 1960 hit "Stairway to Heaven" (which her memory retitled "Climb Up"). One time when she was sick, her mother bought her an LP set of *Madame Butterfly*. And then she would shut herself away and listen. *Music,* as she would write years later, *permeated the room like an odor like the essence of a flower.*

Her mother would also take her back into Philly, stop by Leary's Book Store, and buy her a bag of books for a dollar. "Stuff like *Uncle Wiggily* and *The Wizard of Oz*," she told A. D. Amorosi in the *Philadelphia City Paper.* Then they'd go for a meal to Bookbinders, or Pat's, with the best steak hoagies in town.

She was a happy child, then, nurtured in a loving household. And she looked toward religion, not necessarily for solace, but because she was curious about the source of the strength that it offered people. Beverly Smith was a devout Jehovah's Witness, and that was always a part of her daughter's spiritual landscape. It was her mother who taught Patti to pray, and Patti accompanied her on trips around the neighborhood, distributing literature and canvassing for souls.

It was a sobering experience. Not everybody enjoyed having their weekday evenings or weekend mornings disturbed by the rat-a-tat-tat of a visiting Witness, and not even the presence of a young daughter could shield Mrs. Smith from the anger, scorn, and abuse of those people. Patti was fascinated, not only by the vehemence of the neighbors who chased her mother away, but also by the faith that kept her going back.

But there was something amiss with that faith as well, an inconsistency that Patti could not place her finger on until one day, while talking with a fellow Witness about life in the aftermath of Armageddon, Patti was mortified to be informed that the Museum of Modern Art wouldn't be around any longer.

Neither would her beloved books. Neither would her records, nor most of the people who made them—and that included Little Richard, who gave up rock 'n' roll in 1957 after a vision warned him of his own damnation. He took Voice of Prophecy courses (Seventh-Day Adventist) and was ordained a minister in the Church of God of the Ten Commandments. And even that wouldn't save him.

Patti quit the Witnesses.

At age twelve, she discovered Buddhism, after accidentally bringing divine wrath (or so she believed) on the innocent people of Tibet. She had selected the Chinese-occupied state as the subject of a school project, which asked her class to write regular news reports on the foreign country of their choice throughout the course of a year. She prayed that Tibet would provide newsworthy material for her assignments. Soon after, Tibetans in the capital rose up against their occupiers, Chinese troops violently put down the rebellion, and the Dalai Lama was forced into exile.

"I felt tremendously guilty," she confessed to Stephen Foehr in the *Shambhala Sun.* "I felt that somehow my prayers had interfered with Tibetan history. I worried about the Dalai Lama. It was rumored that his family had been killed by the Chinese. I was quite relieved when he reached India safely. I vowed to always say prayers for his safe-keeping, which I have done." Her flirtation with Buddhism provided her with a spiritual center that her disillusionment with Christianity had temporarily robbed her of.

The previous year, 1958, had seen the birth of Patti's second sister, Kimberly Ann, the fourth and last of the Smith kids. No matter how much she loved the newcomer, Patti was painfully aware of the further strain that she placed on the family finances, especially after the baby developed serious asthma, adding further weight to the already barely manageable medical bills.

One of Patti's most profound memories of the period was of the day a Household Finance debt collector was banging on the front door, trying to pick up the money her parents owed. Her mother told Patti to tell them she was out, then hid herself in another part of the house. "My mommy's in the bathroom," Patti told the visitor. "But she's not home."

Another memory preserves the night that a barn across the road burst into flames following a lightning strike. Patti's youngest sister, Kimberly, had just been born, and "I went outside and I was holding her, watching this barn in flames. Hundreds of bats lived in it, and you could hear them screeching, and see bats and owls and buzzards flying out," she told the *Observer* in 2005. She elaborated in a note published in her collected lyrics book *Patti Smith Complete*: "And Kimberly was shining in my hands like a phosphorescent living doll." The images of that night would become the poem "Kimberly."

But Patti was not yet a poet herself. As she approached her teens, her imagination turned toward the visual arts. It was not a purely aesthetic love; art taught her new ways to confront the challenges of her looming adolescence. "With a lower class upbringing, it was real desirable to have big tits and big ass," she told *Hit Parader*'s Lisa Robinson in 1976. Patti, on the other hand, was so thin—"skinny" and "creepy" as she put it—that her body tormented her. When it was time for her class to be weighed before gym class, she would load her pockets down with heavy metal locks—anything to add a few pounds to her scrawny frame. Until a teacher took Patti to the school library and hauled a few art books out, opening them to the Modiglianis and the El Grecos, giving the insecure young woman for the very first time something physical to which she could relate her appearance. Patti had just one difficulty, as she confessed to *Oui* magazine: "It wasn't easy for a girl who fancied herself the cosmic mistress of Modigliani to sing Tex Ritter songs."

Not all her pursuits were artistic, however. Interviewed by Penny Green for Andy Warhol's *Interview* in 1973, she laughed, "Yes, I'm just a Jersey girl. I really loved that I was from South Jersey because it was a real spade area. I learned to dance real good . . . there was a lot of colloquial stuff I picked up, that's where I get my bad speech from. Even though my father was an intellectual, I wanted to be like the kids I went to school with, so I intentionally never learned to speak good. . . . I thought I couldn't use it on the dance floor, so what good was it?"

She practiced dancing, teaching herself in her bedroom by loading a stack of singles onto her record player and dancing till they'd all played through. Then she'd pile on another batch and dance them away as well.

She enrolled in Deptford Township High School, and although she was perhaps a little disingenuous when she told *Blast* magazine's Michael Gross that "the school I went to was a real experimental school," in her own mind that may have been the case. "It's like a weird school because it was one of these new kind of experimental schools where they sent special children, geniuses. High-strung geniuses whose fathers were head of MIT or something. Retarded kids and lots of Spanish-speaking people. There were a lot of epileptics. It was one of the schools that accepted epileptic children and had a regular program for them.

"My school nobody was weird. Everybody was special in their own way. So I never got a sense of myself being any different than anybody else. I was sort of like a beatnik kid, but so what?"

It was at Deptford that Patti found herself plunging, not necessarily consciously, into the increasingly muddy waters of the nascent civil rights movement. Buoyed by the Buddhist belief system that she was slowly acquiring, she found herself cultivating ever sharper instincts not for the political aims of the upcoming struggles but for their humanitarian goals. She may well have been the first girl in her class to date a black boy following Deptford High's integration, and she was certainly the only one whose parents did not raise hell when they found out.

The fact that she was dating, however, did not mean that she was sexually active. "My one regret in life," she told *Penthouse*'s Nick Tosches in 1976, "is that I didn't know about masturbating. Think of all that fun I could've had!" As a teenager, she said, "I was horny, but I was inno- cent 'cause I was a real-late bloomer and not particularly attractive. . . . Nobody told me that girls got horny. It was tragic, 'cause I had all these feelings inside me. . . . I never touched myself or anything. . . . I did it all in my mind."

All of her report cards, she recalled, complained that "Patti Lee day- dreams too much." They did not have a clue what she was daydreaming about.

Not all of her passions were conventional. Later in her teens, Patti relaxed into writing a series of lengthy poems in which she was arrested, for crimes unknown, by a beautifully blond Nazi sadist, and then tor- tured to death or orgasm, whichever came first. The notion that the two were not mutually incompatible, however, had its genesis in a most unexpected place: in the journals of Anne Frank. Since the 1959 release of a movie based on the young Jewish girl's diary of the years she spent hiding from the Nazis, the media had taken a fresh look at the atroci- ties that were the backdrop to Frank's tale. "I'd read that stuff and I'd get really cracklin' down there," Patti told *Penthouse*.

By sixteen, Patti had decided it was time to put a stop to her yearn- ing. She was reading *Peyton Place*, Grace Metalious's then-shocking novel of the secret lives of small-town America, and one scene stuck in her mind: the one where heroine Allison McKenzie is told that you can tell if a woman is a virgin by the way she walks. It was a horrifying revelation for Patti, because it meant that everybody would know the same thing about her. So she set about cultivating what she described to Nick Tos- ches as "a fucked walk," by watching actress Jeanne Moreau. "You watch her walk across the street on the screen," she decided, "and you know she's had at least a hundred men."

Patti, on the other hand, had not had one, and she sometimes doubted that she ever would. Journalist Richard Meltzer later reflected on the stories she told him during the years when she was best known as a poetess, and he was still laughing about them five years later. Like how she didn't have a birth certificate any more, because the rats ate it, how her father was a gangster and her aunt once spent a hot night with Hank Williams, but best of all, how her father explained the facts of life by telling her, "The erect male penis is put into the female vagina, and you only do that when you're in love." And so, she told Meltzer, the first time a guy asked to fuck her, she said no, because she didn't love him. So he asked if he could eat her instead, and what did Patti reply? She said she'd have to ask her father. Who told her, "Forget it."

When American female teendom became obsessed with having eyes made up like Cleopatra, as played by Elizabeth Taylor; or, later, when the Ronettes sent their distinctive hairstyles soaring into vogue, Patti just shrugged and went back to her books. She once remarked that she read her entire childhood away—that she was far more intrigued by her interior world than the outside. When she did seek out idols, they were the ones her peers may not even have acknowledged: Edith Piaf. Folk singer Joan Baez. Actresses Moreau, Ava Gardner, and Anouk Aimée.

Aimée was the rising star who exploded out of Fellini's *La dolce vita* in 1960 (alongside another of Patti's later icons, Nico), shrouded in black dress and dark glasses, to disguise the black eye that she would soon be revealing. "Anouk Aimée with that black eye," Patti marveled in a 1976 *Circus* interview with Scott Cohen. "It made me always want to have a black eye forever. It made me want to get a guy to knock me around. I'd always look great."

Still, she remained an incorrigible tomboy. "I was always jealous because I wasn't homosexual," she declared at a poetry reading in New York in 1975. "I'd have these dreams that I could steal boys' skins at night, and put them on and pee and stuff like that." In the poem "Piss Factory," she mused on *the way boys smell . . . that odor rising roses and ammonia,* and noted the way their schoolboy legs *flap under the desk in study hall* and *the way their dicks droop like lilacs.*

She tried to remain romantic, to convince herself that her first love would be her forever love. But it didn't work out like that. She was the girl who did the guys' homework for them but was never rewarded with anything more than a thank-you. She was crazy about boys, but she was *one of* the boys, great to hang with, but not to date. She recalled one in particular, the splendidly named Butchie Magic. He allowed her to carry his switchblade. But that was as far as their relationship went. No matter whom she fell for, he was always the most inaccessible, not to mention inappropriate, guy around.

But she was a survivor. She would tell *Rolling Stone*, "I grew up in a tougher part of Jersey than Bruce Springsteen"—raising herself above the last Jersey native to make it big in the mid-1970s. "Every high school dance I went to, somebody was stabbed." Talking to *Penthouse*, she ran through a mental checklist of the "cool people" whom she hung out with in her teens. Most, she declared, were either dead or in jail. "A couple are pimps in Philly."

And at the same time as she struggled to be accepted as something more than the class clown—an appellation that would pursue her into the pages of her high school yearbook—she delighted in her outsider status. In fact, she worked to cultivate it.

"The worst wallflower weirdo" joined the jazz club and fell under the spell of John Coltrane, Thelonious Monk, and Miles Davis. She demonstrated her precocity by trying to get into some of Philadelphia's most legendary nightspots: "I tried to hang at jazz clubs like the Show-boat, just to see the musicians," she told the *Philadelphia City Paper*, "but I was way too young." She owned her own copy of Coltrane's *My Favorite Things*, and when Coltrane played the local nightclub Pep's, she made her way in and was able to stick around for one complete song, the opening "Nature Boy," before she was carded and evicted.

Patti graduated high school in June 1964 and promptly sought out a place at Glassboro State Teachers College (now Rowan University) in Glassboro, New Jersey. The two-year program would ostensibly equip her for a career as an art teacher. She loathed it, and hated even more the fact that she had to work through her vacations to pay her way through its classes, in minimum-wage factory jobs that devoured the only free time she had to look forward to.

"I was really a good girl," she told *Blast* magazine. "I didn't curse and I was a virgin and I didn't drink or nothing when I went to college."

And to Amy Gross, she added, "I was in my Greta Garbo period. . . . I was so innocent. I didn't even know there was a war on. . . . All I knew in South Jersey was black culture."

Her horizons expanded. She would take the bus up Broad Street from her Woodbury home and get out in Camden, New Jersey. She would buy an orange juice and some donuts, then stand and stare at the Walt Whitman Hotel. In her imagination, the great man himself had stayed there. Patti was also in Philly a lot now, taking the bus across the river and spending her Saturdays in morning classes at the Philadelphia Museum of Art.

She also plunged into Philly's Jewish culture—for its aesthetic rather than its religious value. "They were so hip," she told Amy Gross. "They wore black leotards, they had sports cars and all these art supplies. So I went back to Glassboro dressed like a Jewish art student.

"I failed everything—I was so undisciplined."

2

ANNA OF THE HARBOR

A s Patti tried on different personas, she also cultivated an array of life ambitions. She would listen to Coltrane and then write poetry, trusting the freedom of one to unlock the doors to the other. She dreamed of being an actress like Jeanne Moreau or Anouk Aimée. And she looked forward to the day when she would become an artist's mistress, the power behind the throne of creation. One day, she imagined, she would subsume herself behind the requirements of a man who would answer all of her questions, who could tell her what to say and what to think, when to laugh and when to cry. One day. But until then, she would dream—of Coltrane, of Bob Dylan, of William Burroughs. And Rimbaud. Especially Rimbaud.

To Patti, Rimbaud was everything, and had been ever since she first saw his face, one day as she was passing the bookstall that used to stand across the road from the main Philadelphia bus station. A portrait on a book cover caught her eye. She may or may not have heard of the poet at that time, but it didn't matter. It was the photograph that drew her in. He looked a little like her father, a little like Dylan, and a lot like the boyfriend she wished she'd meet. The book was called *Illuminations*.

She picked up the same bilingual French and English reprint that every other budding romantic of the era owned, and once she'd finished devouring it, she devoured the rest of its author's life.

Jean Nicolas Arthur Rimbaud was born in Charleville, France, on October 20, 1854, the son of a veteran of France's conquest of Algeria. The boy's early gift for poetry was rewarded when the *Revue pour tous* published his "*Les etrennes des orphelines*" ("The Orphans' New Year Gifts") in January 1870.

He was unruly from the outset. Despondent when his favorite tutor, Georges Izambard, quit to fight in the Franco-Prussian War later in 1870, the teenager turned his literary talents to the most antisocial ends he could imagine. He drank and stole, and dedicated his pen to vileness and scatology. He grew his hair and abandoned his earlier manners and morals. He moved to Paris and joined the Commune, that short-lived experiment in communism that erupted on the streets of the city following the war's humiliating cessation, and he openly embraced homosexuality, launching into a torrid relationship with an older man, poet Paul Verlaine, that ended only when Verlaine was jailed for two years for shooting at his lover. A bullet hit Rimbaud in the wrist.

Rimbaud blazed with creative rage for just five years, a short span in which he wrote some of the most moving and meaningful of all the poetry now collected beneath the banner of Symbolism. *Illuminations*, published in 1874, was his final major work; two years later, he enlisted in the Dutch Colonial Army and used that as the bridgehead to the world travels that would consume the last years of his life.

He deserted the army in Java, returned to France, and then moved to Cyprus, where he worked in a stone quarry. The following year, 1880, he was in Aden; by 1884, he was in Harar, Ethiopia, running his own export company. There, with a circle of friends that included Ras Makonnen—the father of future emperor Haile Selassie—he seemed to find happiness. But in 1891, returning to France in search of treatment for what he thought was rheumatism, he discovered instead that he was suffering from cancer. Rimbaud died in Marseille on November 10, 1891. His death, Patti mused to herself, was infinitely more interesting than her life.

"I really didn't fall in love with writing as writing," Patti told Victor Bockris. "I fell in love with writers' lifestyles. Rimbaud's lifestyle. I was in love with Rimbaud for being a mad angel and all that shit." She thought of Rimbaud as a boyfriend, she joked to Thurston Moore, laughingly demanding, "If you can't get the boy you want, and you have to day-dream about him all the time, what's the difference if he's a dead poet?"

Young minds often associate poetry with death. Perhaps this is because many of the now so-called classic poets—Lord Byron, Percy Bysshe Shelley, John Keats—succumbed to tragically early and romantic deaths. Byron died of fever at age thirty-six while fighting for Greek independence; Shelley was thirty when he drowned while on a boating expedition; Keats was just twenty-six when he was snuffed out by consumption. Add to these sad statistics their heroically tragic lives and the long shadows that such events cast over their work, and an active imagination can easily connect the dots between torture and art.

Patti also fell for the Spanish poet Federico García Lorca, murdered by Nationalists in 1936 at the outset of the Spanish Civil War. Under the spell of his floridly avant garde writing, and entranced, too, by his professional associations with the painter Salvador Dalí (which bled, with poetically misbegotten passion, into a wholly unrequited love), Patti began composing her own lengthy romances. Most of them, she confessed to Nick Tosches in *Penthouse*, involved "men in love with their dead wives . . . kneeling in the dirt, trying to get their dead wives to show them some warmth."

Only in death, she believed, could true love be revealed.

She was seduced by the ways of life of her poets and performers—and of her artists too. She remained the "cosmic mistress" of Amedeo Modigliani, another tragic victim of the tyrannical hold that a calling to art, no matter how poorly paid, can hold over its victims—the penniless Italian artist died from tubercular meningitis in Paris in 1920. She was fascinated, too, by painter Chaim Soutine, an Eastern European Jewish emigrant who, living in Paris when the Nazis invaded France, somehow evaded the attentions of the Gestapo for three years, only to die from a perforated ulcer in 1943.

But there were exceptions. For Patti, while there was Rimbaud, there was also Bob Dylan. "It was a relief," she confessed to Thurston Moore, "to daydream about somebody who was alive."

When she looked back at her late teens, Patti never seemed certain of when she had first encountered Dylan. It might have been an afternoon in late 1964 when her mother returned home from work and handed her an LP called *Another Side of Bob Dylan*. "I never heard of the fellow," her mom said, "but he looks like somebody you'd like." Or maybe it was at a Joan Baez show a year or so earlier, when Baez introduced a special guest. "She had this fellow with her, Bobby Dylan," Patti told Moore. "His voice was like a motorcycle through a cornfield." Or maybe it was an afternoon when, on a day trip to Manhattan for kicks, and sitting in a cafe in the Village, Patti looked over toward a red door a few houses down and Dylan stepped out.

Maybe it didn't matter where or when she first discovered him. All that matters is that she did. Barreling after the Rolling Stones into her private pantheon of cultural touchstones, Dylan's 1965 hit "Like a Rolling Stone" became one of the first white rock records that ever made her feel alive. But only one of them.

Patti's musical tastes had been rooted almost exclusively in black music, because that, she believed, was where music kept its soul. Now she was discovering otherwise, although it wasn't Dylan who had changed her mind. It was the Stones.

She was at home with her parents on the evening of October 25, 1964, when her father called her into the front room with the incredulous insistence that she had to "look at these guys!" Grant Smith always watched *The Ed Sullivan Show*, and always found something else to comment upon, some performer who caught his eye for good or bad. But this week it was destiny.

they put the touch on me, Patti wrote in a 1973 essay in *Creem* magazine. *I was blushing jelly. this was no mamas boy music. it was alchemical. I couldn't fathom the recipe but I was ready.*

No more than a year into their career, and still coming to terms with the English media's insistence on demonizing them ("Would You Let Your Daughter Marry a Rolling Stone?" was one of the year's most memorable British headlines), the Stones were miming to two songs, "Around and Around" and "Time Is on My Side." But it was the visuals that Patti found so vivid, not the music: Mick Jagger, white turtleneck and tight black trousers, still looking like the slightly hip economics student that he used to be, but all the more alluring for the snatches of shyness that hung around those deep-set eyes. Keith Richards and Brian Jones, besuited and suave, one skinny-legs and moddish, the other haloed blond, and all but ignored by the Sullivan cameras, so you hung on the edge of your seat in the hope of anything more than a long-distance glimpse.

That was my introduction to the Rolling Stones . . . my brain froze. Watching that performance today, with the mind's eye stripping away the baggage that the succeeding decades have piled upon both our perception of the Stones and the liberation of television, it is still possible to see how these five unknown young Englishmen created such a stir, in her loins and in several million others'.

Later, as she heard and saw more, *my pussy dripped my pants were wet and the Rolling Stones redeemed the white man forever.*

The Stones and Bob Dylan may seem a poor fit for Patti's grim collection of idols. But we should remember that at the time Dylan was widely regarded as an imminent casualty and would indeed come within a hair's breadth of fulfilling that prophecy when he crashed his motorbike in 1966 and was forced into seclusion. And every time the rock press compiled its latest list of rock's most likely next fatality, Keith Richards was usually at the top of the pile, even if it was Brian Jones who ended up dead first. Long before Patti had formulated the ambition that would snatch her out of academia, her eye for icons was already trained upon those artists who were, for want of a less cliched expression, too fast to live. Unfortunately, you are never too young to die.

In 1965, Patti was seduced again by a living tragedy: Edie Sedgwick, the superstar consort to artist Andy Warhol, captured in *Vogue* magazine.

Sedgwick, scion of one of New England's wealthiest families, struck Smith immediately. "It was like seeing a black and white movie in person," she recalled to Scott Cohen in *Circus.* Elfin and boyish, wide-eyed and bubbling with innocent beauty, Edie was irresistible. "Twenty-two, white-haired with anthracite-black eyes and legs to swoon over," mooned *Vogue* magazine; "she didn't mess around," Patti echoed. "She was really something. . . . She really got me. It was something weird."

After death took Edie, too, just six years later, Patti would eulogize her in the pages of author Jean Stein's book-length obituary: "Living in

South Jersey, you get connected with the pulse beat of what's going on through what you read in magazines. Not even through records. *Vogue* magazine was my whole consciousness. I never saw people. I never went to a concert. It was all image. In one issue of *Vogue*, it was Youthquaker people they were talking about. It had a picture of Edie on a bed in a ballet pose. She was like a thin man in black leotards and a sort of boat-necked sweater, white hair and, behind her a little white horse drawn on the wall. She was such a strong image that I thought, 'That's it.' It represented everything to me . . . radiating intelligence, speed, being connected with the moment." A decade after she discovered *la* Sedgwick, Patti and photographer Robert Mapplethorpe would draw from those same visual energies to shoot the jacket photograph for Patti's debut LP.

Patti saw Edie in the flesh for the first time in the fall of 1965, when Andy Warhol and his entourage, Edie at the helm, descended upon Philadelphia's Institute of Contemporary Art for Warhol's first-ever retrospective. "Edie was coming down this long staircase," she told Jean Stein. "I think she had ermine wrapped around her; her hair was white and her eyebrows black. She had on this real little dress [and] two big white afghan hounds on black leashes with diamond collars, but that could be fantasy. . . . She had so much life in her. Her movement was fluid, and she was like little queenie. . . . I wasn't into girls or anything, but I had a real crush on her."

Patti encountered her again on a rare visit to New York City; the city was like Oz to her then, a beckoning presence at the end of the bus ride, far enough away to be fabulous, close enough not to be out of reach, and magic enough that she refused to despoil it by visiting it all the time. Neither would she try to gain entrance to the palaces where her idols congregated. It was enough to make her way to places like Arthur's, or the Scene, stand outside on the sidewalk, and just watch the comings and goings.

One night, however, knowing Sedgwick was in the building, Patti cajoled the doorman to let her run inside for a moment; "I think I said I had to use the bathroom." She was, she thought, looking pretty hot that night, in a green woolen miniskirt that would have blown the doors off any South Jersey nightclub. "I didn't look so hot there." But she watched

Edie and her friends as they danced, and that "was the big moment of my life"—even though she wasn't especially impressed by the *way* in which they danced.

They looked like weird chickens, she thought, all angles and elbows and long, dangling earrings. Nobody danced like that in South Jersey; nobody would have even dreamed of dancing like that in South Jersey. Patti knew there and then that she didn't ever want to be like the people she so admired. "I just liked that they existed, so I could look at them."

Back in Philadelphia, the Museum of Art continued to exercise her imagination, and daydreams of her own future in the art world further clouded her work at Glassboro. Her dreams of becoming the power behind an artistic throne, of winning the heart of a struggling genius, coaxing and inspiring him to attain his potential, became an even more vivid lure.

Spinning out fantasies of Edie's relationship with Warhol—for few then would have asserted that his best work was created with her by his side—she dreamed of discovering a Dylan or a Jackson Pollock, or even a Harry Houdini (for what is escapology if not an art form in action that stands in for words), of standing alongside him as he worked for acceptance, and molding his talent to meet it. She had yet to meet that special person, of course. But she floated through life, through her studies, with the growing conviction that someday soon she would.

And then her dreams were shattered, not once but twice.

Patti has never been good at keeping her stories straight. "I was holding a temporary minimum-wage job in a textbook factory in Philadelphia," she recalled in her memoir *Just Kids*. At other times, she described herself as laboring at a baby buggy factory, turning out pushchairs for the glowing moms of the day. Other biographers have named her employer as the Dennis Mitchell Toy Factory in Woodbury, where her duties apparently included assembling the boxes into which baby mattresses were packed.

Whatever and wherever it was, her summer job was poorly paid and shoddily maintained, and filled with women for whom life could and would offer nothing better—or, at least, nothing that they could be bothered to aspire toward.

Patti hated it and was hated in return. Working too fast for her co-workers' liking, she was first tormented, then bullied, and finally threatened. One day, she was cornered in the restroom and challenged to shatter her goody-goody demeanor by letting out a few swear words. When she refused, they threatened to push her head into an unflushed toilet bowl. Patti gave in and unleashed a torrent of the foulest language she could think of, until her tormenters backed away. But, she said, she was devastated, because she had desperately wanted to become a part of their world, and now she had blown it.

Not long after that incident, Patti was nestled somewhere in the building, reading her treasured bilingual copy of Rimbaud's *Illuminations*, when her shift supervisor came up behind her and spotted the French text that ran down every alternate page. The woman demanded to know why Patti was reading a foreign language.

"It's not a foreign language," she replied, pointing to the English text on the facing page that she had been devouring. But her supervisor was not fooled. She knew what she'd seen. And what was that? Communist literature, of course, because in her view (which she shared with an awful lot of people in those days, thanks to the Cuban Missile Crisis and Khrushchev banging his shoes on the table), "if it's foreign, it's Communist, because anything foreign is Communist."

She probably said a lot more than that, but her other words were drowned by the hue and cry that her first remark made, as the rest of the women crowded around to see the real-life commie that was wriggling in their midst.

Patti stormed home, and her final paycheck followed her. She'd been fired for reading a book. It was, she sighed later to Mick Gold of the UK magazine *Street Life*, "a real drag," having to go home to South Jersey and tell her parents she'd been fired, because it wasn't easy to find work in the area at that time. There were a few opportunities. The Columbia Records pressing plant in Pitman had her on their waiting list, and there was the Campbell Soup factory in Camden. She would take whichever came up first and then count down the days until she returned to Glassboro. But she already knew that whatever job she found was unlikely to offer any kind of improvement on life at the Piss Factory. She was not simply unemployed. She suddenly realized that in the eyes of her New Jersey peers, she was also unemployable.

That was the first shock. The second, just months later, was the discovery that she was pregnant.

She was existing on a staple diet of the Rolling Stones' album *Aftermath* and the Beatles' *Revolver* when she got the news of her pregnancy, torn between the twin axes of Lennon's "Doctor Robert" and Jagger and Richards's "Mother's Little Helper," a stupid girl who understood that tomorrow never knows. Somewhere between those philosophical poles, she knew what she had to do.

She made up her mind to carry the child to term and then give it up for adoption.

The father was just a boy, almost three years younger than she was, a high schooler while she was at teacher training college. Not that she would remain there for long, not after the authorities discovered her condition. Nor could she stay at home with her parents, where she had lived for the last nineteen years. "Judgmental neighbors made it impossible for my family," she wrote in *Just Kids*, "treating them as if they were harboring a criminal." Finally, some far-off friends took her in, a painter and a potter who lived by the south Jersey shore and were happy to see the girl through her confinement.

She hated, she wrote in the poem "Female," being *bloated*, feeling like *a lame dog*, wanting nothing more than to *pull my fat baby belly to the sea*.

But she was also aware that the first phase of her life had come to an end, and she realized with a start that she was not too sorry to see it go. Without the pregnancy, she might have drifted on forever, rootlessly dreaming and stargazing from afar, imagining the magic that was off on some horizon, and standing stock still waiting for it to come down and embrace her.

She was never cut out to be a teacher, and the school authorities knew it. By the time Patti fell pregnant, she had been a student at Glassboro College for two years, during which time she succeeded only in being repeatedly instructed to stick with the curriculum, and not to bring her own, distinctly individualistic teaching methods into the classroom. So many dreams, so many ideas, so many fanciful notions. Her pregnancy stripped them all away. But it did not simply transform the dreaming girl into a thinking adult. It forced her, too, to make a very important decision.

If life was beginning, she was going to get started ahead of it. At Easter 1967, Patti's parents came to the house where she was staying and drove her to the hospital in nearby Camden. There, Patti Smith's daughter was born on April 26, 1967—the thirtieth anniversary of the bombing of Guernica during the Spanish Civil War, she later observed. She never saw her again. "I gave [the child] up . . . because I wanted to be an artist—simple as that," Victor Bockris and Roberta Bayley's biography quoted Patti as saying. "I wanted to create and re-create in my own way."

Nine weeks later, on July 3, Patti spent her savings on art supplies— a box of colored pencils and a wooden slate to draw on—and, with whatever was left over from the $16 she'd put together, set off for New York City. She caught the bus to Philadelphia, which was just about as far as she could go, because she'd completely underestimated the cost of a ticket to New York. But, just as she was about to call home in despair, she noticed that the last person to use the call box had left a wallet on the shelf. Inside that wallet was $32. She had her ticket.

3

BALLAD OF A BAD BOY

JULY 3, 1967, was a Monday, but the next day was Independence Day. Anybody who had been given the chance was still out of town, enjoying the luxury of an extra-long weekend. The city wasn't deserted, but it wasn't crazed either, and the bus made good time as it wove through to Port Authority.

Patti already knew her way around. On her previous, deliberately rare visits to the city, she'd made sure to memorize every place she needed, and she knew precisely where to go. Plus, she had a subway map: take the A train to Hoyt-Schermerhorn, then across to DeKalb Avenue. A Jersey friend, Howard "Howie" Michaels, had a brownstone in Brooklyn, while he studied at the nearby Pratt Institute of Art. She would crash with him for a few days while she found her feet, and then her life could begin. Except it didn't quite work out that way.

Her friend had moved on, said the guy who opened the door to her, and the only person who seemed to know where he might have gone was asleep at the back of the apartment. Patti insisted on waking him. The young man whose rest she disturbed later described her as looking like "a creature from another planet," a skinny little thing in dungarees and a black turtleneck, with a funny way of looking at you, like she didn't want you to know she was there. This day, however, he barely spoke a word to her. He simply dressed, walked her a few blocks across the neighborhood, deposited her on her friend's doorstep, then headed back to bed.

The apartment was in darkness, and when the sun set, it remained closed up and black. Night had fallen on her first day in the city, and she didn't know where else to go. So she bundled up in her raincoat, with her little plaid suitcase for a pillow, and went to sleep on the stoop. In the morning, she realized the flaw in her mighty master plan: her friend was in school here, but school was out for the summer. It would be another two months before the streets of Brooklyn were alive with students again. She spent the next day, the next week, a large part of the next month, restlessly searching for a friendly face, a place to stay, a place to work.

She headed back to Manhattan, painfully conscious that every subway token took another bite out of her nest egg, but equally aware that the Village never slept, and it wouldn't let a sister starve either.

The Summer of Love was at its fulsome height. Over on the West Coast, as the radio sang, the kids all danced with flowers in their hair, but the East Coast was no slouch in the cultural stakes either, and New York City was the center of everything. Every park was packed with kids—hippies in the common vernacular, dropouts and dope fiends in the adult opinion—draft dodgers, junkies, and freaks. Free drugs, free love, tune in, turn on . . . peace, man.

If you walked the streets of Greenwich Village from West Houston to Washington Square, past every patch of open space, every corner and every courtyard, you could have been passing through the Twelve Days of Hipmas: eleven leafletters leafletting, ten drummers drumming, nine protest singers protesting, eight radicals radicalizing, and all of them living large on the promise of the teenage dream.

Radio blared the FM of the day. The Beatles' *Sgt. Pepper* was barely a month old and still spinning on every record player. The Doors' "Light My Fire" was on its way to #1; the Association's "Windy" would make way for its ascent. Jefferson Airplane's "White Rabbit" was in the wind, and you saw a lot of copies of *Alice in Wonderland* being studied by the readers on the grass, and a lot of chess matches being fought as well, the players waiting for the chessmen to tell them where to go. Hey, kid—try this, sniff that, feel this, cop that. Patti had never seen anything like it.

Unfortunately, nobody saw her. She spent a night in Central Park, in the shadow of the statue of Alice's Mad Hatter, and the next day she resumed her wanderings. Up and down Fifth Avenue to ask if the stores had any openings. She filled in applications when they did, although she hadn't yet figured out how they'd contact her after that. Maybe she'd just drop in every few days to see if anyone needed her.

Down to Forty-Second Street and Times Square, the neon-lit heart of America's sleaziest soul, where every artery pumped sex and souvenirs. There were X-rated peepshow holes where a pocket full of quarters could buy you twenty minutes in a sticky, lust-filled booth and ragged hookers lurked outside to relieve you of your bills. The occasional door might lead you elsewhere: it was only the storefronts that glowed with seedy grandeur; upstairs there might be a movie house, a library, even a recording studio. In two years' time, John Cale, the man destined to produce Patti's first LP, would oversee the recording of the Stooges' first LP at the Hit Factory, one floor above a Times Square peepshow.

The best Patti could muster was to find herself a job, waitressing at an Italian restaurant called Joe's. But she lost it within three hours after spilling a meal into a customer's lap.

Patti kept walking. She'd left her suitcase in a lockup in Brooklyn, which flushed more cash down the drain, and carried everything she needed in a bundle beneath her arm. She'd more or less given up eating by now; she just pinned her hopes on finding a friend, who'd help her find a home, which would help her find a job. At last, she found a place to sleep: riding the subway from one end to the other, nodding off between stops and her fellow passengers' noises. Or she'd go back out to Brooklyn, where she occasionally bumped into someone she recognized as a friend of a friend, who'd let her use the shower or crash on the couch.

She gravitated to St. Mark's Place, sensing that this East Village street was the epicenter of something, and so it was, ever since Andy Warhol touched down there earlier in the year. Warhol had since moved on; the Dom, the nightclub where his plastic inevitable had exploded through the spring, was under new management, as the Electric Circus. But the boutiques and bars that blossomed in his shadow were still alive and well, and there was always something going on: seven mime-artists miming, six fire-eaters eating, five old queens.

Patti found another job, but this was one she could pull off, at Brentano's bookstore across from the Rockefeller Center on Fifth Avenue. While she waited for her first week's pay—which, of course, was withheld for a week, to keep staff from walking out without notice—she spent her nights in the store itself, stashing herself away in a bathroom, then creeping out when the last door was locked.

But it wasn't just a job or a place to sleep at night. For Patti, Brentano's was also paradise. "Booksellers to the World: All Books, All Languages," boasted Brentano's logo, and it was true. Before the company was subsumed into the Waldenbooks/Borders empire during the 1980s and '90s, it was both a publisher whose Éditions Brentano's imprint was home to the French writers exiled from their homeland during the Vichy period, and a storehouse whose shelves creaked beneath the weight of valued and valuable tomes. There, in that century-old forest of bound paper and carved wood, dominated by the curving staircase and the little wooden benches where browsers could relax, Patti could absorb literary history firsthand.

Other people moved to the city and found themselves devoured by its friendless emptiness. Patti found herself enfolded within its magnanimity. But only one of the people she met during those first weeks in the city would be allowed to see inside of her: an absurdly photogenic young art student named Robert Mapplethorpe.

He was precisely fifty-six days older than she, born on November 4, 1946, at Irwin Sanitarium in Hollis, Queens, and raised in another neighborhood in the borough, Floral Park. His half-German father, Harry, and Irish Catholic mother, Joan, already had two children (there would be three more after Robert was born), but Robert was always the odd one out.

"A mischievous little boy whose carefree youth was delicately tinged with a fascination with beauty" is how Patti recalled him in her memoir *Just Kids*. He was a budding artist before he could even color inside the lines, a skilled one after he abandoned his crayons, and now an art student with so much potential that even his beloved LSD only scratched the surface of his imagination. The first time Patti saw his paintings, she said, they reminded her of Henri Michaux and Richard Pousette-Dart.

They met by chance, one day during Patti's first week at Brentano's, where they discovered that they'd already run into one another once before, on her first day in the city, while she was looking for somebody else. Mapplethorpe was the silent young man who had escorted her to her absent friend's door.

This time, he came into the bookstore with a credit slip from another Brentano's branch, where he worked, and bought a Persian necklace that she'd fallen in love with. They swapped smiles and words but didn't exchange names. That happened a few days later in Greenwich Village, while Patti was enduring the attentions of an unwanted dinner date, a customer from the bookstore whom, in her mind, she was beginning to equate with a potential serial killer. Then she spotted Mapplethorpe walking toward her through crowded Tompkins Square. She rushed over, greeted him as though they were longtime lovers, and waved away her original date.

They began to talk, and at first it may have seemed that they had little in common. They were both artists, Patti later explained to Ed Vulliamy of the *Guardian*, but she was into abstract impression, while Mapplethorpe was working in tantric art. One of the few things they found they shared was their love of poet William Blake (1757–1827).

As a child, Patti had devoured Blake's *Songs of Innocence* and *Songs of Experience*, and for a long time she viewed him as a children's writer. Which "in a way he was—making me aware of the life of a chimney sweep," she told the *Guardian*. "But then I grew with Blake, with his sense of spirituality, of social activism, his visionary experience, his compassion for the flaws in human nature and his own nature." Now, it was Blake who first bound her to Mapplethorpe. "We would spend whatever money we had on books, even if we had nothing to eat, and spent a lot of time together with our Blake books. Both of us had what I'd call a Blakean palette."

And soon she was telling Robert her life story. He enjoyed listening to her tell him stories, so she did. Every night—or almost every night, because on some evenings they were too tired to even try to stay awake, and on others they didn't close their eyes at all—Patti would talk Mapplethorpe to sleep. Sometimes he would request particular tales; other times he would simply tell her to begin and then drift to the cadence of her rhythm and tone. Other times he would ask her to draw what she saw when she looked back into her past, and the sound of her pencil would lull him away. And slowly, over time, she recalled in *Just Kids*, her most precious childhood memories became his.

But Patti's stories could be infuriating as well as comforting. Even attempting to have a simple conversation could wrap you up in her word games; you never knew what she was talking about. "She was on the edge of being psychotic in a schizophrenic way," Mapplethorpe admitted to his future biographer Patricia Morrisroe. "She told me stories, and I didn't know whether they were fiction or nonfiction. If she hadn't discovered art, she would have wound up in a mental institution."

Instead, she wound up crashing with Mapplethorpe at an apartment on Waverley Avenue in Brooklyn that he was already sharing with a college friend, Patrick Kennedy, and Margaret, his wife-to-be. It was not the happiest of domestic arrangements. Apparently, Margaret found Patti to be judgmental, manipulative, angry, and thoughtless; Patti thought nothing of marching naked through the apartment, no matter who else might be visiting—Pat Kennedy's midwestern parents on one memorable occasion.

Patti and Robert spent what little money they had cautiously. Food or a book? A book or a record? Whenever they could, they would bypass such decisions by visiting their parents for a free meal. The elder Mapplethorpes were never taken with Patti, even after Robert told them that they were secretly married; Patti's mother and father liked Mapplethorpe, but they didn't see him much. It was so much cheaper for Patti to make the long hike into Jersey on her own, especially since she could bring the loot back in her bag. And the money they saved, on the fare and the food and anything else she returned with, could be put toward more important things.

Milk or a magazine? Sustenance or a subway token? The Village or Midtown?

It was Mapplethorpe's dream to visit Andy Warhol's Factory, so they did. Located on East Forty-Seventh Street, on the fourth floor of a warehouse buried in the shadow of the Empire State Building, the

Factory glittered beneath the artist's fame and notoriety. Warhol's own art and works aside, in late 1967 the Factory was home to the Velvet Underground, the musical experience that remained a tightly guarded secret among the city's artiest cognoscenti. Their debut album was in the stores, its distinctive Warhol cover art of a peelable banana a vivid contrast to the traditional teenybop-friendly mugshots with which most artists bedecked their LPs, but visitors to the Factory could hear it for free, because there was always a copy spinning on the gramophone there.

"The first time I ever saw Patti was at Andy's," the Velvets' golden-haired chanteuse, the German-born Nico, recalled. "She was skinny, like a rat, but she was from New Jersey and so was Lou [Reed, the Velvets' front man], so that was all right. She didn't speak much; she just stood and watched the people. I don't know if we even knew her name."

Patti and Nico would grow to know one another slowly, and Nico would always speak kindly of her. ("She was a female Leonard Cohen when she moved from writing to singing, and I liked her because she was thin and strong.") For now, however, Nico was as perplexed by Patti and Robert as everybody else. Were they siblings? Were they lovers, and if they were, who was the boy and who was the girl? Were they strangers who had connected? Or connections who liked one another's strangeness? Either way, Nico made up her mind to keep a watchful eye on the Jersey girl and her leonine consort as they hovered uncertainly around the edges of the circus.

For it was a circus, a vast room glazed in aluminum cooking foil, a Silver Factory filled with freaks, and Smith looked as out of place there as she felt. "I was a very naive person . . . and there were so many weird things in New York," she told Amy Gross. "A lot of sexual stuff—not just happening to me, just *happening*—that I had to realize was part of life. I had lived such a sheltered childhood, so family oriented, and all of a sudden I was on my own. And that's when I learned that anything is possible."

Another occasional hangout was the Cooper Union for the Advancement of Science and Art in the East Village. And then it was over to St. Mark's Church in-the-Bowery, just north of the street that bears its name, where Paul Blackburn's recently launched Poetry Project was the already booming center for the city's poetic community.

Loose and unfunded since its official opening on September 22, 1966, said historian Jerome Rothenberg, "the project developed . . . into the closest thing we have to an ongoing, venerable center for poetry, run by poets and open foremost to the full range of visionary, revolutionary, language-centered, spirit-centered arts that poets have both invented and discovered in the newest and oldest possibilities of our human (and animal) natures. . . . It is what Ezra Pound called a vortex—the Poetry Project vortex."

Rothenberg unwrapped his own memories of the Project's first performances: "Beat poets, New York School poets, San Francisco poets, Black Mountain poets, Deep Image poets, Midwest and Southwest regionals, Fluxus poets, Umbra poets, and so on. And from then on: African American poets, Latino poets, feminist poets, Indian poets, Language poets, anti-Language poets, sound poets, silent poets, mumbling poets; even . . . academic poets." Patti was none of these things—not then—and Mapplethorpe had no desire to become any of them. There, as every place else they visited, they were simply observers, hanging on the periphery of the action.

The center of their universe, however, was what Manhattan then regarded as the hippest joint in town: Max's Kansas City. For that was where everybody went. Opened by club owner Mickey Ruskin in fall 1965, off Union Square on Seventeenth Street and Park Avenue, Max's prospered immediately from Ruskin's own long-standing relationship with the city's artistic underbelly, particularly once word got around that Warhol was a regular visitor and the Factory crowd were nightly denizens.

Sex and drugs were commonplace. But it could also be a brutally exclusive enclave. The first time Patti and Mapplethorpe turned up at Max's entrance, Mickey Ruskin refused her entry, she looked so drab and dirty. She was in good company—he once barred Janis Joplin for much the same reasons—and he soon relented. It would take time for the pair to be accepted as even peripheral members of Max's glittering inner sanctum of self-styled superstars, Warholian freaks, and all-purpose artistic weirdoes, but even from the fringe of this exciting new society, they knew, and became known to, the characters that dominated this particular aspect of New York City culture.

The pair would hang out at Max's every night they could, often remaining there until three in the morning. She and Mapplethorpe justified the time by telling each other that they were waiting for "a big break," but she admitted that she wasn't certain what they were even trying to get a break for. It was six months, she later reflected, before anybody even said hello to them.

Today, writers look back on that scene and describe it as one long, calculated hustle. It wasn't. Patti told A. D. Amorosi in the *Philadelphia City Paper*, "Writers focus on the hustling or the trampling over each other for success. Perhaps some is true, but one can't discount youth and idealism. The lifestyles may have been morally questionable but a lot of people were very idealistic."

In November 1967, Patti and Robert found their first home together, an eighty-dollar-a-month apartment that devoured the entire second floor of an old brownstone on Hall Street. Its last tenants, apparently, had been a nest of junkies; the stove was filled with old, used syringes, the fridge was overflowing with mold, and the walls were smeared with blood and graffiti. The young couple took one look at the place and grabbed it with both hands, while the landlord was so happy not to have to refurbish it himself that he gave them half off the required deposit if they would clean and repaint it themselves.

So Mapplethorpe set to work.

They relished their newfound privacy. There in their own apartment, their respective talents stretched out: Mapplethorpe as the chrysalis that would burst open to reveal one of the most gifted photographers of his generation, Smith as a would-be wielder of words who composed her poetry from beneath a photograph of Rimbaud, while their tiny record player pumped out an endless soundtrack of whatever felt right: jazz and rock, Coltrane and the Stones, the Beatles and Motown when Patti took control of it; Tim Buckley, Tim Hardin, and the baroque bombast of the Vanilla Fudge when Mapplethorpe made the decision.

The room was sparse, furnished with the pickings garnered from walking the local streets and carting home anything that looked remotely serviceable or repairable. Old lamps, a battered bookcase, a stained mattress, a ratty rug. Those regular trips back to South Jersey allowed Patti to add some of her old books and records to the ambience.

Mapplethorpe decorated the walls with his art. Patti littered the floor with hers. She had no sense of permanence; whether it was a drawing that her boyfriend adored, or a poem that he admired, sooner or later it would be on the ground, jumbled up with the unwashed laundry, newspapers and magazines, discarded books, and more street scrapings. They ate as well as they could afford to, which generally meant not much, and if there was no money for food, there was certainly none for anything else. So they stayed in nights and listened to music, or drew or read or talked or whatever.

Shortly before Christmas 1967, the pair lost their jobs at Brentano's. Mapplethorpe was laid off; Patti was fired. It could have been a disaster, but it wasn't. Just doors away from the bookstore, the world-famous FAO Schwarz toy store was advertising for staff. But while Mapplethorpe dressed windows and won the applause of his employers, Patti worked the cash register for the Christmas rush only and hated every moment of it.

So she moved on, back to the world of books at Scribner's, a glass-fronted beauty at 597 Fifth Avenue, where one of her few allies from Glassboro College, Janet Hamill, was now working.

Destined to become one of Patti's closest friends, and still a regular guest at her readings and performances, Hamill was another Jersey girl, born in Jersey City and raised in New Milford. She moved to New York City, BA in hand, around the same time as Patti. And like Patti, she hoped to carve herself a niche in the poetic trade by taking a job that brought her closer to her ideal. It was she who had encouraged Patti to apply for the job, and her intervention came just in time. Mapplethorpe quit the toy store shortly after Patti started at Scribner's, complaining that it sapped his appetite for his own work, and Patti became the household's sole breadwinner.

She adored the job. Not only was Scribner's one of the most beautiful bookstores in America, but it also respected its customers and demanded that the staff do likewise. Every weekend, the sales staff were expected to hunker down with the *New York Times Book Review* and read it from cover to cover. Then, when customers came in and asked for recommendations, the person they spoke to would know exactly what they were talking about. It was the kind of work that Patti excelled at. A title moved onto the bestseller list. The staff were told to read it. A new release was creating a buzz. Read it. An old classic was back in fashion. Read it. Read, read, read. And then talk, talk, talk.

Mapplethorpe, meanwhile, dipped in and out of odd jobs. He worked for a time as an usher at the Fillmore East, newly reopened by Bill Graham in March 1968, and came home raving about the first band he saw there: Janis Joplin fronting Big Brother and the Holding Company. Later that month, he scored Patti and Janet Hamill a pass apiece to see the Doors.

But outings like that were a rarity. "We were totally isolated," Patti told Lisa Robinson in 1996. "We were twenty years old, we lived in Brooklyn. . . . I worked in the bookstore. I came to the apartment and we spent most of our time drawing, looking at books, and spending all our time together, hardly ever seeing other people."

Yet their idyll was doomed. Robert was becoming troubled and possessive. She found another lover. Howie Michaels was the painter friend she'd been looking for on her very first day in the city. Now they had reconnected, and when that relationship had blossomed far enough, she announced she was moving out of the Hall Street apartment.

She moved in with Janet Hamill, and Mapplethorpe was devastated. But he also sensed an escape route out of his private dilemma. If you leave me, he told Patti, I'll turn gay.

Her reaction, she confessed in *Just Kids*, was "less than compassionate." She felt she had failed him. And the next time she saw him, dropping by the apartment to pick up some of her stuff, he had wallpapered it with pin-ups cut from gay porn magazines.

Howie Michaels did not stick around long. He knew that in her heart of hearts, Patti still possessed a bond with Mapplethorpe that he and the girl could never share. He moved on just a short time after Patti moved out. But when Patti went to look in on Mapplethorpe next, she learned that he had moved to San Francisco. He came back shortly after, but now he had a boyfriend.

4

DEATH BY WATER

IN MAY 1969, Patti and sister Linda up and flew to Paris. It was a trip they had long dreamed of taking, but the time had never felt right. Now it did. Patti's need to escape her multiple romantic crises was the impetus they'd been waiting for.

For Patti, the trip was very much one of literary discovery. It was her idea to book a room at the Hôtel des Etrangers on the Boulevard Saint-Michel, and she who asked the concierge if they could be given one specific room: the attic where Rimbaud had shared his passion with the poet and inventor Charles Cros. In many people's eyes, Cros was the French Edison, whose achievements were clouded only by his widely publicized (and widely ridiculed) belief that the planets Mars and Venus were both inhabited and that all mankind needed to do to make contact was to erect a giant mirror capable of burning messages into the two planets' surfaces. Such is the historical legacy of a man who *almost* invented the gramophone—that, and a few lines of lust in the average biography of the poet he adored.

Patti was besotted regardless, all the more so after she learned that few people ever stayed in the attic room, simply because it was in the attic. Eighty years had elapsed since Rimbaud stayed there, and that was not very long in the life of a Parisian hotel. "I'm sure I slept in the same bed," she told writer Scott Cohen in *Circus*. "It was like in the movies when they go into the haunted house and they hit everything and there's tons of dust and spiders and the bed is shaped like bodies. It was a tiny bed on a metal ramp. You could see the outline of bodies where the people had slept."

Patti and Linda pounded the Paris streets, seeking out the tiniest references to the poet's visits to the capital, and unearthing other treasures too. Paris in spring 1969 had had a year to recover from the headline-making riots of the previous summer. It remained, however, a hotbed of political dissension and agitation, as worldwide opposition to the American war in Vietnam continued to grow against a backdrop of increasingly horrific news images.

The Smith sisters steered clear of the areas where the students gathered more volubly; Patti has since confessed that even on campus in New Jersey and Philadelphia, she had nothing to say about the war, and no real awareness of it beyond the occasional glance at the headlines. Years later, with her political activism a burning passion, she would revise her memories somewhat, but at the time, neither apathy nor complacency explained her disinterest. She simply had not paid attention. But attempting to explain that to an overexcited audience of hypertense French students—for that was the fate of every American who wandered onto the south bank at that time and made the mistake of speaking aloud—was not a task that either woman relished.

Instead, they spent their time drifting through historic Paris: the graveyards, the boulevards, the sites and scenes that they had only read about back home. At l'Église Saint-Germain-des-Prés, they visited Picasso's *Portrait of Dora Maar* in the garden. Patti was, she said later, too shy to enter the church itself. "Paris to me is completely a city of images," she told Penny Green in 1973. "I always felt that I was in a black-and-white 16 mm film."

The pair paid their way by taking part-time jobs in cafes and restaurants; for a time, they worked as street entertainers, joining a ragged posse of musicians, jugglers, fire-eaters, and mimes and collecting whatever coppers were thrown their way. Linda sang and danced; Patti beat out rudimentary melodies on a toy piano.

She also started to write.

Inspiration struck on the morning of July 4, 1969, when Patti and the rest of France awoke to the news that guitarist Brian Jones had died the previous evening, drowned in his swimming pool while, apparently, a party full of friends looked on. Patti had, she later said, just emerged from a five-day immersion in French filmmaker Jean-Luc Godard's documentary *One Plus One*, a revolutionary tract that included some fabulous footage of the Rolling Stones recording "Sympathy for the Devil"—five days during which the faces of the five Stones were seared even deeper into her mind than they already had been. Now those Stones were four.

She remembered the first and only time she'd ever seen Jones in the flesh, when the Rolling Stones played Philadelphia on November 6, 1965. The band was off and running by then; "Satisfaction" and "Get Off of My Cloud" had proved Mick Jagger and Keith Richards to be as capable songwriters as Lennon and McCartney, only with better-sounding records. Fans of the two bands, the Beatles and the Stones, had already divided themselves down fiercely antagonistic lines: clean or dirty, sweet or savage, "Yesterday" or *right now*. And the only common ground was the screaming little girls.

Patti had not intended screaming, and when she took her seat in the auditorium with the rest of the audience, all had seemed calm and orderly. Then the Stones came out and pandemonium erupted, the entire room pushing toward the stage, and Patti was pushed *into* the stage, crushed against its hard wooden lip and feeling herself being dragged down by the weight.

Desperately she reached out for something to hold onto, to pull herself back to the surface. Her hand connected with Brian Jones's ankle. "I was grabbing him to save myself," she told Thurston Moore. "And he just looked at me. And I looked at him. And he smiled. He just smiled at me."

If she had had any doubt as to who her favorite Rolling Stone was before that night, there was no question any longer. And now Brian Jones was dead, and as if that was not nightmarish enough, there was the sense that somehow she might have saved him. For in a vision, or a dream, or a premonition, call it what you will, she had sensed that Brian Jones was in danger, that Brian Jones was hurt, that Brian Jones was about to sink beneath the surface, just as she herself was going under at that concert.

And just like her, his hand was outstretched for something to grab on to. She had grasped his ankle and pulled herself to safety. He had reached out and she wasn't there.

The night after Brian Jones died, the day that she learned he was gone, Patti set to work on what would become the first poem she wrote in her own true voice, a rock 'n' roll mass set to a rock 'n' roll rhythm. It wasn't anything she'd ever heard of anybody else having done. Maybe Dylan and Van Morrison had come close occasionally, and the Doors' Jim Morrison—at that moment, probably the biggest star in American rock—might have strayed even closer. But she wouldn't have cared if the whole world had pulled it off before. "I wasn't trying to be 'innovative,'" she told Lisa Robinson in 1976. "I was just doing what I thought was right, and being true to Brian."

And she was being true, whether she would have seen it this way or not, to the nature of the hall of fame that still hung in her mind: the idols who died before their time, the artists for whom the weight of art was far too grand to bear. Two years ago, in her first days in New York City, John Coltrane had died. Next year, Jimi Hendrix and Janis Joplin would join him; the year after that, Jim Morrison. Patti would eulogize them all, and then add them to the arsenal of imagery that she was slowly, and only half-consciously, constructing around herself.

It was late July 1969 before the Smith sisters returned to the United States from their Parisian sojourn—pulled home, said Patti, by a series of increasingly portentous dreams about their father. The pair had scarcely communicated with their family all the while they were in Paris, the occasional letter or postcard drifting leisurely across the ocean to wash up at the American Express office, maybe a collect phone call or two. Patti had written and received far more letters from Robert Mapplethorpe than from her family, but that did not mean they were out of her mind completely. She had ignored the visions she'd had of Brian Jones; she was not going to make the same mistake again.

The women returned home just days after Grant Smith was taken into the hospital, the victim of an unexpected heart attack, and just as the doctors delivered the news that he would survive.

So, Patti had decided, would she. The broken heart that Mapple-thorpe had sent her away with was repaired by now, and he, too, was back in New York and regretting the precipitous manner in which their relationship had shattered. The day Patti turned up on his Delancey Street doorstep was the day he broke up with his latest boyfriend—and the day, too, that the pair decided that they had wasted too much of their lives already, struggling along amidst decay and indecision.

They quit Delancey Street after a neighbor was murdered just across the hallway from them, and moved on to the Allerton Hotel on West Twenty-Second. Down among the druggies and the derelicts, it was about as low as any hotel could go, but Patti and Mapplethorpe had somehow sunk even lower.

Never too careful about his health, and especially disdainful of his dental requirements, particularly his ulcerated gums, Mapplethorpe had developed a serious infection while Patti was in Paris. He was now in terrific pain, spinning between unconsciousness and delirium. Patti recalled these weeks in the poem "Sister Morphine," titled for a song that Marianne Faithfull wrote with the Rolling Stones (in mid-1969, it was the B-side of her latest single) but inspired wholly by Mapple-thorpe's suffering: *i checked into the alton house with my friend, in pain. his nerve was exposed and he laid for several days on the bumpy rusting cot draining and weeping.*

They couldn't afford a doctor, and they couldn't afford their rent, either. Just weeks into their tenure, they made a midnight getaway, Patti all but carrying the still-sickly Mapplethorpe down the fire escape and across town.

It was time, Patti decided, to go for broke. If they were to be artists, they needed to live like artists. They'd still be starving, but at least they'd have style. And there was only one address in Manhattan where starva-tion and style went hand in hand. The Chelsea Hotel.

Quite possibly the most famous hotel in America, and certainly the most famous in the American art scene, the Chelsea was built in 1883, when for a short time its twelve floors established it as the tallest building in New York City. Planted on West Twenty-Third Street between Sev-enth and Eighth, it was originally designed as luxury cooperative before becoming a residential hotel in 1905. In the decades that followed, Mark Twain, O. Henry, Sarah Bernhardt, and Thomas Wolfe numbered among its residents, and it was their patronage that gave the Chelsea its reputation.

By the early 1950s, the Chelsea had degenerated into a virtual flop-house, its doors open to anybody who could afford a room for a night—and with its prices kept deliberately low, that was a lot of people. It was in a dangerous neighborhood as well, one where even a not-so-innocent passerby was as likely to get mugged as mug someone else.

But the hotel's aura lingered on. Poet Dylan Thomas stayed there during one of his New York City visits, and the Chelsea was a magnet for the Beats as well: Jack Kerouac, Allen Ginsberg, and Gregory Corso all lived there for a time; William Burroughs wrote *Naked Lunch* there. And by the time manager David Bard handed the running of the hotel over to his son, Stanley, in 1957, the Chelsea was on the up-and-up again, at least as far as its best-known clientele was concerned.

During the mid-1960s, Warhol's Factory regarded the Chelsea as a second home, with Gerard Malanga, Brigid Polk, Ondine, and Nico all resident there. Warhol's movie *Chelsea Girls* was partially filmed there, at least until Stanley Bard kicked the crew and their cameras out and the movie had to be finished on a lookalike film set. Lou Reed wrote the movie's title theme, a haunting ode to the hotel's most colorful denizens.

Leonard Cohen lived there for a time, and wrote one of his best-loved songs, "Chelsea Hotel #2," about the night he spent there with Janis Joplin. Joni Mitchell was a resident, and she emerged with "Chelsea Morning." If any simple pile of brick and mortar was capable of inspiring the arts, it was the Chelsea.

And Stanley Bard knew it. He listened while Patti outlined the dreams of glory that awaited Robert and her, smiled as she handed him her art portfolio as collateral for the rent they would not be able to pay, and allowed her to barter the promise of future fame for a room key.

It was a tiny key for the tiniest room in the hotel, a pale-blue tenth-floor shoebox with just enough room for a twin bed, a sink and a mirror, a chest of drawers, and a portable television. For now, though, that was all they needed. With Reed's musical tribute echoing in their ears, and the ghosts of so many other past residents flitting through their consciousness, the couple knew they had found their niche. They had found their workplace.

Patti's first order of business, however, was somewhat more mundane: to nurse Mapplethorpe back to health, borrowing antibiotics from any friend who might have some lying around his or her medicine cabinet, mixing and matching whatever remedies she could find, until his fever broke and his temperature dipped and he was capable of consuming more than chicken soup.

Once he was back on his feet, they began to explore their new playground, inside and out.

Max's was opening to them as well. After so many nights by themselves in the corner, their persistence had finally paid off. Danny Fields, a hardwired hustler who had crammed an incredible life into his twenty-seven years—journalist, A&R man, manager, and even, for a time, Edie Sedgwick's loft-mate—was the first to acknowledge them, inviting them to join him at his table one night and putting into words the questions that, unbeknownst to Patti and Mapplethorpe, had been exercising a lot of other people's minds over the past months: Nobody cared who this couple were, really. What fascinated them, just as it had fascinated Nico, was, *What* were they? In an environment where everybody's business was everyone else's, and a person's sexual proclivities could be as grand an introduction as their professional or personal abilities, the quiet couple who sat in a corner, sipping Coke and sharing a salad, attracted a lot more attention that they ever realized.

"People didn't know what to make of them," Nico confirmed. "Robert was so beautiful, he had to be gay, and Patti was so dark, she had to be beautiful. But nobody knew, because they were shy, so shy. We would watch them watching us, and everyone would look away if they thought they'd been seen. But they were fascinating, and finally Danny started talking to them, and that meant that other people could as well."

The couple accepted Fields' invitation, and they opened up to him. Patti spoke of her poetry and drawings, Mapplethorpe of his photography, and both confirmed the energies that they derived from each other.

Other people started to notice them. Filmmaker Sandy Daley lived a few doors down on the tenth floor of the Chelsea, in an apartment that had once been occupied by Jackson Pollock. Ten years Patti's senior but as free a spirit as the era demanded, Daley was the first person to capture the couple's gaunt, haunted beauty on celluloid. She filmed Robert, cradled in the arms of a male friend, having his nipple pierced while a largely unseen Patti maintained a constant dialogue of random observations and thoughts, for her film titled, fittingly enough, *Robert Having His Nipple Pierced*.

Daley was constantly encouraging Mapplethorpe's work too. While Patti was at the bookstore by day, the filmmaker would sit and enjoy long conversations with him, on art, photography, film. Then, when Patti came home, the discussions would broaden to include her aspirations, too.

Patti was still pursuing her part-time dream of painting, although the harder she tried, the more she seemed to realize that it was pen not brushstrokes that inspired her, and that an image she might struggle to capture in many hours bent over the easel came a lot easier to her if she just wrote it down. *for a while i drew,* she later wrote in the prose piece "Doctor Love," *but some found out about it and i feared i'd be classified as an artist. i was afraid they'd find a place for me in their society.*

The poetry that she had picked up, abandoned, resumed, and then replaced so many times over the years since childhood was pushing back into her heart. The difference was, this time the voice it used was her own. No more convoluted Spanish dramas; no more following in the footsteps of her foreign-language masters. No more Communism! She wrote as she thought, and having determined that her thought processes themselves were worth preserving, she made her decision: "I had gone to Paris to find myself as an artist," she was quoted as saying in *Patti Smith: An Unauthorized Biography,* "but I came back to New York filled with words and rhythms."

She was writing furiously now, squirreling away her poetry for a time when she felt comfortable enough to publicize it. In the meantime, however, as the doors to recognition began to open, she went to work unlocking more. A meeting with Bobby Neuwirth, one of Bob Dylan's closest friends during the mid-1960s, one of Edie Sedgwick's many lovers, and still a fixture on the New York City music scene, sparked friendship, and he became one of the privileged few to be permitted a glimpse inside her notebooks.

They met at the Chelsea Hotel, of course. One day as she stood in the lobby, clutching her notebook, a voice behind her called, "Hey, poet!" She turned, and the look on her face must have said something, because Neuwirth immediately carried on: "Well, you look like a poet. Do you write like one?" Patti recognized him instantly—she had watched the Dylan documentary *Dont Look Back* often enough, with Neuwirth the dark-humored presence that forever lurks at the master's side—and was promptly flattered.

They talked; they became friends, Neuwirth nurturing the un-schooled talent, the talent accepting his advice and criticism unflinch-ingly. He rewarded her devotion with barely qualified admiration, talking about her work in ways that nobody ever had and recognizing, Patti real-ized, qualities that she had not even sensed herself. "He was the one who really pushed me into writing poetry and kept inspiring me to keep the music in the poetry," she told Lisa Robinson in 1976. "He said we needed a poet." Neuwirth drew her into the circles that he now habitually moved in, as a friend and occasional confidant to the likes of Kris Kristofferson and the Winter brothers, Edgar and Johnny, as they passed through New York City and invariably wound up rooming at the Chelsea.

But it was Janis Joplin who fascinated her the most. Joplin was in town for a show at the Wollman ice skating rink in Central Park. The gig was canceled when the heavens opened up, and it was rescheduled for August. But while she was in New York, Patti laughed later, it was Joplin who showed her how to drink. How to *really* drink.

The two women's conversations, however, rarely revolved around either drink or music. Patti was in full cry now, chasing down that most elusive of themes that had always fascinated her: the moment where pri-vate self becomes public image, without the person even being aware of it. Joplin's greatest regret, Patti said, was that she could not reveal herself as a fragile person, that she needed to keep up the appearance of the hard-bitten boozer.

Other guests passed through the Chelsea, and Patti seemed to meet them all. "Sometimes people say to me, 'oh, you knew all these famous people.' Well, none of us were famous," Patti reminded *Interview*'s Christopher Bollen. "And even the people who were supposedly famous and had some money didn't seem much different from the rest of us. I mean, if you sat in a room with people like Janis Joplin, they had arrogance, but they didn't have bodyguards or paparazzi around them or tons of money. What I'm saying is, that line between us and them was easy to walk across. It was just that the greatness in their work was undeniable, and their arrogance or indulgences were more palatable. Still, they were human beings."

Harry Smith, the great folklorist, filmmaker, and occultist whose painstakingly collected archive of traditional American music influenced Bob Dylan, Joan Baez, and a host of other folkies, was living just a few floors below. Patti met him for the first time on her first day at the hotel, and soon she was spending evenings in his room, crushed in among the heaps of papers, boxes, and general clutter that constituted Smith's manifold collections (and through which he had carved narrow corridors of living space), and singing to him in that strange, reedy whisper that put so many other people in mind of the ghosts that crackled from forgotten 78s. He repaid her, as he did so many of his other friends and benefactors, with a brief cameo in his latest movie, *#18 (Mahagonny)*, an eleven-hour-plus collage of imagery, portraits, and street scenes that he spent two years shooting (1970–1972), and another eight editing down to its final running time of 141 minutes.

She met the Allman Brothers, deep southerners riding the first phase of their eventual superstardom, and closing her eyes decades later as she wrote the liner notes to her album *Twelve*, she could still picture them, "a group of gangly boys gawking at the freaks populating the lobby of the Chelsea Hotel," while she looked on, a midtwenties girl in a straw hat and polka-dot dress.

James Hamilton photographed her, looking every inch a rock star in her own right, with Rod Stewart at a press reception for Stewart's band the Faces. With a wine bottle clutched in her needle-thin hand, and the other hand folded thoughtfully to her mouth, she watched as Stewart held forth from the seat next to hers. "She was crazy about the Faces," Hamilton recalled for his photo book *You Should Have Heard Just What I Seen*.

She ran into Allen Ginsberg, who thought she was a boy. (She would later recount the story to fellow poet Ed Friedman, who would share it with Legs McNeil and Gillian McCain in *Please Kill Me: The Uncensored Oral History of Punk*.) Ginsberg, it seems, was using all his wiles to induce her to join him in his bed, and Patti was exhausting all of hers trying to discourage him. Until finally, she snapped, exasperated. "Look at the tits, Allen. Notice the tits." Patti would always love Ginsberg, not only because he was a great poet but also because he was a New Jerseyite.

William Burroughs was still there, filling the hotel with his peculiar presence and his habitual uniform of hat and black cashmere overcoat. Soon, every impressionable youngster who passed through the Chelsea was affecting the same distinctive look, with Patti at the head of the line. "He was so neat," she said in Robinson's 1976 interview. "Burroughs showed me whole new tunnels to fall through. . . . He was never too crazy about women, but I guess he liked me because I looked like a boy."

While Burroughs's influence at the Chelsea remained strong, in recent years Andy Warhol's presence had begun to shift elsewhere. The artist himself had faded from his old visibility after the disgruntled feminist Valerie Solanas shot him in 1968. Now he was happier remaining back at the Factory. The fragile beauty of Edie Sedgwick was long gone; the curve of Warhol's movie career now enveloped some of the most glamorous drag queens the city had ever seen: Candy Darling, Holly Woodlawn, and Jackie Curtis. His women now were the kind that few other men would knowingly fantasize over, although Warhol himself loved to slyly remind people that when Candy was at her best, it was impossible to believe she was a man.

These remarkable characters formed the core of another exclusive group, Charles Ludlam's Ridiculous Theatrical Company, nominally based at the Sewer, a gay club on West Eighteenth. It was for this company that Curtis, in particular, would fashion bizarre little plays around the mores and immoralities of her own lifestyle. Wayne County, a Georgia native destined to become one of the most provocative rock performers of the age, spoke for many a starstruck ingenue when he admitted that the Ridiculous crew's *The Life of Lady Godiva*, with Jackie Curtis in the title role, completely realigned his life. "I was never the same after seeing [that]. When I first came to New York, I was just a little hippie queen."

Patti was never going to make such a vibrant transition. But Curtis noticed her regardless, hanging around at Max's nightly, and as the playwright put together her next production, *Femme Fatale: The Three Faces of Gloria* (partially titled for the Lou Reed composition "Femme Fatale," which was in turn written about Edie Sedgwick), she earmarked the scrawny poetess for a role.

A tangled masterpiece of improvisation, *Femme Fatale* developed out of Curtis's relationship with the underground actors John Christian and Penny Arcade, both of whom were originally scheduled to appear in the play. Christian, however, was forced to drop out after he was afflicted, he claimed, with such severe agoraphobia that he could no longer leave his apartment. Curtis shrugged and offered Patti his role, without even stopping to ask if the newcomer could act; nor, according to another of the team, actor Leee Black Childers, caring that Curtis and Patti had never particularly hit it off.

Patti won the playwright's heart, however, by throwing herself into the latest game to intrigue the cast of the back room at Max's, another Curtis invention called the Outrageous Lie. The rules were simple. You told the most outrageous lie that you could, on the premise that little lies are easily caught, bigger ones can sometimes survive, but a truly outrageous one will become a part of your personal mythos forever. That was the thing about the outrageous lie: not even the other contestants should be certain whether or not it was actually a lie.

Maybe Joan Crawford really did give Wayne County that brown silk jacket that he wore whenever he could.

Maybe Cyrinda Foxe really did carry the scars from a run-in with the Hell's Angels.

Maybe Nico really did study with Lee Strasberg and hang out with Marilyn Monroe.

And maybe Patti Smith, laboring through her teenage pregnancy, really did get kicked so hard by her unborn child that a tiny leg burst out of her stomach and hung there still kicking till the doctor could jam it back in again.

Any girl who could live through an experience like that, reasoned Curtis, had to have something going for her, and he recommended that Tony Ingrassia, *Femme Fatale*'s director, cast his own eye over her. Ingrassia, too, felt she had a part to play in the production.

Patti had never set foot onstage before—not since that childhood opera, anyway. But you'd never have guessed it. Already most comfortable in the trademark black-urban-guerrilla chic of her later public fame, she was majestic and magnetic, cool, mean and hard-bitten, radiating an intensity that could not have been further from the burlesque grind and exaggerated sexuality of her costars.

With another Warhol associate, Mary Woronov, adding further star power to what was already a spellbinding underground bill, *Femme Fatale: The Three Faces of Gloria* opened at the La MaMa Experimental Theatre Club on East Seventy-Fourth Street on May 6, 1970. The following month, shortly before the play transferred to the upstairs room at Max's, *Gay* magazine's Everett Henderson described it as "an uneven, amusing, boring, hilarious, weird, simplistic study of lots of old movies, gangster riffs and the Sharon Tate murder. . . . I do not dare judge the performances or the direction. Anthony Ingrassia . . . successfully got the actors on stage and whipped them through a suitable number of convulsions . . . energetically play[ing] projections of themselves as stars. . . . If you are fed up with the slick, stainless steel emptiness of Uptown garbage like *Company*, . . . it may amuse or irritate you, thrill you or bore you, but it is robust and it is alive."

The success of *Femme Fatale*, and her part in that success, did not close Patti's eyes to her main pursuit, however. Nor to her continuing ability to magnetize the people she most needed to have around her.

Her own adopted family had expanded by one after she and Mapplethorpe befriended a teenaged junkie named Jim Carroll. He was twenty years old, but, Patti assured him, he possessed an infinitely older soul.

The young man was already establishing a reputation as a poet, and in just a few months the *Paris Review* would cement his position among the city's literary elite by publishing an excerpt from his book *The Basketball Diaries*, an autobiographical account of falling off the rails at one of the city's most exclusive private schools, Trinity. Carroll had served a stint in Rikers for possession of heroin; by spring 1970 he was living at the Chelsea, penning the poetry that would become the Pulitzer-nominated *Living at the Movies*.

Inevitably, he and Patti met just outside the Chelsea, although Carroll had seen her around before that, "checking me out" at Max's Kansas City or watching his readings at St. Mark's Church. According to Carroll's account in *Please Kill Me*, Patti and Mapplethorpe were fighting as Carroll came into view, but the battle stopped the moment she spotted him. "Hey, you're Jim Carroll, right? I'm Patti."

They small-talked for a moment, and then Patti asked if she could drop by his room the following day. She had a book about Native Americans that she wanted to give him.

"Sure," Carroll began. "I'm in room . . ."

"I know what room you're in," she replied.

"Already he was pretty much universally recognized as the best poet of his generation," Patti told the *New York Times*' William Grimes in 2009. "The work was sophisticated and elegant. He had beauty." The wiry blond also became her confidant and sounding board for at least as long as their relationship lasted, a tempestuous era that Carroll later celebrated in his book, *Forced Entries: The Downtown Diaries, 1971–1973*.

Moving into the West Twenty-Third Street loft that Patti and Mapplethorpe had started renting as an "art factory" but that quickly supplanted the Chelsea as their home, he followed Bobby Neuwirth into the select band of people with whom she'd share her poetry. She'd been seduced, Carroll said, not only by the fact that he, too, was a poet, but also by his heroin habit. "I think she would have been disappointed if I'd *stopped*," he told Patricia Morrisroe.

But an even more powerful figure was approaching, one who would finally offer Patti the strength to stop dreaming about her ambitions and start living them.

Sam Shepard, three years Patti's senior, had arrived in New York City in 1963. He'd worked as a bus boy around Greenwich Village while he insinuated himself into the city's lifeblood. He was a musician, a playwright, an author, an actor, and over the course of the next five years, each of these ambitions drew him into its soul.

The band he played drums for, the Holy Modal Rounders, made something of a local impact even before they landed a track on the soundtrack to the film *Easy Rider* in 1969. Shepard was a fixture off-off-Broadway, leading the Theatre Genesis—another of the artistic endeavors that called St. Mark's Church home—to glory. He collected Obies, the *Village Voice*'s greatest theatrical award, like other actors collected reviews: by 1970, he had won half a dozen.

If there was any man on the arts scene at that time who could have given Patti Smith a glimpse of her own future glory, it was Shepard.

5

THE AMAZING TALE OF SKUNKDOG

PATTI WAS DATING Todd Rundgren, the brilliant young Philadelphian who had escaped the clutches of his last band, the Nazz, to launch a wildly idiosyncratic solo career from the upstate New York headquarters of his manager Albert Grossman—the same Albert Grossman who had once managed Dylan and now handled Joplin. Bobby Neuwirth had introduced Patti to Rundgren, and now Rundgren introduced her to Sam Shepard, backstage at a Rounders gig at the Village Gate. His own relationship with Patti wound up soon afterward.

Patti quickly discovered that Shepard was married, with a young son, no less, but their attraction, she insisted, was so pronounced that neither she nor Sam had any choice in the matter. They were destined to be together, for however long they could last. Together they visited the Italian gypsy tattooist Vali to be engraved with permanent reminders of their romance: a lightning bolt for Smith, the Native American symbol of a hawk moon for Shepard. And just to ensure that permanence, Sandy Daley filmed the entire process.

Days they spent discussing their work; nights would see the pair descend upon Max's, "have a lot of rum and get into trouble. We were hell-raisers.

"Sam loved my writing more than anyone I ever knew," Patti told Patricia Morrisroe. "He made me value myself as a writer." He also encouraged her earliest forays from poetry into song. "It had never occurred to me to sing," she told Ramsay Pennybacker of the *Philadelphia Weekly*. "You know, he asked me to write song lyrics to one of his plays, *Mad Dog Blues*. I said, 'I don't know how to write song lyrics.' And he said, 'You write them all the time!'"

He bought Patti her first guitar, a 1931 Gibson acoustic, and she taught herself to play along to a handful of Dylan songs. Meeting new people, especially musicians, she would ask them if they wanted to see a really neat guitar, then bring it out to show them. That guitar has probably been tuned by more famous fingers than any other instrument on earth. Even Bob Dylan would get his hands on it one day.

Shepard now encouraged her to take the next step—to make her debut as a performing poetess. Throughout the summer of 1970, Patti had delivered impromptu poetry readings to whoever cared to stop and listen as they passed through the lobby (and other rooms) of the Chelsea. In February 1971, she booked her first official event, at the St. Mark's Poetry Project's regular Wednesday-night reading.

The performance might have gone quite differently had she not met guitarist Lenny Kaye just a few weeks before. Interviewed on the Rocktropolis network in 1997, Patti recalled, "I read an article he wrote about a cappella music in 1970 and was so taken with it, I called to thank him for writing it and we became friends." Soon she was showing up every Saturday night at the Village Oldies record store on Bleecker Street where Kaye worked. He would crank up the oldies, the Deauvilles and the Moonglows and company, and the two of them would simply dance. "So that's how we got friendly," Kaye reflected in *Please Kill Me*.

Born three days before Patti, on December 27, 1946, Kaye was the nephew of songwriter Larry Kusik, composer of "A Time for Us" from *Romeo and Juliet* and "Speak Softly Love" from *The Godfather*. With connections like that, Kaye's musical career had started promisingly: under Uncle Larry's tutelage, Kaye cut the single "Crazy Like a Fox," released in early 1966 under the pseudonym Link Cromwell. Unfortunately, his star had been in decline ever since. There was no follow-up, and Kaye was now performing around the bars with a band, the Zoo, and supplementing his income with freelance music journalism. He broke into *Rolling Stone* in May 1969, with a review of the oddball Lothar and the Hand People's first album, a smorgasbord of theremin-led lunacy; now he was writing reviews for *Fusion* and *Crawdaddy* too, and editing the music column for the men's magazine *Cavalier*.

Patti, too, was looking to break into music journalism, and their early conversations revolved around the introductions that Kaye could bring her. But he was fascinated by her other writing as well, and as he looked through her treasured notebooks of poems, and felt the rock rhythms that percolated so naturally through her verse, a crazy notion began to coalesce.

Her poetry reading was already scheduled, and Patti knew that it would be the easiest thing in the world for her to just get it over with, take the podium and spout her poetry, one more in the long line of hopefuls who haunted St. Mark's. Or she could *perform*—and what better way to brush away the cobwebs than to elevate her poetry to the plateau she envisioned when she wrote it?

Would Kaye be interested in accompanying her on three or four poems? He would.

On February 10, Kaye joined Patti for her debut performance. Her Factory friend Gerard Malanga was the "headline" act, recruited by Robert Mapplethorpe to give Smith her break. And the audience that night spilled far from the customary gathering of beatniks and nobodies who normally swelled the attendance into double figures.

Sam Shepard, naturally, was there. So was Bobby Neuwirth, accompanied by Edgar and Johnny Winter, and another of Patti and Mapplethorpe's friends, Steve Paul, founder of the Scene nightclub. Bookstore owner Terry Ork, whose eponymous record label would become one of the key documents of mid-1970s New York City, was there, as were Danny Fields and journalist Lisa Robinson. Jim Carroll turned up accompanied by some boys that Patti described as fashion models—because that was what people thought they looked like.

Allen Ginsburg arrived with John Giorno, whose Giorno Poetry Systems was the loudest voice in the universe of New York City poetics. Mutual friends from the Ridiculous Theatrical Company, Malanga's cohorts from the Factory . . . they all piled out that evening, and nobody really knew what to expect from the skinny girl who cleared her throat to remind the audience, "Anytime if you can't hear me, tell me, because I don't want to beat off alone up here, it's really dumb." The bespectacled guitarist sat grinning beside her.

They didn't know what to expect, but she gave it to them regardless, her speech littered with a nervous overuse of the word "like": "If, um, anytime like you can't hear me like tell me because like, um, OK, um . . . Today is like, um, Bertolt Brecht's birthday and, um, February 10, and in tribute to [him] first thing I want to do is like, um, is just a little version, my version of like one of his great masterpieces. Oh, fuck, I don't even got it.'Mack the Knife.'"

It was Bob Dylan who had introduced Patti to Brecht in the first place, back in 1965. Studying her copy of his newly released *Bringing It All Back Home*, she'd begun taking note of the records that littered the floor of the cover photograph. One was by singer Lotte Lenya, wife of Brecht's songwriting partner Kurt Weill and the custodian of the two men's works. Patti was intrigued. More than thirty years later, she explained the fascination to Ed Vulliamy of the *Guardian*. "I wanted to listen to whatever Bob was listening to, which then opened a whole world to me, of Bertolt Brecht and Kurt Weill. And in particular the way in which Brecht's work blends art and activism, and the strength of his characters. It's this idea: that power can come from below, from the people."

Lenny Kaye kicked up a barely amplified rhythm on his guitar, and Patti caterwauled, uncertain but convincing regardless, through Brecht's "Mack the Knife." You could hear her confidence building as the song went on, and when she did call a halt with an off-mike "OK," the audience immediately responded with a ripple of bemused but genuine applause.

Patti was not the first poet to grapple with rock 'n' roll. Ginsberg had been moving in that direction for years, even before he recorded a clutch of songs with Bob Dylan the previous year, while Anne Sexton had toured with a full-fledged jazz rock band, Her Kind, during the late 1960s. And then, of course, there was the dribble of rockers who saw themselves as poets too: Jim Morrison in America, Marc Bolan in England, and so on. They were different, though, because they operated on stages that could handle the cross-pollination: Bolan haunted the hash-hazed dens of psychedelic London, where whimsy and fantasy were part and parcel of the multimedia celebration; Morrison had a full-fledged promotional machine to ram his poetic aspirations down his audience's throat. And Sexton's first live performance was at a rally for Eugene McCarthy at Boston's Fenway Park in July 1968, while her tours tended to visit museums and galleries as much as established concert and poetry centers.

But Sexton's motives were not that far from Patti's fledgling dreams. The band, Sexton averred in a summer 1971 interview with Barbara Kevles of the *Paris Review*, "opens up my poems in a new way by involving them in the sound of rock music. . . . People flock to Bob Dylan, Janis Joplin and the Beatles—these are the popular poets of the English-speaking world." Patti may not have seen matters so clearly or so calculatedly. But she understood them all the same.

"Mack the Knife" over, Kaye stepped away. Now Patti stood alone, smiling uncertainly, looking out at the luminaries gathered to watch her. Her next reading, she declared, was dedicated to "crime," and then she sped on, through unaccompanied renditions of her own creations—all composed as poems, but now teetering on the edge of something inherently musical too: "Oath," "The Devil Has a Hangnail," "The Wait for You," "You're the River," "A Saint in Any Form," "The Murdered Boy," and "White Lightning," before Kaye reappeared for a keening "A Fire of Unknown Origin" and the wild "Don't Hang Me Up, Jesse James," dedicated "to all my favorite guys, including Bobby Neuwirth, who really helped me with my shit."

"Prayer," "a little prayer I made up," followed, coyly dedicated to François Villon. "He was really neat because he was a poet but he was a murderer too."

The climax of her performance, however, was "Ballad of a Bad Boy."

"This is for Sam," Patti said quietly, before she and Kaye launched into a rhythmic riff and swaggering chant that came so close to predicting the pair's future that the modern listener spends the entire performance anticipating the moment that the rest of the band will kick in. They don't, but the tuning dial was already racing toward Radio Ethiopia, and no matter who the history books are currently crediting with the blueprint for New York City punk rock, "Ballad of a Bad Boy" really was Year Zero.

I wept on a stock car / I captured the junkyards / and I sped thru the canyons . . . wrecking cars was my art.

A "negative effect" rippled through the room, she told David Fricke of *Rolling Stone* in 2004, as Kaye unleashed "his sonic interpretation of a stock car race." The audience shifted and grumbled; expressions turned exasperated; eyes and ears averted themselves. Poetry, those angry faces seemed to say, was about the power of words, not the needling of noise.

Patti disagreed. "I took that [negativity] as a positive sign."

Despite the presence of so many poets in the audience, Patti continued to feel like an outsider, a voice on the fringes of even the New York underground's left-field sensibilities. And although she knew the traditional routes into their world, she eschewed them. Conventional poetry readings bored her; she would rather play a rock 'n' roll show, to a rock 'n' roll audience, than endure another night of studious academia in front of her so-called peers.

That is the route she took. It was a grueling apprenticeship, she said. Nobody was interested in what she had to say, and she knew that if she had a fifteen-minute slot, ten of them would be spent arguing with the audience. But it was exposure and it was experience.

Her immediate plans, however, moved away from music and verse. One evening, which ultimately stretched over two, Patti and Shepard sat down to write together, passing a typewriter back and forth to create a play that Patti titled *Cowboy Mouth*, from a line in Dylan's "Sad-Eyed Lady of the Lowlands." Part autobiography, part wishful thinking, the play is the story of Slim and Cavalle, two lovers—"two big dreamers," Patti told Robb Baker of *After Dark*—whose life together has deteriorated to the point of wastefulness, a state of affairs for which Slim blames nobody more than Cavalle.

He seeks redemption by asking her to tell him about the life of the French poet Gerard de Nerval, a supposed madman who would walk the park of the Palais Royal, with his pet lobster on a pale blue ribbon. He liked lobsters, he claimed, because they didn't bark. He also had a pet raven, to whom he taught the words *J'ai soif*—"I'm thirsty"—and when Nerval died, hanging himself on January 25, 1855, with a relic that he insisted was the Queen of Sheba's garter, the raven circled his body, calling out those same words.

Other times, Cavalle bemoans her lot in life: savage memories of a childhood spent in therapy, and the bitter pill of having grown from an ugly duckling into an ugly duck. "I never got to be the fucking swan. I paid all those dues and I never got to be the fucking swan."

A third character, the Lobster Man, is introduced, a would-be rock 'n' roll savior, all glam and leather, who soon transforms into the same kind of martyr as the poets Cavalle waxed so lyrical about: the play ends with Cavalle delivering a monologue, while the Lobster Man takes a gun and shoots himself in the head. It was, Patti mourned, the true story of her life with Shepard: two people who came together in love but were destined for "a sad end. . . . We knew we couldn't stay together."

They headed straight into rehearsals for the play anyway. Actor Robert Glaudini was cast as the Lobster Man—but the playwrights themselves took on the roles of doomed lovers Cavalle (Patti) and Slim (Sam). "It was just a play between us," Patti explained to Robb Baker. "We had lots of alchemy, because we had written the play, we were sayin' our own lines. Lots of light comin' out of that stage." Alongside another Shepard short, *Back Bog Beast Bait*, the play was set to open at the American Place Theater, at St. Clement's Episcopal Church at 423 West Forty-Sixth Street, on April 29, 1971.

Patti's latest transition from poet to stage actress was not seamless. According to the program issued for that opening-night performance, the theatrical union Actors' Equity had forced her to change her name before registering, to avoid being confused with another actress named Patti Smith. She became Johnny Guitar. In addition, claimed the program notes, "she goes abroad twice a year to sing in bars, wearing a black dress and leaning on pianos. She says her best number is 'My Funny Valentine.' She also says, 'I ain't no actress.'"

Cowboy Mouth was scarcely a success, not even to its cocreator Shepard. Just weeks earlier, he had taken the stage at the same theater with his wife, O-Lan, in another of his plays, *Mad Dog Blues*, and it was no secret among those who knew of his extramarital romance that O-Lan's character was at least partly based on Patti. Now here was Patti in person, playing herself while Sam did the same, and it was more than Shepard could tolerate. It was difficult enough to live certain elements of his own life sometimes, without then reliving them on stage.

A few days earlier, Shepard had been asked to join the Holy Modal Rounders in Vermont. He wasn't sure at first whether he wanted to leave New York City. But one night of *Cowboy Mouth* made up his mind for him. Without a word to Patti, he fled north and, from there, took his wife and son to London.

Patti consoled herself by delving deeper into her writing, both poetry and journalism. She landed another reading at St. Mark's, opening for Jim Carroll, and found herself headlining the show instead when Carroll was busted for possession in Rye, New York, and detained half the night by the local sheriff. She was invited to introduce a few other readers, too. She wrote her first (and only) review for *Rolling Stone* in the August 19, 1971, issue, lavishing praise on Todd Rundgren's newly released *Runt* LP but neglecting to mention that they had been lovers. "Like Mozart," she wrote, "Todd Rundgren never wanted to be born; his mother labored hard to put him here and he's fought hard to singe his musical autograph in the progressive pages of rock & roll."

Another friend stepped forward.

Three years earlier, Sandy Pearlman had been a writer for *Crawdaddy* when he had the idea of putting a band together to perform a series of musical poems he had written, *Imaginos*. Since that time, the band he created, Soft White Underbelly, had morphed into the Stalk-Forrest Group, but it was about to change its name again, to the Blue Öyster Cult, and set out on a career pioneering a seismic brand of militaristically mystical metal. Pearlman would remain their manager, and looking to expand his stable of clients, he was pushing Patti to delve deeper into rock 'n' roll as well.

His dream of pairing her with a keyboard player and composer named Lee Crabtree collapsed when Crabtree committed suicide following a row with his parents over an inheritance from his grandfather. So Pearlman suggested Patti join the Blue Öyster Cult instead, as a behind-the-scenes writer if not a performer. Patti never took him up on the offer, but she did start dating the band's keyboard and rhythm guitar player, Allen Lanier, igniting what would become the most permanent relationship she had ever known. She and Lanier would remain partners until 1978.

Other opportunities arose. She talked with promoter Steve Paul about the possibility of putting together a band with another of his clients, guitarist Rick Derringer; they even took a few promo photos together. Patti stepped back from this project as well. She wanted to perform, but she wanted to do so completely on her own terms, with a musical collaborator whose own ambitions walked hand-in-hand with hers. Not a yes-man per se, but somebody who would allow her to lay down the law when she saw fit to do so, while at the same time putting forward ideas that she would wish she'd thought of herself.

Steve Paul moved on to offer Iggy Pop a berth in Derringer's band (he, too, turned it down). The Blue Öyster Cult moved on to sign with Columbia Records and become the most significant American metal merchants of the 1970s.

And Patti moved on as well. In September 1971, she appeared for the first time before cameras being held by somebody who was not a close friend or associate. The BBC was in New York City, shooting a documentary about the Chelsea Hotel and interviewing its most familiar—or persistent—denizens.

With her feathered hair, silver jewelry, and a beguilingly engaging smile, archetypal hippie chick Patti was among those who eased their way into shot, performing a short poem for the cameras that, to the surprise, perhaps, of everybody she told, made it into the final cut. Just six lines long, "my little prayer for New York" is performed by a clearly shy and obviously nervous young woman, batting her eyes at the camera and gazing upwards from beneath her bangs.

New York is the thing that seduced me
New York is the thing that formed me
New York is the thing that deformed me
New York is the thing that perverted me
New York is the thing that converted me
And New York's the thing I love, too.

Compared to much of the rest of the documentary, her verse takes its significance only from the retrospective identity of its performer. But it is strangely affecting as well, an acknowledgement not only of the magnetism of New York City but also of the hold that the city has on so many imaginations. And it was that hold that Patti wanted to infiltrate for herself. Other performers became a part of New York City, but that was a one-way street. She wanted the traffic to run in both directions.

September 1971 also saw the Detroit-based rock magazine *Creem* publish three of Patti's poems, at the same time recruiting her as one of their occasional freelance contributors. "For Bob Neuwirth," "Autobiography," and "For Sam Shepard" (the last a slightly revised "Ballad of a Bad Boy") all appeared in that issue, making this her first true step outside of New York City. The magazine's nationwide distribution allowed readers across America to experience Patti's writing firsthand, and Sonic Youth's Thurston Moore spoke for many when he recalled for Robert Matheu and Brian J. Bowe's book *Creem: America's Only Rock 'n' Roll Magazine*, "The first time I ever heard of Patti Smith was in *Creem* . . . when they ran her poetry. Those pictures of her with the short Keith Richards hair and the cigarette—they completely made you stop in your tracks. What is that? It read so good and looked so good, it made me realize that that's what I wanted to do. I want to go to New York and see that."

She was writing occasional pieces, too, for *Rock* magazine, a monthly competitor to *Rolling Stone* that took itself very seriously indeed—certainly too seriously to entertain a writer who, dispatched to interview Eric Clapton, commenced her inquisition by asking him for his six favorite colors.

Finally, she received a call from tiny publisher Telegraph Books, run out of a storefront on Jones Street by writers Andrew Wylie and Victor Bockris. They wanted to publish the first collection of her poetry.

In his 1999 biography of Patti, Bockris outlined her appeal to Telegraph Books: that she provided, for the first time, a voice for a generation that was still attempting to adjust to the violence that had marked the end of the 1960s, violence that shattered the hippie dream that was the hallmark of the decade's final years. The fatal stabbing at the Rolling Stones' Altamont Free Concert in December 1969, the Manson murders that shocked the world earlier that same year, the continued war in Vietnam, the US government's increasingly heavy-handed response to domestic protest, "the increasingly dangerous drug scene that had changed from something peaceful and friendly to something violent, dangerous, and criminal"—all of these things were battering a generation that had been persuaded, however fleetingly, to dream of a man-made utopia. Patti Smith, Bockris reasoned, was the voice that could help them survive the storm.

She may not, Bockris continued, have been aware of this calling, and may not have been prepared to answer it. But he and Wylie glimpsed her potential regardless, and they would do their level best to encourage her to answer it.

Gerard Malanga made the necessary introductions, although Bockris has also insisted that it would have been difficult for anybody on the New York City arts scene of the day *not* to be aware of Patti Smith. He wrote in *Patti Smith: An Unauthorized Biography*: "For a short time in the spring and summer of 1971, she was high on the list of New York's 'Hot 100' who were going to Make It, and was turning down offers right, left, and center."

This is probably an exaggeration. Yes, she had succeeded in her handful of public readings to date, before an audience composed largely of friends and associates. Yes, she was making some headway in the world of rock journalism. But they were baby steps at best, and if Patti's personality was sufficiently urgent that the people she encountered were not quick to forget her, she was scarcely the first young up-and-comer to have that effect on people. Any offers that Patti was receiving at this time were being made by would-be entrepreneurs who were in the exact same position she was: just starting out on the first rung of their chosen ladder and casting around for anybody who could help them move a little higher. Which is precisely what Patti was doing when she accepted Telegraph Books' offer.

Fronted by an indelibly atmospheric black-and-white photograph taken by New Yorker Judy Linn (destined to become one of the young Patti's most dedicated chroniclers), Patti's first book of poems, *Seventh Heaven*, would emerge as a forty-seven-page collection of twenty-two poems, dedicated to actress Anita Pallenberg. It would be published the following spring as a limited run of fifty signed and numbered first editions, alongside a regular run of one thousand copies selling at a dollar apiece.

Writing it was simple, or so Patti later laughed in the *New York Times Magazine*. Speaking with writers Tony Hiss and David McClelland in late 1975, she explained, "I'd sit at the typewriter and type until I felt sexy, then I'd go and masturbate to get high, and then I'd come back in that higher place and write some more."

By now more than a year had passed since her first St. Mark's reading, and Patti sensibly opted not to include in her book any of the verses performed there, nor those that might have been glimpsed in *Creem*. Instead, she included her tributes to her sister Linda, actress/singer Marianne Faithfull, aviator Amelia Earhart, and actress Marilyn Monroe, under her married name, Marilyn Miller. The collection also featured her odes to French martyr Joan of Arc and one of the actresses who have portrayed her, Renee Falconetti, and her elegy to Edie Sedgwick, written just days after the news of the beauty-no-more's drug death on November 16, 1971.

I'd like to see / her rise again / her white white bones / with baby Brian Jones.

Patti refused to rest while she awaited publication.

Christmas Day 1971 saw her return to the Poetry Project, to run through a dozen verses, including several ("Mary Jane," "Renee Falconetti," "Death by Water," "Seventh Heaven," and "Amelia Earhart") that were scheduled for inclusion in *Seventh Heaven*. Again it was a well-received performance—less immediately incendiary than her debut, of course, because people now had some notion of what to expect, but better attended.

Just days after that, she began packing her bags for her next trip to Europe. John Calder, one half of the London poetry press Calder and Boyars, was about to publish the first-ever British anthology of Telegraph Books writers, and arranged for Patti, Bockris, Wylie, and Malanga to visit London in the new year, to perform a reading for Better Books, the city's premier underground bookstore.

It was an evocative collaboration. Calder was the first publisher to make William Burroughs available in the UK; Better Books was the first British venue ever to host a reading by Allen Ginsberg, in 1965. The store's address of 94 Charing Cross Road was as familiar as any in the world of modern poetry, and seven years after writer and musician Tom McGrath predicted that Ginsberg's debut would be remembered as a pivotal moment in the history of English poetry, and perhaps even England itself, so another turning point arrived as Patti Smith prepared to take the stage.

Or so Patti's admirers would later say.

Calder booked a small but well-appointed Soho theater for the occasion; decked out in bright red plush, the venue was, as its address suggests, more familiar with the screening of porn films at that time, but its intimacy lent itself well to both the reading and the audience. Bockris would recall 125 people turning up for the event, including the English poet Michael Horovitz (*not*, as is often claimed, the American Michael Horowitz) and Eric Mottram, the editor of the British magazine *Poetry Review*. On the other hand, the possibly more objective British rock critic Nick Kent, who also attended the event, recalled there being no more than fifteen people in the room for Patti's recital.

Either way, one suspects that Malanga's association with Warhol was a greater draw for the audience than the unknown Patti Smith. Indeed, the greatest impact she had yet made on the country was the previous October, when a decidedly uncomplimentary topless still from *Robert Having His Nipple Pierced* appeared on the cover of the local listings magazine *Time Out*. In later years, similar images—the fruits of her early photographic sessions with Robert Mapplethorpe—would come to haunt Patti, as would-be critics seized upon them as evidence of a less-than-salubrious past. At the time, however, the uncaptioned photograph of a heavily-made-up Smith, clad in a beret and wielding a hammer, barely even offered titillation to whoever picked up a copy.

But Bockris would proclaim her short (ten or so minutes) performance a triumph. He'd recall the lost-little-girl act with which Patti first seduced and then cajoled the crowd, and laughingly reflect upon the moment of panic that apparently racked her as she took the stage and announced that she'd forgotten to pack the one piece that she intended reading that night and would have to rely on her memory alone.

As Bockris remembered in *Please Kill Me*, "she told this poemlike story, and she said, 'I haven't finished writing this yet, but it goes like this. 'The boy looked at Jesus as he came down the steps.'" Then, as if she recalled the effect that a similar confession had at her first St. Mark's reading, she paused after six minutes to declare, "Gee, uh, I forgot it."

By which time, Bockris reported in *Patti Smith: An Unauthorized Biography*, "she had the audience completely mesmerized. Afterward, some of the awed poets who stayed afterward told [us] that the Telegraph Poets, as we were billing ourselves, had changed the London poetry scene overnight."

Reading through the British poetry press from the weeks and months that followed, one deems it highly unlikely that they had. British and, in particular, London poetry was a highly insular creature at that time, conscious of the impact that the likes of Ginsburg had had in the 1960s but anxious if not desperate to draw away from that influence, too—to establish itself as a separate creation that owed nothing to its American cousins. The idea that even the collective weight of Malanga, Smith, Bockris, and Wylie could redirect thought processes that were already so entrenched was one that only the most naive mind would entertain.

Nevertheless, the visit was victorious, and before it wrapped up, the crew indulged themselves with a photo shoot outside the home of poet Ezra Pound in Kensington. Patti also found time for an unscheduled reunion with Sam Shepard. Then it was back to New York City and Patti's third assault on theater-land, at the La MaMa Experimental Theatre Club in March 1972.

The play *Island* was written and directed by Patti's *Femme Fatale* director, Tony Ingrassia, and stage-managed by Leee Black Childers, and it essentially served as a large-scale reunion for one of the most controversial theatrical troupes of the day, the cast of *Andy Warhol's Pork*. That play's six-week run in London had granted the crew transatlantic notoriety, and now Geri Miller, Cherry Vanilla, Tony Zanetta, Wayne County, and Jamie Di Carlo were back on home soil to present *Island*, which Zanetta would later describe as "probably Ingrassia's best play." It was the story of a bunch of freaks having a picnic on the deck of a Fire Island beach house, at the same time that a US naval destroyer is making its way toward the island, apparently to arrest all the weirdoes besmirching that particular socialite paradise.

"As the play progressed," recalled Cherry Vanilla in her memoir *Lick Me*, "the destroyer got closer and closer to shore, and the action got more and more chaotic. A luncheon scene with all fourteen of the play's characters seated around a huge picnic table, ferociously eating, drinking, passing dishes, and delivering scripted lines amid a cacophony of improvised ones, though a bitch to enact, was a prime example of Ingrassia's genius—or madness."

Vanilla's role was that of a sex-crazed hippie who fucked everyone in sight. County played a transvestite revolutionary ("a few of us were really typecast in *Island*," Vanilla quipped), and Patti was cast as a wired and wiry speed freak whose lines revolved primarily around the fact that Brian Jones was dead.

It was a dry, brittle role, and somehow it seemed to fit her personality. Certainly Patti made little impression on her costars. "Maybe it was shyness," Vanilla remembered on another occasion, "but she didn't mingle with the rest of us at all, which was unusual for actors in a production." There was, she continued, "no big negativity or nastiness, no big deal, no drama." She just didn't say much, so nobody said much to her. "I always gave her the benefit of the doubt, that she was just shy around us," she concluded.

The world of *Island*, with its colorful cast of freaks, was far from the universe in which Patti was now more accustomed to circulate. Jim Carroll, for one, thought she was wasted in theater, even in a production as loosely choreographed as *Island*. "Even though there were no real lines, and she was free to improvise as much as she wanted, she was still restricted by the outline of the play and that wasn't what Patti was about."

Patti agreed with him. At the same time that *Island* was winning plaudits from across the off-off-Broadway crowd (and was even being considered for a Broadway slot, to be directed by Jack Hofsiss), she knew that she was approaching the end of her career as a theatrical performer. "Everybody was asking me to do stuff," she recalled in her 1976 interview with Lisa Robinson. "I was dispersing myself all over New York."

Spring 1972 brought another reading at St. Mark's, and in August, one more return to the stage, playing the role of Jane in the New York Theater Ensemble's production of playwright Hal Craven's *Thunderstorms New York Style*. It was a short-lived venture, just an end-of-month six nights at the East Second Street venue, but it capped a remarkably hectic few weeks, in which she also caught the Rolling Stones when they played at Madison Square Garden and sat down for her first-ever full interview (with Victor Bockris) for publication in a Philadelphia arts magazine.

She could disperse herself no more. "I went into hiding," she told Robinson. "It was the right thing for me to just sit down and find out what was going on inside me—I'd been working on the surface for so long. I was never phony, it's just that I was moving more on an image basis than on a heart or soul basis."

Nevertheless, her first instinct was to remake her image once again. She decided to teach herself how to become a girl. She went shopping for dresses and jewelry; she learned to walk in high heels, and she modeled in front of the mirror wearing silk stockings and garter belts. Hours, she told Amy Gross, were devoted to "sitting around completely self-conscious with all this stuff . . . trying to figure out what all this girl stuff meant."

But to truly figure out what it all meant, she'd need help from an unlikely source. For the next step in her self-examination, Patti would return to Paris with sister Linda—to commune, she said, with the spirit of Jim Morrison.

6

PICASSO LAUGHING

PATTI NEVER REALLY believed that Jim Morrison was dead, a lack of conviction she shared with a surprisingly large number of people. As soon as the first reports of his demise came in from Paris, where he had moved in spring 1971, mystery had surrounded his passing. How it happened, who saw it happen, who saw the body—all of these questions were up in the air, and Morrison's friends back in Los Angeles could not help but remember all the occasions when he had mused aloud about the possibility of simply vanishing, of placing his entire life and career behind him and simply disappearing into anonymity.

"How do you even know he was in the coffin?" asked bandmate Ray Manzarek when he heard about the sealed box and the unannounced funeral that laid the Lizard King to rest. "How do you know it wasn't 150 lbs of fucking sand? We'll never know the real truth now. It's all gonna be rumors and stories from here on out."

Morrison was the third rock 'n' roll star to die in less than nine months, following Jimi Hendrix in September and Janis Joplin in October. Joplin had died less than a year after she and Patti met for the first time, overdosing on heroin and alcohol at the Landmark Motor Hotel in Hollywood—one of the boys to the day she died. It was like a biblical plague, or at least the end of an era, and along with everyone else, Patti struggled to make sense of the cull. But when Jimi and Janis died, they stayed dead. Morrison, on the other hand, was out of his box and running around before the soil had even settled on his all-but-unmarked grave.

The first sightings were reported within days, although most were certainly mere misidentification. American singer-songwriter Elliott Murphy relocated to Paris that same summer, busking around the Metro, "and there were so many guys who looked just like Morrison in his later bearded stage."

Morrison appeared in San Francisco, and gave Bank of America teller Walt Fleischer the thrill of his life by cashing some checks there. He spent some time in L.A., hanging around the gay bars in full black leather. He was spotted in Tibet, living the life of a monk. He was in Australia, limping around on a recently broken leg.

He was in Africa, he was in Israel, and he was definitely in the American Midwest, where he developed a taste for dropping in on local radio stations in the early hours of the morning, secure in the knowledge that the only people listening would be a handful of insomniac truckers and the local hippie acid case who'd been having fantasies like this ever since another round of rumors insisted that Paul McCartney had perished in an automobile accident.

So Jim Morrison was not dead, he had simply disappeared, and Patti's latest trip to Paris was timed deliberately to catch the first anniversary of Morrison's *disappearance*: July 3, 1972. But she would still make her way to his graveside first. She dreamed, she said, that he would rise from the ground, or wherever else he might be hiding, to sing a duet with her. She thought "What's Wrong with Me" would be a suitable selection.

Patti and the Doors went way back. After Robert Mapplethorpe scored her tickets to their 1968 appearance at the Fillmore East, she had bought all their albums and listened to them ceaselessly, knowing that the words that Morrison wove were reflected in the rhythms that drove her own creative beat. She read his lyrics and learned from his style; she built on his vision and saw her own taking shape. And when she arrived in Paris and found Morrison's grave, *there was nothing. a dirt site in section 6*, she wrote in *Creem* in June 1975; *no headstone no vibration no flowers no feeling. just a little plastic plaque with the word AMI friend the only thing Jim Morrison ever wanted.*

Morrison did not show up, but a rainstorm did, a pounding Parisian downpour that turned the soil of the cemetery into clinging mud and blanked out even the most hopeful of imaginings. Patti stood for two hours, drenched to the skin and growing increasingly miserable before she arrived at perhaps the one conclusion that Morrison would have offered her, had he been able—or willing—to do so: Stop looking to the heroes of your past for approval. Look to yourself and your future. As she left, she said, she passed Rimbaud's grave. She barely gave it a second glance.

Patti returned from Paris reborn, shaking off the ashes of her past personae. Not one of them, she now knew, was more than a cloak that could disguise her; it was time to delve deep into her own psyche in search of the spirit that she shared with Jim Morrison.

There could be no more excuses. There could be no more heroes. She was the only idol she would ever need.

The reinvention began immediately. Her latest quest to understand "girl stuff" didn't matter anymore. She no longer needed the accoutrements. She had no need for overt femininity. It was not the reality of womanhood that was opening up in her mind, but the options that it opened to her. Not as a hard-faced peasant woman, not as a mystic gypsy princess, and certainly not as a pouting pussycat creation who would devour the attention of the outside world through looks and demeanor alone—heaven knew there were enough of those around already, including many of the women who would later take it upon themselves to criticize Patti's appearance and behavior—but as a woman in herself.

A century earlier, Patti took to reminding people, Rimbaud had predicted that the next wave of great writers would be women, and speaking at a time when female authors tended to occupy themselves with feminine pursuits, he was certainly stepping out onto a limb. But the intervening hundred years had proved him correct. "He was the first guy who ever made a big women's liberation statement, saying that when women release themselves from the long servitude of men, they're really gonna gush," Patti declared in one of her poetry performances. "New rhythms, new poetries, new horrors, new beauties. And I believe in that completely."

Patti's second collection of poems, *kodak*, published toward the end of 1972 by the Middle Earth Press of Philadelphia, would emphasize this conviction. The nine poems, spread across seventeen pages, are dominated by Patti's vision of womanhood triumphant, including a reprise of "Renee Falconetti" alongside another piece in honor of artist Georgia O'Keeffe: *great lady painter / what she do now / she goes out with a stick / and kills snakes.*

Even the title piece, a plea from a killer to French documentarian Georges Franju (director of *Le sang des bêtes*—"The Blood of Beasts"— shot in a Paris slaughterhouse), leaves the reader in no doubt as to the nature of the stalking horror that mercilessly eyes its victim. Quotes the murderer, *my initials are PLS and I'd be pleased to leave my monogram.* PLS—Patti Lee Smith.

Patti left behind her own mark—"PATTI SMITH 1946"—stenciled on the wall of her West Twenty-Third Street loft, when she and Robert Mapplethorpe moved out in late 1972. The time had come for the two to part company, at least as roommates. "Separate ways together," was how she described it in *Just Kids*; "we went our separate ways, but within walking distance of one another." Mapplethorpe moved across the road from one of John Lennon and Yoko Ono's properties on Bond Street; Patti moved into an apartment on East Tenth with boyfriend Allen Lanier. Being apart from Mapplethorpe would be difficult at times, especially with Lanier out of town so much as the Blue Öyster Cult's career picked up speed, but they both had their own lives to build around their careers, and now they could watch each other grow.

To coincide with the publication of *kodak*, Patti booked three public performances at the Mercer Arts Center, a club/hangout that backed onto the old Broadway Central Hotel and was establishing itself as an alternative to the now gruelingly fashionable Max's. Patti's friend Jane Friedman was acting as her manager by this point, and it was Friedman who was in charge of booking the Mercer's acts.

The Arts Center was a magnificent environment. Built around three stories' worth of rooms, it offered rehearsal space, crash pads, and anything else an aspiring artist might require. It also featured a boutique stacked with bizarre plastic miniskirts and the distinctly left-field couture that would soon inspire a visiting Malcolm McLaren to open his Sex boutique in London; a kitchen kitted out with video machines, on which all comers were invited to show their latest creations; and so much more. At the Mercer, the likes of the New York Dolls and Wayne County's Queen Elizabeth cut their performing chops, and Friedman was swift to offer Patti a berth on its stage, in the club-like surroundings of the Oscar Wilde Room.

It was a bold move on Friedman's part, and an even more courageous one for Patti to accept. Despite the Arts Center's all-encompassing mission statement, audiences expecting an evening of degenerate rock 'n' roll, a la the Dolls' most excessive press reports, were ill prepared for the lone woman who emerged with nothing more musical than a toy piano, a trumpet, and a megaphone. As her performances became more regular, her ten minutes were as likely to be devoted to shooting down hecklers as reciting her verse.

Sometimes she would laugh and either win or shame the heckler into silence. Sometimes she would curse and hope that the audience would curse with her. Sometimes she would ignore it, and "sometimes I'll seduce him to do it more." She told English journalist Charles Shaar Murray in 1976, "I'm just reacting. I don't have a stage act—I don't have a stage *persona*. I don't turn on a separate set of reflexes when I get on the stage. I'm the same person I am here. In fact, often I'm better here than I am up there. . . . Sometimes I really dig people who give me a hard time, because it's friction, but it's *reaction*."

She would execute dances and tell jokes. There were times when she felt more like a stand-up comedian or a late-night TV host than a poet, but that suited her. She had never wanted to be a simple poet anyway—a point that Allen Ginsberg would make in 1973, when he characterized her work as a hybrid, conscious or otherwise, of "the Russian style of declaimed poetry, which is memorized, and the American development of oral poetry that was from the coffee houses. . . . Then there's an element that goes along with borrowing from the pop stars and that spotlight, too, and that glitter."

It was Ginsberg, too, who first predicted that Patti could become a national figure; maybe not a superstar, and probably not even a household name, "but it would be interesting if that did develop into a national style. IF the national style could organically integrate that sort of arty personality—the arty Rimbaud—in its spotlight with makeup and T-shirt."

Right now, however, she was bottom of the bill at the Mercer, her ten-minute recitals prefacing performances by the likes of Ruby and the Rednecks, Moogy and the Rhythm Kings, and Teenage Lust, with Patti often feeling fortunate if she could complete a poem or two. But that would change. By early 1973, Patti was more or less a fixture on the weekly bill, and would even be facing down the Dolls' most partisan audience, as that band set about shoving themselves into a limelight that really didn't seem that keen on acknowledging them. In New York City, David Johansson, Johnny Thunders, and company were widely regarded as the city's next big export. To the rest of the world, they were a joke.

Patti continued to flit across the Manhattan arts scene. January 1973 saw her undertake another of her sporadic theatrical ventures, when she appeared at St. Mark's Theatre Genesis, playing the part of Dixie in Sam Shepard's new play *Blue Bitch*. She also appeared in lingerie designer Fernando Sánchez's latest fashion show, modeling furs on the runway.

On April 2, 1973, Patti reunited with guitarist Lenny Kaye for five nights opening for drag queen Holly Woodlawn at Reno Sweeney. A cabaret launched the previous year by songwriter Lewis Friedman and Eliot Hubbard, Reno Sweeney was what writer Vito Russo called "the center of the universe during the now-legendary cabaret revival of the early '70s. Everybody who was anybody either played its famous Paradise Room or sat in the audience to watch." This list included Jim Steinman, Nona Hendryx, Phoebe Snow, Quentin Crisp, Jackie Curtis, the Manhattan Transfer, and many more.

Holly Woodlawn's performance slipped exquisitely into the cabaret milieu; for Patti and Kaye, on the other hand, playing to an audience of self-conscious sophisticates was one more challenge to meet. It was one at which they succeeded. The first time the future Joey Ramone saw Patti perform was at Reno Sweeney, and he was entranced.

Days later, the duo were at Kenny's Castaways, a Village club where they shared the bill with Gunhill Road (a New York City three-piece recently signed to Mercury Records) and the wild folky-jazz hybrid of

Cathy Chamberlain's Rag'n Roll Revue. Patti had her act down now. She would read a poem, then when it was finished, she would screw up the piece of paper she'd written on and toss it onto the floor. Or she'd pick up a chair and smash it against a wall. Anything to grab the audience's attention, anything to provoke a reaction.

And it worked. After two years of pushing ever harder at what she perceived were the barriers that separated poetry from rock 'n' roll, at Kenny's Castaways she finally achieved the breakthrough she demanded, in the form of a shocked review from the *Village Voice*. Patti was, the reviewer insisted, "in the vanguard of cultural mutation; a cryptic androgynous Keith Richards look-alike poetess-appliqué."

Yet it was not her appearance that shocked so much as her repertoire: "You Don't Want to Play with Me Blues," "Anita Pallenberg in a South American Bar," the death-laden "A Fire of Unknown Origin" and the Dylan-littered "Dog Dream"—*have you seen / dylan's dog . . . the only / thing allowed / to look Dylan in the eye*—all were machine-gunned into an audience that was uncertain whether to applaud or excrete. She introduced "Redondo Beach," written in one sitting after a row with sister Linda: "Needing time to think, I took an F train to Coney Island and sat on the littered beach until the sun rose," she remembered in *Patti Smith Complete*. "I came back, wrote the draft and fell asleep."

But it was the concluding "Rape" that caught the most attention, just as Patti and Kaye knew it would when they selected it to crown their collection of garage-hewn verses. "Rape," peeping inside *bo's bodice. lay down darling don't be modest let me slip my hand in. ohhh that's soft.*

"Rape," glamorizing, humorizing, humanizing that most brutal crime.

"Rape," then and probably now as well, the most discomforting poem Patti Smith ever wrote. And she knew it.

But she was unrepentant. She would compare herself to a novelist, slipping in and out of the characters she was writing about. Depicting a rapist required her to become, in her mind, a rapist; "Rape" itself, she explained to Amy Gross in *Mademoiselle*, was the end result of reading everything she could lay her hands on about Richard Speck, the killer who raped, tortured, and murdered eight student nurses in Chicago, in one night in July 1966. Writing the poem six years later, Patti "just lurked about the room for a while, letting the saliva come out of my mouth, till I felt like Speck."

I'll never forget how you smelled that night. like cheddar cheese melting under fluorescent light.

But people should not take it so seriously, she said. Her verse was filled with jokes and wordplay. *I'm a wolf in a lamb skin trojan*, for example. Or her descriptions of her victim as a pretty shepherdess, and *beep beep sheep I'm moving in.*

Not for the first time, Patti shrugged. "I think of myself not as male or female or rapist but as a comedian."

On July 3, 1973, Patti marked the second anniversary of Jim Morrison's death with a reading at friend and filmmaker Jack Smith's loft, at Greene Street and Canal. Back in the early days of the Playhouse of the Ridiculous (sire of the Ridiculous Theatrical Company), Jack Smith had designed many of that ensemble's most dramatic costumes, and his influence remained a tangible slice of the underground arts scene. Most of the summer, however, was spent preparing her third poetry collection for publication, this time under the aegis of Andreas Brown, owner of the legendary Gotham Book Mart.

Like so many other writers and artists of the past fifty years, Patti was ranked among the Gotham Book Mart's most regular customers, not necessarily because she bought a lot of books there, but because she spent as much time as she could browsing within that narrow, crammed space, pouncing upon titles that she may never have heard of—or titles only she had heard of, for the Book Mart's specialty was rarities and limited editions.

The artist Edward Gorey was another familiar face there, his darkly sinister cartoons strangely at home amid the friendly tumble and jumble of the Book Mart. Gotham would publish many of Gorey's best-loved works, particularly toward the end of the artist's life. Brown worked with Patti, on the other hand, at the dawn of her career, lining her up alongside the other poetic giants that crowded the Gotham catalog: Allen Ginsberg (who once worked as a clerk there), Edith Sitwell, W. H. Auden, Dylan Thomas, and so forth.

The volume was *Witt*, and it featured twenty-two poems that remain among Smith's best known. Scarcely surprisingly, given its impact that spring, "Rape" was included; so were "Georgia O'Keefe" [*sic*] and "Prayer." Another piece, "To Remember Debbie Denise," would so enthrall boyfriend Allen Lanier that he would soon be setting it to music and, in 1976, recording it for the Blue Öyster Cult's *Agents of Fortune* album.

But *Witt*, like the volumes that preceded it, was never destined to see anything remotely approaching a mass market. All Patti's books had been produced by small presses, with the emphasis on "small"; in those days, when word of mouth was by far the most effective marketing tool for any aspiring writer, their circulation was limited to no more than any "fan club" the author had already accrued. Both *Witt* and *kodak* had initial runs of no more than one hundred copies. Patti's renown remained no more than a whisper, even down those corridors that acknowledged poetry as a force to be reckoned with.

Within her sphere, however, she was slowly gathering a very vocal following, including author Nick Tosches. By the time of *Witt*, he wrote in 1976, she was "feared, revered, and her public readings elicited the sort of gut response that had been alien to poetry for more than a few decades. Word spread, and people who avoided poetry as the stuff of four-eyed pedants found themselves oohing and howling at what came out of Patti's mouth. Established poets feared for their credence. Many well-known poets refused to go on after Patti at a reading, she was that awesome."

The source of this fascination lay in her delivery, a sense of timing that did indeed have far more in common with rock 'n' roll than with the studied metier even of the so-called rock 'n' roll poets, Jim Morrison paramount among them. For they were still attempting to add a rock vibe to poetic delivery—to shoehorn their poetic vision into musical surroundings, while retaining what they regarded as the individualist purity of both forms. The result was often stultifying, usually laughable, and ultimately little more than a hollow impersonation of the original.

Patti threw off such constraints. Perhaps because she never intended to create a hybrid, when one coalesced regardless, it did so organically. There was no sense that she was trying to push boundaries or force the audience of one medium to accept and appreciate the other. She was, simply, writing, and if her upbringing as a child of the rock 'n' roll years informed her words with a rhythm that was not normally associated with unaccompanied verse, then that was because she spoke to, and for, herself.

Even as her fame became palpable, even as audiences at the shows she opened suddenly seemed to comprise almost as many Patti Smith fans as anybody else, still she adhered to the writing and performing process that she had marked out at her first reading, and only honed and purified in the two and a half years since then.

A sense of self-consciousness was creeping in, however, together with the knowledge that, having isolated the beginnings of an audience, she needed to expand its horizons while at the same time encouraging it to extend its own expectations. That was what prompted her to title her next performance Rock'n'Rimbaud, a play on words that would come to the aid of any number of lazy headline writers as the next few years unfolded.

Appearing with Kaye at Le Jardin in the Hotel Diplomat on November 10, Patti turned in her longest performance yet, a marathon of twenty-four poems that looked all the way back to "Ballad of a Bad Boy" and forward to "Rape," and concluded with two dedications to Rimbaud. The reading was punctuated by snatches of song: the Julie London chest-beater "Cry Me a River" and the old Hank Ballard lament "Annie Had a Baby."

It was these moments that caught a lot of people's attention. The future Richard Hell saw her, and though he watched the performance in astonishment, the audience, too, astounded him. "They just would go nuts for her," he recalled in Please Kill Me. "Patti would just reel this stuff out and it was so hot and she was so sharp, but she was so sweet and vulnerable at the same time. She was the real thing, there was no mistaking it."

Not everybody agreed with him. Chris Stein, guitarist with the bar band the Stilettos (but soon to form Blondie with the Stilettos' Debbie Harry) was one of many who were prepared to write the Smith and Kaye duo off as a novelty act or at best some kind of humorous deconstruction of conventional rock 'n' roll. Kaye rarely allowed the volume of his guitar to disturb him, even when it was clearly drowning out Patti's voice; she in turn thought nothing of turning around in midflow and telling him to turn it down. It was anarchic, primitive, and, if you were so disposed to think in those terms, amateurish, a joke performance that had nothing in common with the more earnest endeavors taking shape elsewhere around the city.

For New York City was beginning to stir, the Dolls' death-or-glory assault upon the hearts and minds of America prompting any number of other young rockers to reach beyond the tried and tiring conventions of the big-time music industry, in search of something different, something real. Richard Myers and Thomas Miller, a pair of poets toying with the notions that would see them reinvent themselves as Messrs. Hell and Verlaine. The Stilettos and Luger. Wayne County and that other *Pork* graduate Cherry Vanilla, stepping out from the shadows of her new role as David Bowie's publicist to thrill Max's Kansas City with her own vision of Oz.

Such stirrings were far from Patti's playground, yet the duo continued to receive bookings that nudged them deeper into those bands' territory, culminating in their own debut at Max's, six nights opening for folkie Phil Ochs. The shows ran from the day after Christmas to New Year's Eve, and included a benefit for activist Abbie Hoffman midway through the run.

At Max's, Kaye now remained onstage for the entire performance, and Patti took full advantage of his presence to press home the musical qualities of her voice. Looking back at these early performances in 1976, *New York Times* columnist John Rockwell would describe her as "a chanting poet who lifted her words beyond language with the power of music. From the first, she used the idiom of rock, but she wasn't so much a rocker as a poet-shaman who used rock to make a statement." It was a reference that Doors fans in particular might have viewed with either fascination or disdain; Jim Morrison had certainly received similar notices from awestruck admirers.

But at the time, not every observer was so impressed. *After Dark* magazine's Robert L. Weinter suggested that Patti should remain in her living room and entertain her admirers there. But Rockwell would have one final rejoinder to make: "The art was raw, bizarrely theatrical, populist. But it was art, nonetheless."

And it was becoming artier, because it was also at Max's that Patti embraced the final piece of her jigsaw.

Lenny Kaye had recently been commissioned by Jac Holzman, the head of Elektra Records, to create a two-LP study of garage Americana. The *Nuggets* compilation was destined to become one of the most influential collections of its (or any other) ilk; its subtitle, *Original Artyfacts from the First Psychedelic Era 1965–1968*, scarcely does justice to the music and energies wrapped up inside. Kaye would now be inserting those same energies into his and Patti's repertoire.

With *Nuggets* by their side, both the finished album and the pages-long wish list of songs that didn't make the final cut, Patti and Lenny "chose songs that were basically three chords, so I could improvise over them. 'Cause I didn't wanna just do 'songs.' I didn't wanna do lame approximations of songs," she explained to NPR's Terry Gross. "We did what we called 'fieldwork,' so we'd pick songs that had basically three chords, and just sort of used 'em as a springboard."

Later, writing the liner notes for her first album, Patti would seize upon the notion of "three chords merged with the power of the word." If there was any single recipe for what she and Kaye were creating in 1973, that was it.

Three chords merged with the power of the word.

7

HA! HA! HOUDINI

PATTI WAS BACK at Reno Sweeney on December 9, 1973, where journalist Lisa Robinson awaited, poised to pen the first review to deliberately accentuate Smith's femininity over any other aspect of her performance.

Of course, Robinson made reference to a set list that was deliberately tailored for the cabaret audience (a tribute to Ava Gardner, "Speak Low"; a dedication to Frank Sinatra, "I Get a Kick Out of You"). But she also commented upon Patti's dress—a black satin pantsuit and white satin blouse, topped with a black feather boa—peculiar observations to make of a poetess. Few people, after all, ever commented on Adrienne Rich's outfits when she gave public readings. But they were appropriate too, a reminder of just how close, and how swiftly, Patti was moving toward both a rock 'n' roll audience and a rock 'n' roll sensibility, and of the new pressures that she would face once she did.

It is both tedious and cliched to look back today with disapproval on what in the early 1970s the media still termed "women in rock." Any criticisms of the period can be made only with the benefit of hindsight; it was what it was. On the American mainstream, the all-female band Fanny was still being regarded as something between a musical novelty and a four-headed sex toy; in Europe, Detroit rocker Suzi Quatro was turning out in leather catsuits and being patted on the head for showing that girls could look tough. There were more scathing performers in the underground, of course, but there was a very good reason why they were still in the underground. Because the overground simply couldn't wrap its head around the fact that an artist could be a performer first and a woman second, and it didn't particularly want to.

Patti was aware of this, but right now she had no intention of fighting against it, and may even have been aware of the futility of attempting to do so. Ingrained opinions can rarely be altered by words alone; a fighting example alone can effect change. And that is what she and Lenny Kaye set about creating, consciously or unconsciously, when they began spreading the word that they were looking for a piano player to join the act.

It was not an easy decision to have made. The idea of allowing a stranger entry into their world was anathema to the approach that had served them so well so far: the pure, organic growth of friends helping out, drawing in their own friends, the word of mouth spreading through a tightly knit circle and then reaching out through their recommendations to recruit like-minded spirits. Advertising for a new face meant throwing the duo's own vision open to the scrutiny and suggestions of any number of strangers, most of whom—Kaye knew from his experiences auditioning musicians for his own past bands—would be drawn less by any awareness of what he and Patti were doing and more by the assumed glamour of simply "joining a band."

It would be a difficult slog, and they had done their best to avoid it. The first advertisements only went out once they exhausted their own circle of friends and acquaintances and finally admitted that the easiest of alternatives, a friend of a friend named Eric Lee, simply wasn't going to work out. He sat in with the pair for a week, and he was a great pianist. But he was uncomfortable with the sheer weight of sexuality that clung to Patti's words.

The search began. Patti was back from a short vacation in Mexico, and manager Jane Friedman had offered them audition space in the Times Square office of her company, Wartoke. But auditions turned up nothing but one barrelhouse boogie boy after another, all wandering in with much the same ambitions: a would-be Elton John, a wannabe Keith Emerson, an imitation Billy Joel. Some even arrived bearing their own portfolios, packed with the songs that they could bring to the nascent group. All of them, Patti recalled in her 1976 *Penthouse* interview, seemed to glaze over the moment that she and Kaye started talking "all this cosmic bullshit to them, like 'Well, what we want to do is go over the edge.'"

"Fine," the latest applicant would reply. "Do you wanna hear me play 'Rocket Man'?"

The process was hopeless, and as it wore on, the pair began to doubt whether they would ever find what they were looking for. Certainly they were under no illusions when a devastatingly pretty boy named Richard Sohl walked in, togged up in a sailor suit. (It was a look, amusingly, that Russell Mael of Sparks had experimented with during that band's earliest days but discarded quickly enough.) Sohl looked, Patti and Kaye giggled to themselves, like Tadzio from the movie *Death in Venice*.

At least he arrived with recognizable credentials. He was Danny Fields's lover, and it was Fields who suggested he look in on the audition. He was also, Patti recalled, "totally stoned and totally pompous," and when Kaye delivered the "big cosmic spiel" that even he had grown tired of repeating, the newcomer just looked at him through hooded eyes and snapped, "Look, buddy, just play."

"We felt like *we* were the ones getting auditioned!" Patti continued in that monumental *Penthouse* interview. "So Sohl said, 'Whadya want? Ya want some classical?' He played a bunch of Mozart. 'Ya want some blues?' He played a bunch of blues. The fuckin' guy could play anything! So we started talkin', and it turned out that he'd been raised as a Jehovah's Witness, which I had been, too. We'd both rebelled against the same shit, and that helped. So we just brought him in."

The audition behind him, Sohl would not wear the sailor outfit again—but the *Death in Venice* association stuck. His new bandmates rechristened him DNV, for the movie's (almost) initials.

DNV was born Richard Arthur Sohl, on May 26, 1953, in New York City. Intensely private and touchingly frail, by 1974 he was already beset by the heart problems that would see him pass away before his fortieth birthday. But he was indeed as prodigious as Patti recalled, as a player and as a personality, and when he played, as she wrote in the verse that she dedicated to him, "Sohl," it really was as if *a cluster of glories erupted from his skull.*

He certainly brought an entire new dynamic to the act, a stately musicianship that was equally capable of weaving pretty melodies beneath the rant and scratch of his bandmates and leading them into new realms of discordance and dissonance. Classically trained but forever bucking against that discipline's strictures, he really could play anything they asked, and if they didn't ask, he'd play something different regardless, just to see what might happen.

Rehearsing through the spring at the Wartoke office, the trio developed an almost psychic bond with one another, an understanding that did not even require eye contact to be transmitted between them, a fire of unknown origin, *sweeping through the hallway like a lady's dress . . . riding down the highway in its Sunday best.*

But it was not just their own musical compatibility that sparked the trio's creativity. The outside forces that Patti had first witnessed converging around the twin centers of Max's and the Mercer were continuing to swirl, only now they were centered upon a newly opened club called CBGB OMFUG (Country, BlueGrass, and Blues and Other Music For Uplifting Gormandizers).

When it came to location, CBGB had nothing whatsoever going for it. It was simply a bar on the Bowery, as rundown as every other storefront in that then-blighted district, and as likely to be lined by the area's indigenous homeless as it was any cash-paying customers. An earlier business on the same site, recalled English journalist Mick Farren, was renowned for possessing "the worst drag queens on the planet"; they had since moved on, to be replaced by cheap drinks and great burgers, but still CBGB was little more than a long, thin closet, its dimensions further constricted by the bar and tables that hung on either side of the alley-like dance floor.

Even Patti, who came to love the place, called it "basically a hole in the wall," and the first night she visited, she recalled, the audience was more of a trickle than a flood. Within weeks, however, CBGB would be flooded with both onlookers and participants.

"The sense of self and new energy was instantaneous," Patti enthused, recalling the venue's heyday for David Fricke in 2006. "The confidence it inspired was strong, and the sense of community was immediate. William S. Burroughs lived down the street. He came all the time. We gave him a little table and a chair, and he'd sit there. All of our friends came— Robert Mapplethorpe, Jim Carroll. CBGB was the neighborhood—the artists and poets and musicians—and we all inspired each other."

In years soon to come, the phenomenon that inspired so many at CBGB would be christened *punk rock*. That first night that Patti was in attendance, though, it was something else entirely. It was art, it was anger, it was boredom ricocheting from arena to club, it was even (as owner Hilly Kristal was wont to tag the music oozing from his establishment) *street rock*. But it wasn't punk rock.

That term, if you went by the pages of the music press, was reserved for the snotty singer-songwriters who'd been emerging elsewhere on the sub–big time mainstream. Hindsight might be outraged, but there are writers around the United States who still remember (and were maybe even responsible for) the point when Nils Lofgren was called "punk," Bruce Springsteen was "punk," Graham Parker was "punk," and the unfathomable racket leaching from the underbelly of New York City was just the out-of-tune strummings of so many no-name wannabes. It was only when you dug a little deeper that you realized just how many of them there were, and just how stylistically different they all were.

Wayne County, the Dolls, Teenage Lust, and the synth and vocal duo Suicide continued to strut their sordid variations on an unsalable theme of glam rock. CBGB, on the other hand, had an eye toward grimier and gruntier talents, those who weren't so keen on dressing up, and who were maybe a little more arty-smarty as well—a pack that was led by a band called Television.

By the time decade-old friends Tom Verlaine and Richard Hell formed Television, they had already run through a number of juvenile collaborations. Hell's poetry magazine *Genesis: Grasp* was one. Another was the Neon Boys, a proto–progressive rock band completed by another of their school friends, Billy Ficca. Attempts to add another guitar player to the Neon Boys lineup repeatedly failed, however, despite the likes of Blondie's Chris Stein and the future Dee Dee Ramone trying out. The band folded with just a six-song demo to its name, then regrouped briefly and equally unsuccessfully as Goo Goo.

Another year would elapse before the trio reunited under the aegis of Terry Ork, manager of the Cinemabilia bookstore, where Hell and Verlaine both worked. It was Ork, too, who introduced the band to Richard Lloyd, a guitarist who perfectly fit Verlaine and Hell's specifications; the quartet was christened Television and debuted at the Townhouse Theatre on March 2, 1974. And it was Ork who suggested the band take a leaf out of the early New York Dolls' book and find a small club to play on a regular basis. Verlaine promptly went out and discovered CBGB; the band would play there for the first time just five days later, on March 31.

Patti already knew Richard Hell vaguely; they met sometime in early 1974, with Television's first CBGB gig already looming. Away from his musical interests, Hell was also publishing small-press poetry books under his own Dot Dot Dot imprint. Andrew Wylie, one half of the old Telegraph Books team, wrote the first volume, *Yellow Flowers*; the mysterious Theresa Stern composed another, *Wanna Go Out?*, and friends alone realized that "she" was actually another collaboration between Hell and Verlaine. Now Hell was wooing Patti into adding her work to the Dot Dot Dot imprint, and when he invited her down to Television's CBGB debut, he assumed that their discussions would carry on around the show. He was wrong.

Patti and Lenny Kaye arrived at the show fresh from the press preview of the latest Rolling Stones movie, *Ladies and Gentlemen, the Rolling Stones*, much of which had been shot at the same Madison Square Garden gig that they had both attended two years earlier. They were hopped up already, then, but when Television took the stage, any notion that the Stones would continue on as some kind of musical figurehead was first dampened then dismissed. "When I heard them, I felt like I'd met my kin from whom I'd been separated all my life," she remembered in her interview with Ed Vulliamy. "I immediately wanted to work with them."

Compared with what Television would become—the gorgeous spiraling leads and lyrics that were etched into space by their masterpiece album *Marquee Moon*—the early Television was scratchy, blurred, monochromatic. Hell and Verlaine were both powerful front men, which set up its own brutal dynamic on the stage, as each edged the other in search of the spotlight and neither was prepared to give an inch. The songs that they were writing jarred, too: scarred urban nightmares from Hell, more symbolic, ethereal visions from Verlaine. They did not adopt their pseudonyms for nothing!

But it was that very dichotomy that grasped the watching handfuls, and that sent Patti into paroxysms of both lust and longing. According to Terry Ork, the first thing she told him at the end of the show was how much she wanted—physically wanted—Tom Verlaine. According to the words she wrote for Lisa Robinson's *Rock Scene* magazine, however, there was more to her passion than that. "Boycott rock & roll on TV. Who wants an image of the image. Rock & roll is not Hollywood jive . . . [but] the rhythm and alchemy of hand to hand combat. . . . Already a new group has begun an attack. Starting from the bottom with completely naked necks. A group called TELEVISION who refuse to be a latent image but the machine itself! The picture they transmit is shockingly honest. Like when the media was LIVE and Jack Paar would cry and Ernie Kovacs would fart and Cid Caesar [*sic*] would curse and nobody would stop them cause the moment it was happening it was real. No taped edited crap."

No tighter than they needed to be, but still looping their garage riffs through the exquisite guitars of Verlaine and Lloyd, Television teased and squeezed out a set that effortlessly coiled both Hell and Verlaine's poetic ambitions around riff and rhythm. It was nothing like anything Patti and her cohorts had been doing, or even anticipating. But Patti felt a connection there regardless, one that was only strengthened when she returned home and found herself sitting up all night with Mapplethorpe, Kaye, and Sohl, talking about Television, but also about the directions in which their own music might go in the wake of all that Television portended.

There were no deep dreams of forming a musical movement at that time, nor even of keeping up with the new kids in town, for every one of them was certain that once the media glimpsed Television, the band would become as widely feted as Patti already was. What Television offered was simply the knowledge that it was time to raise their own sights even higher—to place the poetry clubs and cabarets behind them and move into a more conventional rock setting. They talked of expanding the lineup even further, of transforming themselves from a trio to a band. They spoke of amplifying the silent music that already ran beneath the best of Smith's poems. But most of all, they spoke of cutting a record.

And soon, as Patti watched the television news, she would discover what that record ought to be.

For the past two months, America's news media had been captivated by the saga of Patty Hearst, heiress to the newspaper fortune of the same name. Nineteen years old and blessed with the kind of beauty that every girl next door should possess, on February 4, 1974, Hearst was snatched from the Berkeley apartment that she shared with her boyfriend. Her kidnappers were members of the Symbionese Liberation Army, a hitherto all-but-unknown left-wing guerrilla group fighting for the rights of California's poor.

Their ransom demand was simple: the Hearst empire should donate $70 in food to every deserving case in the state, and when analysts pointed out that such a gift would cost the company somewhere in the region of $400 million, then that only amplified the SLA's message even louder. Could it really be true that the most glamorous state in the union, the most powerful, sun-kissed, and full-of-itself part of the entire United States, was home to so many needy people that it would take $400 million just to feed them for a week?

The Hearst family would finally distribute some $6 million worth of food around the Bay Area, and most analysts expected that to satisfy the kidnappers. But when the time came for Patty to be released, the SLA balked, saying first that the food was of such poor quality that it barely counted, and then that Patty was so disgusted by her family's perfidy that she was now an SLA member herself. She had one message for the world. "Tell everybody that I'm smiling, that I feel free and strong and I send my greetings and love to all the sisters and brothers out there."

Just two weeks after Patti and Kaye first saw Television at CBGB, on April 15, 1974, Patty Hearst—or Tania, as she now styled herself—was photographed wielding an M1 carbine during an SLA raid on a San Francisco bank. An even more powerful photo would follow, a shot of a fatigues-clad Hearst standing with her legs spread, gun in hand, before the SLA's banner, a nine-headed serpent. It was, and it remains, a magnificent image, the ultimate romantic portrait of an urban guerrilla: beautiful, stylish, methodical, cool. Hearst's own story would reel on for two years longer before she was captured, and for decades more of accusation and denial, triggering a small sea of books, biographies, movies, and portrayals. But for that one frozen moment in April 1974, Hearst was arguably the most famous and notorious, adored and pitied, loved and loathed woman in America, and if the traditional image of a 1960s student crash pad is dominated by a portrait of Che Guevara, a decade later Patty Hearst had replaced him in both style and substance.

And Patti Smith, gazing at the photograph as it was transmitted from the newspapers to the poster stores and on to every right-thinking radical's bedroom wall, couldn't help but wonder what was really going on inside the girl's mind, now that she was on the run.

Patti was part of a generation of young people who were growing increasingly aware that their heroes would always let them down in the end. But this image of Patty Hearst transcended all those fears, because it transcended heroism itself, to become an image and an icon. Hearst herself could be caught or killed; she could say what she liked in defense of her actions. But the poster told no lies—she was an avenging angel. And the verses that Patti wrote about her that month, and then fed back into a stylized revision of the Jimi Hendrix hit "Hey Joe," would become the psalm that summoned her to earth.

Or maybe, as Patti would giggle, she simply liked hearing the newsreaders talk about Patty, because she could pretend they were speaking about her instead.

With its strong topical focus, "Hey Joe" was the obvious choice for Patti's debut single. With an equally strong grasp of her personal self-mythologization, so was "Piss Factory," a poem Patti wrote about her experiences working at the textbook (or was it baby buggies?) factory back in New Jersey, and into which she wrote her first slice of prophesy, too: *I'm gonna get out of here I'm gonna get on that train and go to New York City and I'm gonna be somebody . . . I'm gonna be so bad, I'm gonna be a big star. . . . Oh watch me now.*

The first half of that prediction had already come true. Maybe this little record would help achieve the second.

Robert Mapplethorpe had agreed to set aside a thousand dollars to cover the recording and manufacturing costs. Patti could have recorded the single anywhere. New York City was littered with tiny hole-in-the-wall recording studios; move out of the city, and the suburbs and beyond would be cheaper as well. But she had no interest in doing things on the cheap.

She knew that there was only one place where you could record a version of a song made famous by Jimi Hendrix. You went to the studio made famous by Hendrix: the Electric Lady complex that he had built on West Eighth Street. There, at least according to the musicians who had passed through since the guitarist's death, his spirit still hung around, ever ready to add a helping hand to any musician whom he deemed to be worthy.

Patti had been there once before, on August 26, 1970, attending the first true rock 'n' roll party of her life as a guest of Jane Friedman. It was the studio's grand opening party, but Patti was simply too nervous to go into the main room. So she sat on the stairs outside—where she discovered that the party's host, Jimi Hendrix, didn't really want to brave the throng either. So they sat on the stairs and just chatted, about his music, about his plans, about his immediate schedule. He told her about the new music he was intending to make once he returned to New York from his next scheduled visit to London. Music that he would never make; less than three weeks later, Hendrix was dead.

"Hey Joe" opens with Patti alone, a few lines of introduction before Richard Sohl's stately piano slowly mourns the opening bars. Lenny Kaye's bass and a guesting Tom Verlaine's guitar follow as the pace picks up. Even compared to the sounds that the trio had been making in the rehearsal studio, the final recording makes clear that Patti Smith had moved into an entire new musical dimension, one in which her musicians didn't simply accompany and counterpoint her words but became one with them. They created a seamless whole that was so unlike *anything* that had ever masqueraded as rock and poetry that by the time the poem reaches its conclusion—Patti as Patty spitting defiance with a carbine between her legs, *nobody's little pretty little rich girl . . . nobody's million-dollar baby*—the listener too has become a part of the performance.

More than thirty-five years after it was recorded, "Hey Joe" remains one of the high-water marks of 1970s rock as it moved toward the brave new worlds of punk and the new wave. At the time, picked up on the black-labeled 45 that was self-released on Smith and Kaye's own label, Mer (from the French for "sea"), from the tiny network of New York City–and–elsewhere stores that were sentient enough to even know it existed, "Hey Joe" was simply spellbinding. Nobody knew then what it portended, that the remainder of the decade would be carved from within the shadow of its very existence. But everyone who heard it knew that something that powerful would never wither on the vine.

By contrast, "Piss Factory" sounds rushed and hectic, a mood ideal for the pell-mell nature of the poem itself, but one that Patti felt obliged to excuse when she was asked about the sessions. The lion's share of their studio time, she explained, was devoted to recording and mixing "Hey Joe." "Piss Factory" was run though, recorded, and mixed in an hour.

With its first single in the can, the three-piece group made its live debut at the Greendoor on May 18, 1974. The real test, however, lay two months ahead, when Patti would finally make her headlining entrance to Max's Kansas City. There she would determine the wisdom, or otherwise, of all that they had been working on in the rehearsal room: the layering of rhythms and melodies behind songs that she had been performing as poems for over three years; the fusion of her work with that of other artists.

"Hey Joe" was not her sole hybrid song. She grafted her poem "Oath" onto the song "Gloria"; the poem's opening lines, *Jesus died for somebody's sins / but not mine*, completely redefined Van Morrison's original ballad of a bad girl. The song had been a big hit for Van Morrison's first band, Them, back in 1965, and since then it had gravitated into the repertoire of almost every garage band in the country, by virtue of a slobberingly simple rhythm and a chorus chant that grabbed every voice in the room: *G-l-o-r-i-a*. It was Lenny Kaye's idea to do the song in the first place; according to Patti, she had never wanted to perform it. "I didn't really have any interest in covering 'Gloria,'" she admitted to Terry Gross. "But it had three chords and I liked the rhythm, and we just sort of used it for our own design."

The trio also worked up a version of the old Motown classic "The Hunter Gets Captured by the Game"; with their song "Land," they interpolated songwriter Chris Kenner's "Land of 1000 Dances"—a hit for Wilson Pickett—into a brutal tale of homosexual rape in a locker room; and they realigned "Time Is on My Side" to prove that it was. Individually and collectively, the band was creating "a battleground for all kinds of adolescent excursions," explained Patti on *Fresh Air*. "So that's why we picked songs like that."

They believed all their selections were a natural extension of what had gone before, but they also realized that, for the first time, they were crossing the divide between art and commerce, starry-eyed idealism and bull-headed populism. Observers drawn by Patti's reputation as a poet would wince as Kaye struck up his electrics behind her and her poetry morphed into song, while the know-nothing tourists who flocked to Max's shrugged and mumbled about Jim Morrison's leather trousers.

Max's had changed dramatically since the days when Andy Warhol could describe it as "the exact spot where pop art and pop life came together in the '60s." Or, rather, Max's clientele had changed. It was more of an industry hangout now—still a place where people went to be seen, but one where there seemed to be a lot more looking than was ever worth looking at. It was a part of the tourist route, with the stars securely roped off behind however many walls of bouncers they could bring.

Enough so-called stars still passed through, though, to ensure that Max's retained that slither of subversive glamour that had attracted Patti and Mapplethorpe five years before. The club's booking policy, too, remained haute. Bob Marley played his first-ever US shows there, opening for the then equally unknown Springsteen; Aerosmith, Billy Joel, and Garland Jeffreys passed through. But Max's was also a testing ground for local talent, and home to established local heroes as well. When the Mercer Arts Center had been forced to close in 1973, after its ceiling collapsed during an Eric Emerson and his Magic Tramps rehearsal, the party—the New York Dolls among them—moved the few blocks up to Max's Kansas City, and the fates continued to conspire from there.

Patti's group was booked at Max's for four nights running, July 12–15, 1974. Sohl later described the earliest Max's shows as tentative, exciting more for the performers' own uncertainty and nervousness—"How would we be accepted?"—than for the performances themselves. Their confidence grew, however, as the residency ran on. When the three came offstage following the fourth and final night, it was in the knowledge that, while there would always be dissenters, the supporters would outnumber them every time.

"It could have been our Newport Folk Festival," Sohl continued, referring to the night nine years earlier when Bob Dylan took the stage before his core constituency of folk-music fans and blew their heads off with a wall of unrepentant electricity, only to have the roars of disapproval all but drown out his rock band. Instead, "people seemed to like it."

More than that, people seemed to acknowledge, agreeing with the musicians themselves, that the shift was necessary—not only if Patti was to pursue any form of stardom but simply because the day was gone when an artist could afford to sit still through his or her career, content to weave around the same circle of arenas, exhibiting to the same admirers. Besides, it was not as though Patti had deliberately set out to seduce a rock 'n' roll crowd. True, her poem "Work Song" did insist *I was working real hard / to show the world / what I could do.* But it was the crowd that had courted her, opening its doors and inviting her in, apparently understanding that she had a lot more in common with its own aims than many who were already inside, including some of rock's most storied superstars.

Within days, Mickey Ruskin had rebooked Patti for another twenty shows: two a night between August 28 and September 2, 1974, and eight more on the same schedule the following week, September 6–9.

Meanwhile, Television was celebrating the release of its own first record, cut in stark emulation of Smith's example. The band had been through the fires of record company interest, and had even been paired with Brian Eno for a handful of demo recordings. But Tom Verlaine was never satisfied with what other ears heard in the music he made, and when Richard Hell left for Johnny Thunders's new band, the Heartbreakers, Verlaine resolved to forgo the record companies and release the group's debut single under the independent label Ork Records, which Terry Ork formed specifically for that purpose.

Recorded on a 4-track borrowed from the Mumps' drummer, Jay Dee Daugherty, "Little Johnny Jewel" was hypnotically haphazard and arrogantly ambitious, with Verlaine's strangled gulp of a voice as dislocated as the glacial riff. The track stretched to more than seven minutes in its original form, so it was sliced down the middle and spread across both sides of the record for single release.

But, for all that future critics would compare Television to a new wave Grateful Dead, the song's almost endless guitar noodles have more in common with Philip Glass than Jerry Garcia, and its appearance on 45 provoked gasps of disbelief from both without and within. Lou Reed asserted that it had no chance of becoming a hit (not long after Tom Verlaine was reported to have confiscated the batteries from Lou's tape recorder at a Television gig). And Television's own Richard Lloyd was so opposed to the release that he promptly quit the group. But he returned three days later—and "Little Johnny Jewel" went on to sell twenty thousand hand-bagged copies by word of mouth alone. It was the correct choice after all.

Patti, needless to say, loved it. She also delighted in the fact that Verlaine had written one of her childhood nicknames, Winghead, into the lyric. The kids at school had called her that because her hair stuck out at strange angles, and she'd loathed them for it. Verlaine made it sound kinda sexy.

In another echo of her past, a revival of *Cowboy Mouth*, the play she wrote with Sam Shepard back in 1971, was running in a small theater in the West Village, Unit 453 in Westbeth's Exchange for the Arts. Across town, Patti was developing a reputation that in some circles rivaled Shepard's own.

Her name even traveled to the UK, as *Melody Maker*'s New York City correspondent, Chris Charlesworth, warned readers, "She's a bitch straining at the leash in most of her songs, all of which are prefaced by some kind of unusual story." It was "her ability to hold the audience's attention" that he perceived as "her main selling point: drift away and you'll miss something you wish you hadn't." Testily, fans may have noted that Genesis, too, prefaced its songs with some kind of unusual story, but if anybody was expecting any further similarities before a Patti Smith performance, they were swiftly disabused.

Patti's new status was embodied in another piece of poetry from her past, lines from "The Ballad of Hagen Waker" that she might never have dreamed she would experience for herself: *That capricornous fever / of being higher than the crowd / as for the crowd / they are ecstatic.*

You know, she had written, *it's often I'm glowing in the dark.*

Her schedule remained hectic. The trio staged their latest Rock'n'Rimbaud events, one at the Riverside Plaza Hotel in New York City on October 27, 1974, another within the palatial surroundings of the Roosevelt Hotel's Blue Hawaiian Discotheque two weeks later. At the November 10 Rock'n'Rimbaud, the musicians were joined for the first time by a fourth member, folk guitarist Sandy Bull.

Bull is widely proclaimed one of the fathers of world music, an incredibly eclectic musician whose talents stretched from riotous Chuck Berry covers to hypnotic Middle Eastern rhythms, from classical favorites to salsa and beyond, all played out on such instruments as oud, sarod, six-string bass, and pedal steel. He had been tremendously popular throughout the 1960s before a drug habit forced him into virtual retirement.

An old friend of Bobby Neuwirth, Bull was just beginning to reemerge from his addictions when Patti, Kaye, and Sohl began considering augmenting their lineup even further. But he was never seen as a full-time recruit to the group; billed as a special guest for the evening, he joined them onstage for the opening "All the Hipsters Go to the Movies," then disappeared until the final number, an impassioned "Land." His presence, however, only hardened the trio's determination to stretch out even further, a mood that their next adventure only amplified.

Days after the Roosevelt Hotel gig, the trio flew to Berkeley, California, to play a show at Rather Ripped Records, the self-styled "best little record store you ever saw." (The shop's full name, quoted in its advertisements, was I'd Rather Be Ripped Records, but signage to that effect would not have sat well with the authorities around the Northside neighborhood.) Taking the stage in her white Keith Richards T-shirt, Patti drew the small crowd close and then closer still. "Kids are more maniac in Berkeley than anywhere else in America," she told Lisa Robinson in *Hit Parader* in 1977. "Even more than CBGB. It's just so incredible. . . . They'll scream and do interpretative dancing. They don't give a shit about being cool."

From Rather Ripped, the trio moved on to San Francisco and the Fillmore West—at least according to one of the most intriguing legends in their mythology. As the story goes, promoter Bill Graham offered them a spot at the Fillmore's latest audition night, which the band celebrated by inviting Jonathan Richman, the Boston songwriter who was in California recording his first album at the time, to sit in on drums. Patti recites this same tale (with no more detail than that) in *Just Kids*. Unfortunately, the Fillmore closed its doors in 1971 and would not reopen until the 1980s. With nobody else appearing to have any memory of the occasion—Richman merely answered "no" when he was asked about it in the 1990s—this would seem to be one of those little legends that gets glued into history without anybody questioning whether it actually occurred. In this case, it probably didn't.

The group did, however, make it down to Los Angeles for a couple of shows at the Whisky a Go Go, opening for the British funk-rock band Fancy, which was launching its first-ever tour in the wake of the hit single "Wild Thing." It was an experience that Patti would preserve within the ever-developing text of what was already being singled out as her landmark poem, "Land."

"Land" started life, she would tell Tony Hiss and David McClelland in 1975, as a poem about "a carnival of fools in a city where you can't see the stars, but I gave it a New York ballad rendition—you know, let's keep on laughing, let's keep on dancing. Then, as I got more confident, it was Scheherazade: 'Welcome to the Palace of a Thousand Sensations. It hopes you will *lose* it here, baby.' Then it got real sadistic. . . . Then it was Arabia, Mexico, UFOs, razors, jackknives, horses, and in some notes I wrote last December 16—the 701st birthday of the great Persian mystic poet Jalaluddin Rumi—Jim Morrison, Janis Joplin, and Jimi Hendrix."

Jim Morrison was added to the mix in response to Patti's Los Angeles performance. "I felt the rhythms of L.A. and understood the Doors' album *L.A. Woman* for the first time. So Johnny the hero of 'Land' became very intimately linked with Morrison," she explained to Mick Gold of *Street Life*.

"Johnny got in trouble, I was in trouble on the stage, Morrison had some trouble on stage. Kids used to scream at Morrison wanting him to do his hits. He was very torn apart and frustrated, because he felt himself to be a blues guy and a poet, but he was promoted more as a sex star. That's cool too, but he didn't know how to shift from one to the other. He didn't want to sing 'Light My Fire,' he wanted to sing 'Horse Latitudes.'"

He was never able to make that transition. So she would make it for him.

8

NEO BOY

"**THE FIRST TIME** I heard Patti Smith—and I've heard a *lot* of people, been in music all my life—she just had a magnetism," CBGB proprietor Hilly Kristal recalled. "She may not have been a singer, but she sure sounded like one. She stayed on pitch, she bent the notes just right, she sang real well. She communicated. The life was simple for her. It was all new. She was doing something that she'd probably wanted to do all her life. She was excited by her own feeling that it was happening for her. She loved it. I heard the same performance over and over, and she was one of the few people I *could* listen to over and over."

Patti played her first-ever CBGB show at the end of December 1974, right around the time that a passing journalist asked if she still wanted to become a famous poet. She would prefer to be remembered as a great rock 'n' roll star, she replied, and she meant it.

"Which," said Ivan Kral, "is pretty much where I came in to the picture."

Ivan Král (he later dropped the accent from his last name) was born in 1948 in Prague, then the capital of the Iron Curtain nation of Czechoslovakia. Fifteen years later, in 1963, his parents Karel and Otylie left their homeland for a new life in New York, where Karel was appointed a journalist and translator at the United Nations. Ivan and his brother Pavel followed them in 1966, and, in the near-decade since then, the family had built an entire new life in the West. Because they could not return home.

Karel had been among the most vociferous critics of the 1968 Soviet invasion of Czechoslovakia. Now he was forever watchful of reprisals, and had been assigned an FBI guard to protect him from the still-vengeful Communists. Regularly, the mailman would deliver innocuous-looking invitations for him to speak at grandly titled European conferences, none of which existed as anything but a means of luring him back within reach of the Státní Bezpečnost, Czechoslovakian secret police.

He didn't fall for their tricks, but other dissidents were not so lucky. Karel told his son about the Czech tennis player who was picked up while visiting his girlfriend in Romania and dragged back to Prague to try to lure his father out of hiding. And later, as Ivan's musical career promised to take him back to Europe to tour, his father would have just one warning for him. "Do what you have to do," the old man said. "But I'm not going to bail you out. If anything happens, you're on your own. There's nothing I can do for you."

Ivan had already tasted fame in Czechoslovakia, as a member of the teenage rock band Saze. The group's "Pierrot" had topped the Czech charts shortly before he left the country. Now he was working in the mail room at industry mogul Allen Klein's ABKCO empire—where the affairs of state revolved around the latest happenings in the world of the Beatles and the Rolling Stones—and spending his free time haunting the clubs and nightspots of New York City.

He ran through a handful of small bands, then in 1972 formed Luger, a tight and glamorous group that was constantly being tipped for big things. Unfortunately, Kral reflected, his bandmates—guitarist Mister Paulin, bassist Jon Thomas, and drummer Shayne Harris—were too easily seduced by the modicum of local fame that had already come their way. "They thought they were stars; they would rather go to Max's and pose than rehearse, so I decided to fold the band."

That was fall 1974, and he did not have far to look for his next project—or, at least, certainly not as far as he expected. He journeyed to the West Coast to see if he could make a fresh musical start out there, and worked for a time with Shaun Cassidy's band Longfellow, but he soon returned to New York City and promptly joined what was left of the Stilettos, as Debbie Harry, Chris Stein, Fred Smith, and drummer Billy O'Connor morphed into a new band, Blondie.

It was a short-lived experience. The band recorded some demos for journalist Alan Betrock, but gigs were few, excitement was elusive, and publicity was minimal. While Patti Smith, Television, and the newly emergent Ramones were devouring local column inches, Blondie remained stubbornly unheralded and unknown. By Christmas 1974, Kral was desperate to find another gig.

He played a couple of auditions for a new band that David Bowie's old guitarist, Mick Ronson, was building with drummer Hilly Michaels, and that probably would have been a good fit. But then he heard that Patti Smith was auditioning, and that was all he needed to know. For months, he and his friend Jay Dee Daugherty, the 4-track-owning drummer with the Mumps, had been catching Patti's shows and wondering why she didn't just form a full band. Now she was, and Kral wanted to be a part of it.

Richard Sohl shuddered as he recalled the auditions that the band held for a second guitar player, beginning a few days after Christmas 1974 and then continuing on the other side of Patti's New Year's Day appearance at St. Mark's Poetry Project. "About fifty guitar players came down," he said, and more than a handful of them impressed them.

There was, however, always one drawback. Too many guitar players would spend their audition talking to either Kaye or Sohl, either ignoring Patti or, at best, treating her as some kind of adornment to the main business. Even when they learned that she not only sang but also wrote the lyrics, she remained an outsider in their eyes. Sohl remembered one player who, having thrilled everybody during the audition, then blew it all by taking the guys to one side and suggesting they lose the chick. His exact words were "She can't sing and she looks like shit."

The audition itself was not an easy prospect. "Our thing then was to play 'Gloria' for forty minutes and see who dropped out first," Sohl continued. "All of those guys didn't understand what we were doing."

But then, Patti told Nick Tosches in *Penthouse*, "Ivan Kral came in. This little Czechoslovakian would-be rock star. . . . We did ['Land'] and it went on so long I thought I was gonna puke. But Ivan was so nervous he wouldn't stop, and we figured that was really cool." What they appreciated most, though, was that Kral meshed so seamlessly with their existing sound, even as he enhanced it. They were a rock 'n' roll band at last—but they were still themselves.

"I think my background helped us click," Kral mused, an observation that Sohl was swift to acknowledge: "We all sympathized very strongly with the fact of Ivan's exile. I think all of us felt in some ways that we were exiles; we played in that outsider status."

Patti also came to see him as the guardian angel of the group, someone who was constantly aware of her onstage needs and would do whatever he could to make her look good, even at the cost of his own performance. Patti had recently introduced a stylized revision of the Who's "My Generation" into the repertoire, replacing the familiar *Things they do look awful cold / I hope I die before I get old* refrain with a bellowed *I don't need that fucking shit / Hope I die because of it*; Kral had a crucial guitar part to worry about, she marveled, but he'd always take the time to make sure her microphone was ready.

Days after Patti's latest appearance at St. Mark's (where the audience was made privy to, among other jewels, her uproarious description of ancient Egyptian soothsaying), the January 30, 1975, edition of the *Soho Weekly News* announced Kral's arrival into the band in the kindest terms: "The very talented Ivan Kral, formerly of Luger, has joined Patti Smith's band on guitar and bass." The following week, the group was in Philadelphia, opening for ex-Animal Eric Burdon at the Main Point.

Nobody in the band doubted that they were rising fast. Even though they still weren't earning much more than five dollars each a night, every show they played was swamped with curious journalists; every time they opened a magazine, there was another mention of Patti.

The gang of four—Patti, Kaye, Kral, and Sohl—were all but permanent residents of CBGB. They would hang in the audience to witness whatever was unfolding on the stage or take the stage themselves, then depart for other hot spots to see and be seen. Four nights coheadlining CBGB with Television, February 13–16, were followed by a reception for the Blue Öyster Cult, whose *Tyranny and Mutation* album was about to be released. Smith's "Baby Ice Dog" was one of its highlights. And when Kral and friend Amos Poe decided to capture New York City underground on film in spring 1975, inevitably they went to CBGB to shoot. They emerged with *Blank Generation*, one of the crucial celluloid documents of the age, a flickering black-and-white record of every key act to call CBGB home.

The accolades continued to pour in. Bruce Springsteen ambled up to Patti one evening to announce that he'd fallen in love with her from her picture in *Creem*. *Creem* itself was mourning Patti's decision to quit writing for the magazine because she simply no longer had the time. Her final article, "Jukebox Cruci-Fix," would appear in the June 1975 issue, looking back on rock 'n' roll's dead from Vladimir Mayakovsky, the anarchist poet, through Johnny Ace and Buddy Holly, and on to her account of visiting Jim Morrison's grave. But it ended with the pledge that *we don't look back*, and a hand-scrawled postscript: "This is my last article."

Patti even earned the admittedly dubious honor of a hilarious parody by Wayne County, onstage at Max's one night, just days after her own appearance there on April 1. Donning Patti's trademark stage wear, a white shirt and suit pants, and riffing loosely on her signature work "Land," County launched into a merciless roast not only of Patti's love of Jim Morrison but also of the song's enigmatic equine references (*Horses! Horses! Horses! Horses!*). County raged, *Wildebeest! Wildebeest!* then slipped into a set of poetics that might not quite have been up to Patti's usual standard but left no listener in doubt about their inspiration.

> *Jim Morrison is in the bathtub.*
> *The water is soapy, the water is soapy.*
> *And Jim, he stepped on a bar of Ivory Soap, and it's hard when*
> *   you step on a bar of Ivory Soap.*
> *And he slipped and he fell and he hit his head on the soap dish,*
> *   and the water went through his nostrils, and up to his eyes,*
> *   and passed down his chest and into his lungs.*
> *He was dying, and he started to die, and then Jim Morrison lay*
> *   there, and before he died, he sang*
> *I'm forever blowing bubbles.*

Publicly, Patti ignored the taunt; the group was too busy to care. But they would never play Max's again, and suspicious minds do lay the slight at the door of her hurt feelings. But perhaps it had more to do with the changes to Max's itself. Mickey Ruskin had sold the club in late 1974, and while new manager Tommy Dean swiftly reopened the joint and did his level best to recreate the old scene, for many of those who loved the original pile—and, more importantly, loved the Ruskins who ran it—it wasn't Max's any longer.

Especially now that CBGB had stepped into the breach.

With Television once again the opening act, Patti Smith (as the band itself would be known for the next eighteen months) headlined the venue for sixteen nights in April, two shows each evening. It remains one of the key events in the club's long history: the scene's two most consistently intriguing groups, side by side across a weekend residency that made a legend of the venue and stars-in-waiting of the acts. Written reports of the shows that tore out of the Bowery that season were describing them as epochal before anyone even dreamed what the epoch might turn out to be. British journalist Charles Shaar Murray of the *New Musical Express* wrote, "Patti Smith is a Heavy Cult Figure . . . an odd little waif figure in a grubby black suit and black satin shirt, so skinny that her clothes hang baggily all over her, with chopped-off black hair and a face like Keith Richards' kid sister would have if she'd gotten as wasted by age seventeen as Keith is now. Her band . . . play like a garage band who've learned a few '30s licks to go with the mutated AM rock. . . . Her closing tour de force ['Land'] was undoubtedly the most gripping performance that I've seen by a white act since the last time I saw The Who."

Hindsight can only applaud such commentators' foresight and be grateful that, on one night at least, the audiotapes were rolling. Across the three-hour recording that preserves the show for posterity, every song that subsequently accompanied Patti Smith and Television to glory receives a primal and near-definitive rendering. If one listens with the benefit of hindsight and age, it is clear that it was not what the bands did that night that matters. It was what they represented. Yes, Television's "Marquee Moon" was a little clumsy in places; sure, Patti's "Space

Monkey" could have been tighter. But you can sense the sweat pouring down the walls, the floor-to-ceiling congestion that packed the narrow bar, and the manic determination with which the two bands confronted the potential that everyone said they possessed, before they transformed it into a tangible asset.

Like hearing an audience recording of a very early Sex Pistols show, or Syd Barrett's Pink Floyd before they had their first hits, this is not a simple audiotape but an *experience*, a vérité rendering that even captures the sound of the surreptitious taper, wondering whether his microphone is working. Smith's poetic interludes were spellbinding, Verlaine's guitar was incendiary, and it really doesn't matter that the intro to Television's "Poor Circulation" would one day be grafted onto "Torn Curtain," or that Patti's "Redondo Beach" was taken so fast that it almost out-discos "Heart of Glass." You can't quite smell the toilets or taste the cheap beer, but the bootleg ensures that this night at CBGB is reborn regardless.

Although CBGB was fast becoming a rock shrine, not everybody was impressed with it. "All I can remember," Johnny Ramone said, "is they never had a door on the dressing room, and you played and you wouldn't even get a free beer." Joey Ramone was kinder: "CBGB helped make the Ramones. It gave us a place to play when there probably wasn't another club in the world that would book us, but it also helped us become a part of a community. When we played, we'd look out at the audience and everybody would be there: Patti and her group, Tom [Verlaine] and Television, the Shirts, the Marbles, everybody. And when they played, we'd be there for them." Indeed, the Ramones would join Patti Smith in utterly surpassing their original role as club regulars to become virtually synonymous with the venue.

Patti Smith and her band were never especially close with the Ramones, but still Joey recalled them as being "good friends to us." Other groups on the scene, however, failed to share Ramone's munificence. Stiv Bators, newly arrived in New York City from his native Cleveland, had little time for Patti Smith, an opinion born out of the fact that she had little time for his band, the Dead Boys.

"What Patti Smith did was, she weighed everybody up, to see whether they could be useful to her or not. Useful, meaning, could her

career benefit from being associated with them? So Television, Richard
Hell, Talking Heads, the art types, they were her friends, but the Dead
Boys, she wouldn't give us the time of day, because being photographed
with us, or being seen at one of our gigs, wouldn't be good for her
image. That was all she cared about. All Patti Smith cared about was
what would be good for Patti Smith. Not her band, not her fans, not her
music. Herself."

Debbie Harry, whose Blondie had been hoping to keep Ivan Kral for
themselves, was likewise fiercely antagonistic toward Patti Smith, all the
more so after the media began contrasting the two women's night-and-
day approaches toward appearance and demeanor. Whether she liked it
or not, Harry was on a collision course with the role of "punk sex symbol" that would define her contribution to the next five years of rock
history. Patti, on the other hand, was just Patti.

And Harry never forgave her for recommending that Blondie should
just give up trying before it was too late. *Patti Smith: An Unauthorized
Biography* quoted her as recalling, "She told me there wasn't room for
two women in the CBGB scene and that I should leave the business
'cause I didn't stand a chance against her! She was going to be the star."

Ultimately, of course, there would be room for them both, and if
Blondie did in fact turn out to be the bigger commercial attraction,
Sohl, at least, would shrug away any comparison. "We came out of the
same place, but we were never going in the same direction," he said
gently. "Blondie made some great records, but they weren't records that
we would ever have made, and I'm sure they'd say the same thing about
ours."

Work toward Patti and the group's first album was already under way.
The previous fall, they had recorded some demos for RCA under the
guidance of journalist and A&R man Stephen Holden. RCA had passed
on the band, but now the group had a different suitor: Arista, the new
label launched by former Columbia Records chief Clive Davis, which
was already carving a swath through the established label hierarchy with
a combination of smart signings and hot acquisitions. Ownership of
the now-defunct Bell label gave Arista both the Bay City Rollers, the
hottest teenaged superstars of the age, and Barry Manilow, destined to

become the housewife's choice for an entire generation. A raid on RCA had brought both Lou Reed and the Kinks into the Arista family, and now Davis was looking to add Patti Smith to the roster.

Davis had first seen Patti for himself when he visited CBGB in the company of Lou Reed, and the experience left him reeling. "Sometimes, in the music business," he wrote in *Vanity Fair* in 2010, "you're lucky to be in the right room on the right night and see an artist do something that is completely unexpected and yet somehow inevitable. Believe me, it happens very few times. But it happened the night I walked into that club on the Bowery."

According to published reports, he offered Patti $750,000 for seven albums. More important than that, he pledged that he would support her as an artist, not a random hit-making machine. At the end of April, Patti signed on the line.

The *New York Times* announced the deal first. "Since Mr. Davis is eager for star acts and since Miss Smith is nothing if not a potential star, one can expect a massive promotional push for her," John Rockwell wrote. "All of which means that anyone who wants to see Miss Smith in the ambiance in which she has heretofore flourished—the seedy little club—had better hurry down to CBGB."

Patti and the band played their last few shows at CBGB, then spent May 1975 in rehearsal. By the time they returned to live work, for a WBAI-FM radio concert on May 28, they were already being billed as Arista recording artists. But Patti had no intention of standing on ceremony for either her label or the concert's broadcasters. "I've been told to watch my language," she announced, and within three minutes had dropped her first "fuck," "to prove the station can't censor the people's slang. All we care about is food for the people."

"Fluid" is the term that best describes the concert's set list. By now, Lou Reed's "We're Gonna Have a Real Good Time Together" was the group's established opener, six years after Reed wrote it for the Velvet Underground and then left it unreleased. Smith snatched her version from *Live 1969*, the recently released collection of vintage Velvets live recordings that she'd reviewed for *Creem* in September 1974. (Reed would reclaim the song in 1978, for his *Street Hassle* album.) Undulatingly tender, "The Hunter Gets Captured by the Game" was still on show, as were "Gloria" and "Redondo Beach." "Birdland" had been one of Patti's poems, but the group had developed it into a song over their time at CBGB. The concert also featured "Distant Fingers," a gorgeous cowrite between Patti and boyfriend Allen Lanier, and "Break It Up," a slab of mystic imagery copenned by Tom Verlaine.

Nobody was yet certain how many of these would make it onto the band's upcoming debut album, though, because the band still had one final refinement to make. They had been called to account on more than one occasion for the muddled sound that sometimes beclouded their performances. And once Kral joined the group, there was so much more going on onstage that they needed to know the PA was in good hands; they could no longer entrust it to each venue's usual operator, who might or might not have a clue what he was even meant to be listening to. So Patti decided to recruit their first sound engineer. At Kral's suggestion, they turned to the Mumps' Jay Dee Daugherty.

And when they decided they needed a drummer as well, Daugherty was already there. "I've always had Lenny because I need someone to lean on," Patti explained to *Sounds*' Jonh Ingham in May 1976. "But what if one night we were both in trouble? So we got DNV. And if DNV was in trouble then we were both in trouble, so we needed another one"—Ivan Kral. "One night we were all in trouble and we said, 'We've got to get a drummer to keep this thing all together.'"

Jay Dee Daugherty was born in Santa Barbara, California, on March 22, 1952. He moved to New York City in 1974 with the Mumps, and for a time they were regarded as one of the city's most promising combos. But while so many other groups rose, the Mumps fizzled out.

Daugherty made his debut with Patti at Paul Colby's Greenwich Village club the Other End, on June 26, the night that Patti paid tribute to the Rolling Stones, who were in town to play a week of shows at Madison Square Garden. She unveiled her Keith Richard T-shirt during "Time Is on My Side," and Stephen Holden's review of the performance in *Rolling Stone* celebrated her passion: "She exudes an inimitable aura of tough street punk and mystic waif, in whose skinny, sexy person the spirits of Rimbaud and William Burroughs miraculously intersect with the mystic qualities of Jim Morrison, Jimi Hendrix, the Stones, the Velvet Underground, the Marvelettes and Mary Wells, to name but a few."

In the *Village Voice*, James Wolcott honored her honesty: "When Lenny Kaye was having difficulty setting up his guitar between numbers, Patti paced around, joked around, scratched her stomach, scratched her hair—still Kaye was not quite ready. 'I don't really mind,' she told the audience. 'I mean, Mick would wait all night for Keith.'" And everyone waited for Hendrix, which is why she would later align the two, Lenny and Jimi, in the prose piece "Konya the Shepherd"—dedicated to Kaye, the boy who *was kissing the sky, night after night, star upon star.*

That same night, however, the *Village Voice* also remarked that "even those [onlookers] somewhat used to her galloping id were puzzled by lines like, 'You gotta a lotta nerve sayin' you won't be *my* parking meter.'" For what Patti knew, but the crowd didn't, was that Bob Dylan was in the audience that night, giving the room, wrote Wolcott, "an extra layer of electricity and Patti, intoxicated by the atmosphere, rocked with stallion abandon. She was positively *playing* to Dylan, like Keith Carradine played to Lily Tomlin in the club scene from *Nashville*."

It was the first time Dylan saw Patti perform, and author Sid Griffin speculates on his impressions in his 2010 book *Shelter from the Storm.* "Smith offered several facets which chimed with Dylan. Firstly, the use of poetry in her act. Secondly . . . Smith and her band's extemporized songs eschewed the default settings of orthodox rock'n'roll jamming"— a discipline that Dylan had never successfully mastered. And finally, the fact that she was "audibly and visibly influenced by him. . . . For Dylan to stumble upon Patti Smith and her band on stage at the Other End must have been akin to Ramblin' Jack Elliott witnessing the young Dylan in Greenwich Village for the first time in 1961."

Nobody knew it at the time, but Dylan was piecing together what would become the Rolling Thunder Revue, checking out the morass of musicians who, as word of Dylan's visibility spread, were now descending on the Village in hope of catching his eye. Rolling Thunder was an absurdly grandiose project: He intended to tour small clubs and theaters in the American Northeast with upwards of two dozen musicians, in a four-hour show that allowed everyone to take his or her own solo turn before they all came together to back Dylan's own performance. Bobby Neuwirth was recruited to marshal the sprawl of backing musicians and lead them through their solo numbers. An all-star band rounded up Joan Baez, T-Bone Burnett, Ramblin' Jack Elliott, and Roger McGuinn; scheduled guests would include Allen Ginsberg, Bette Midler, and Joni Mitchell. Sam Shepard would be along for the ride, documenting the unfolding madness for a book; filmmaker Howard Alk would be shooting the affair for a feature film.

Mick Ronson, the English guitarist, had already been recruited to the Rolling Thunder ensemble, and he was there the night Dylan met Smith. "Dylan was looking for names, but not anybody; they had to be people he could sense some kind of link with, and Patti was getting a lot of press calling her the new Dylan or the female Dylan, and Bob was intrigued by that."

Dylan came to the dressing room at the end of the set, looking a lot healthier than legend usually alleges, and a lot better humored as well. When the photographers wheeled to take his picture, the *Village Voice* reported, Patti gleefully pushed him to one side. "Fuck you, then take *my* picture, boys." Dylan laughed and stepped away.

"We were like two pit bulls circling," Patti told Thurston Moore in *Bomb* magazine. "I was a snotnose. I had a very high concentration of adrenaline."

"Any poets around here?" Dylan asked.

"Poetry sucks," Patti replied.

"It was neat that I got to see Dylan," she told Dave Marsh of *Rolling Stone*, "got to spend any time with him before I did my record." But "we never discussed nothing. We never talked. I mean we *talked* . . . You know how I felt? I been talking to him in my brain for twelve years, and now I don't have nothing to say to him. I feel like we should have telepathy by now. Me and my sister don't talk."

So when Dylan called Patti the following week, July 3, and invited her to meet him at Gerde's Folk City, the Village bar where his own early career had unfolded, she initially thought that he was simply asking her out for a drink. In fact, Ramblin' Jack Elliott told Sid Griffin that "[she] came as Bob's date."

It was only once she arrived, and saw the crowd milling around the room, that she realized the evening was to be a little less intimate than that.

Mike Porco, who had run Gerdes since the beginning and was long ago titled "the father of New York folk" was celebrating his birthday that night, and half of the folk scene, it seemed, had turned out to celebrate with him. What better occasion could there have been for Dylan to also announce the Rolling Thunder Revue?

Tom Waits was there, as were David Blue, Dave Van Ronk, and Commander Cody and His Lost Planet Airmen. Joan Baez opened the evening with a solo rendition of one of Patti's favorite Dylan songs, "One Too Many Mornings"; Roger McGuinn performed "Chestnut Mare," while Patti watched and thought of horses. Bette Midler sang a couple of songs from her newly completed—and Dylan-aided—next album, and then, according to Patti, she "came over and threw this glass of beer in my face!" Still astonished two years later, she told journalist Barry Miles in March 1977, "[She] just walked up! I never met her before. It was like a John Wayne movie!"

Dylan wandered over, pushed Patti toward the stage. The room was watching. She had nothing prepared, had not even dreamed that she'd be expected to. But she stepped up to the microphone, then turned to guitarist Eric Andersen and told him to play a droning E chord and not let up till she was done. "I just made up this thing. I looked at Bob and made up this thing about brother and sister. But while I'm doing it I start thinking about Sam Shepard . . . and so I told this story, really got into it, made this brother and sister be parted by the greed and corruption of the system."

She finished, then leaned back to Eric Andersen. They conferred for a moment, then nodded, and the guitarist strummed the opening bars to his own song "Sweet Surprise." The pair duetted, and Patti was beside herself with excitement afterward. "I did a good job and a lot of people liked it. I was real proud."

She was even prouder when Dylan revealed his real reason for asking her down that night. Everybody else on the stage that evening was a part of the tour, he told her. She didn't want to be the odd one out, did she?

She turned him down.

"There was no space for me on that tour, and he knew it," she insisted to *Hit Parader*. "But at that point, it was so early in my career . . . and he felt that I should be exposed to the public. I thought it was real sweet of him."

Mick Ronson explained, "The problem was, she wanted to bring her own band on the road, and that wouldn't have worked because the whole point of Rolling Thunder was everybody using the same group of musicians." (Emmylou Harris, one of the guests at the still-ongoing sessions that would compose Dylan's next LP, *Desire*, would turn down a similar offer for the same reason.) "But I think he still wished there'd been some way he could have brought her along."

Dylan was not offended. Perhaps hoping that he could still change Patti's mind, or maybe just extending the hand of friendship, he invited her back to the club on July 5, to take the stage for a dry run of what she could experience every night if she joined the tour: a heavyweight band comprising Dylan on piano, Ronson on guitar, bassist Rob Stoner, and Bobby Neuwirth handling guitar and mandolin.

Patti was in high spirits that night. Far from her own band and audience, she relaxed into a full set of lightweight folk songs: "Goodnight Irene," "I've Been Working on the Railroad," and sundry other old favorites.

Another day, journalist Larry Sloman was stunned to walk into a Rolling Thunder rehearsal at SIR Studios to find Ramblin' Jack Elliot playing a Grateful Dead song onstage, with bassist Rob Stoner "thumping along on bass, [and] Patti Smith . . . wandering around the rear, directing the music with grandiose sweeps of her arms."

Everybody around her knew that Patti was sorely tempted by Dylan's offer, and that the presence of so many old friends on the tour buses—Shepard, Neuwirth, Ginsberg—tugged at her more than she might even have admitted.

But it wasn't to be, and afterward, she admitted to Thurston Moore, she feared that Dylan would never speak to her again. But a few days after she delivered her final refusal, she was walking down Fourth Street when she bumped into him as he headed toward the Bottom Line. He paused, and reached into his pocket to produce one of the photographs taken of the pair of them, now splashed across the cover of the latest *Village Voice*.

"Who are these two people?" he asked, smiling broadly. "You know who these people are?"

9

CHRIST! THE COLORS OF YOUR ENERGIES

A RISTA BOOKED THE band to go into the studio in August. For a time, there had been talk of them traveling down to Miami's Criteria Studios to record with producer Tom Dowd, as he rode the success of his recent work with Eric Clapton and the Bee Gees. "I didn't know anything about producers and just picked Tom Dowd because I admired him," Patti recalled to Lucy O'Brien in the *Independent on Sunday.*

But then a more suitable choice crossed her mind: John Cale, the legendary cofounder of the Velvet Underground who had already stamped his mark on some of the most important recordings of the last few years. After contributing as a performer to the Velvets' first two albums, he produced the debut LP by the Stooges and three albums by Nico. He handled what would have been the Modern Lovers' vinyl debut, had the oil crisis not forced their record label at the time to dump them midway through the sessions. And, as if to complete the circle, he had almost formed a band with Ivan Kral shortly before the guitarist joined Patti.

None of which had anything to do with Patti's decision to bring him on board. "My picking John was about as arbitrary as picking Rimbaud," she told Dave Marsh. "I saw the cover of *Illuminations* with Rimbaud's face, y'know, he looked so cool, just like Bob Dylan. So Rimbaud became my favorite poet. I looked at the cover of [Cale's 1974 album] *Fear* and I said, 'Now there's a set of cheekbones.' . . .

"The thing is . . . in my mind I picked him because his records sounded good. But I hired the wrong guy. All I was really looking for was a technical person. Instead, I got a total maniac artist. I went to pick out an expensive watercolor painting and instead I got a mirror."

That discovery was still to come. For now, Patti was simply overjoyed to have obtained Cale's services for the record—so overjoyed that when he first got a call from Patti and her manager, Cale was left wondering what she even wanted. In his autobiography, *What's Welsh for Zen*, he recalled, "I said, 'Does she want me to produce a record? Does she want me to get into bed with her?'" And Patti and Jane Friedman, on the other side of the speaker phone, roared.

Cale had seen Patti perform before, he told the *Independent on Sunday* years later, so he understood how much her act depended on both her physicality as a performer and her "use of language . . . the way images collided with one another." As her producer, his first question would be, "How do I contain this energy? How do I capture it on a record?" Such dilemmas are the reason why live albums have a quality that studio discs can never attain, and why a great live act often makes a lousy studio band. Cale's goal was to ensure that Patti made the transition more smoothly than most.

A few weeks before the first studio date, he had Jane Friedman book the group a show in Woodstock so he could see them perform away from their usual audience. It was an awkward request; *he* might have been curious to discover how the band functioned in front of a room full of strangers, but Patti and the band had no interest at all. Besides, Patti was adamant that she hated the countryside.

But that was only the first of their problems. A small and unsuspecting audience stared in disbelief as Cale missed most of the first set when he passed out at the side of the stage. He came to in time for the second set, but spent a lot of that throwing up. "That meant the second set was better than the first," Cale excused himself afterward, but he clearly wasn't overly concerned about endearing himself to the band or, at least, to the band's sense of self-perception.

"How did you like them?" Clive Davis asked Cale at a meeting the following day. "I fell asleep," Cale replied. "Jet lag, Clive, jet lag."

"As soon as I got into the studio with Patti," Cale wrote in his autobiography, "the flirtatious girl on the telephone had been replaced by a female General Patton." But he was willing to put up with that. From the moment he heard her "electric voice" during that first telephone conversation, he'd known he wanted to work with her. He knew, just as his fans did, that some of his best work as both a producer and a recording artist in his own right was cut around the strengths of a powerful female vocal: Nico on the first Velvet Underground album and then across the three albums he had produced for her since then; Judy Nylon making a cameo on Cale's own "The Man Who Couldn't Afford to Orgy."

Patti fell into the same orbit as those women, as Nico remembered. "John always reacts well to strong women. I don't know what kind of relationship he had with them outside of the studio. But in the studio it is a physical thing, sexual, John pushing toward his orgasm and the woman pushing toward hers. On my albums we were like two lovers even when we weren't lovers. You can hear it in the arrangements—we are fighting for our own satisfaction but pushing for each other's as well.

"It was the same when he worked with Judy [Nylon would later become part of Cale's live band] and Deerfrance [Nylon's successor in that same group] and it was the same when he was working with Patti. They fought like animals, but the music sounded like they were fucking like animals as well."

Patti "should have married John Cale," Nico laughed to biographer Richard Witts. "They could live in a gingerbread house and make gingerbread children." They didn't, of course; there was never any possibility of that. But Nico's words ring true regardless, when considered in light of both the final fruits of the recording sessions and the participants' own recollections of the sessions themselves.

Cale began by observing that the band was playing out of tune "because their instruments were warped." Before they recorded a single note, he suggested, they should replace their battered tools. Hardly surprisingly, the band agreed. "You had to make them feel that they were really good musicians to allow room for Patti's poetry to come through," Cale explained in *What's Welsh for Zen.*

He was not certain, though, precisely "what persona this record was going to have until I had her improvise against herself. Then I could see how she had managed to make use of so much from Lou Reed and Dylan in the music." The difference, he surmised, was that Reed's improvisations "came primarily from psychological insights, whereas Patti's were attuned to the rhythms of Welsh Methodist preachers"—an observation, of course, that only a Welshman could make. He also realized that if Patti was going to succeed with a record-buying audience, he would have to help her channel "her aggressive, challenging voice" away from the live stage and into the studio.

Patti herself stood in his way. "I knew nothing about recording or being in the studio," she continued in that joint *Independent on Sunday* interview. "I was very, very suspicious, very guarded and hard to work with, because I was so conscious of how I perceived rock 'n' roll. It was becoming overproduced, overmerchandised, and too glamorous." Patti saw it as her duty to stem that tide, and she would eventually realize that Cale was on her side. "But I made it difficult for him to do some of the things he had to do."

One night, she laughed, they drove Cale so crazy that he was falling asleep at the desk and banging his head on it in a bid to try to stay awake. But "instead of throwing his hands up or being pissed at me, John got even crazier and more obsessive. It was like having two crazy poets dealing with showers of words. . . . There's a certain beauty in it that wouldn't have happened without John."

Or as she put it to Susan Shapiro in *Crawdaddy* at the time, "He's a fighter and I'm a fighter, so we're fightin'. Sometimes fightin' produces a champ."

At other points, Cale's influence was merely cosmetic. For instance, he convinced Patti to drop the mock-Caribbean tone she adopted when performing the reggae-inflected "Redondo Beach" in favor of a more lackadaisical but ultimately more convincing tone. He also suggested that they add strings to the record—such embellishments had worked on several of his own past albums, his love of the Beach Boys shining through a lot of his work (not least of all "Mr. Wilson," on his last LP, *Slow Dazzle*)—but Patti refused to countenance such a suggestion.

She did, however, welcome the participation of several musicians outside her own band. Tom Verlaine was called in to supply the anguished guitar lines that highlighted his cocomposition "Break It Up." And Allen Lanier, who penned music for two of Patti's poems on the album, "Kimberly" and "Elegie," would perform the languid tones of the latter, a poem written to mark the death of Jimi Hendrix, which Patti insisted be recorded on the fifth anniversary of the guitarist's death: September 18, 1975.

That day was their last in the studio, and Verlaine had already been booked to record his part on the same day. According to Cale, the friction between Lanier and Verlaine was palpable (he credited it to Patti's supposed romantic involvement with both men). The result was "one of the most explosive sessions" of them all, with an atmosphere "so tense it was frightening." Frightening, that is, to everybody apart from Patti, who had what Cale called "a mother hen thing about getting all her boys together." When Verlaine and Lanier inevitably sparked, "she thought that was very sexy."

Contentious to the end, the *Horses* sessions finally wrapped. Straight from the studio, Patti and the band headed uptown to the City Center, to take part in a three-day convention for the Arista label. A host of their labelmates were also on display, at an event that Clive Davis had, rather brilliantly, decided to open to the general public as well as the industry suits who normally populate such happenings. Barry Manilow, Loudon Wainwright III, Martha Reeves, and Gil Scott-Heron were also on the bill, but it was Patti Smith who would be headlining, in the minds of both the assembled multitude and the label head himself. Those other acts would undoubtedly go on to sell plenty of records. But Patti was selling a lifestyle.

Patti's set was short, just four songs—"Birdland," "Redondo Beach," "Break It Up," and "Land"—plus an encore of "Free Money." But the results of six weeks in the studio were clear to all. "Birdland," in particular, had taken flight; already flirting with the ghost of Charlie Parker, now it consummated the marriage, and a lot of that was down to Cale.

"There's a lotta inspiration going on between the murderer and the victim," Patti explained to Dave Marsh. "And [Cale] had me so nuts that I wound up doing this nine-minute [version] that transcended anything I ever did before."

Tighter than ever before, the band and their vocalist had melded now into a seamless whole. Journalist Lisa Robinson, reviewing the evening, called the performance "stupendous, a truly exciting moment"—and coming from a writer who had seen Patti perform on so many previous occasions, that was high praise indeed. "Everyone connected with Arista records was ecstatic," Robinson concluded.

That new cohesion, too, was Cale's doing. "What John did for us was to make us aware of each other," Patti acknowledged to Chris Charlesworth of *Melody Maker*. "He said that we were really nebulous and weren't that close, and I thought we were, y'know? But, after that recording, we really broke past everything, got to know each other's fragile stuff. We're like brothers and sisters."

When it came time to shoot the album's cover art, another member of Patti's artistic family was inevitably behind the lens: Robert Mapplethorpe. He photographed the four band members, of course, and their portraits were applied to the album's back cover. But for the front-cover image, Mapplethorpe took a portrait of Patti alone, her black suit jacket slung over one white-shirted shoulder, her hair a tangled mess, her expression not severe but not inviting, either.

It was simultaneously sexless and sexy, emotionless and exciting, deeply androgynous and irresistibly feminine. "The singer's eyes pierce her compatriot's lens," wrote Amy Hanson in 2010, "and you can almost hear the lyrics to the album's closing 'Elegie.' 'There must be something I can dream tonight / The air is filled with the moves of you.' She might have written those words for Jimi Hendrix but they are just as appropriate here."

It was quite unlike any photograph that any "female musician" had ever displayed across the cover of a debut LP.

"People have made a lot of stuff about the *Horses* cover," Patti reflected to journalist Michael Bracewell. "But a lot of what we do is bred on innocence. How people interpret it is up to them. I thought of myself as a poet and a performer, and so how did I dress? I didn't have much money; I liked to dress like Baudelaire. I looked at a picture of him and he was dressed, like, with this ribbon or tie and a white shirt. I wasn't thinking that I was going to break any boundaries. I just like dressing like Baudelaire. . . .

"I know people would like to think that we got together to break boundaries of politics and gender, but we didn't really have time for that. We were really too busy trying to pull enough money together to buy lunch."

Clive Davis headed the long line of observers who loathed the photograph, and from his office at the top of the Arista hierarchy, he pleaded with Patti to change her mind about using it. She refused, and when *Horses* was released on November 10, 1975, it was Mapplethorpe's portrait of Patti that gazed out from the record racks—and ultimately became one of the most revered images of the age. It would not only garner artistic acclaim, appearing high on *Rolling Stone* magazine's list of the top one hundred album covers, but also shape the way Patti herself was perceived—by audiences, by fans, by the still slowly unfolding "punk rock" scene that would embrace her, both musically and visually, as one of its most crucial, vibrant figureheads.

As for the album itself, it is nigh on impossible, from our current vantage point, to appreciate just how *Horses* divided the establishment upon its original release.

In America, the most influential voices seemed to like the record. Griel Marcus told *Village Voice* readers that Patti "has made an authentic record that is in no way merely a transcript once-removed of her live show." John Rockwell of the *New York Times* warned that "it will annoy some people and be dismissed by others," but insisted that it was "an extraordinary disc, and every minute of it is worth repeated rehearings." Later, in *Rolling Stone*, Rockwell reiterated his praises, calling the album "wonderful in large measure," and he had a high old time acknowledging the homage that Patti herself admitted was paramount in her music: "All eight songs betray a loving fascination with the oldies of rock." Patti and her band might have been breaching musical frontiers toward which rock had never cast more than a passing, folk-inflected eye. But she had made a great record, simple as that.

Across the ocean in the UK, however, Patti's importance was the source of no end of controversy.

The people who liked Patti loved her. Manchester-based television host Tony Wilson made several attempts to book the band onto his late-night music show *So It Goes*, and was unequivocal in his admiration for what she represented. Writing in her 2010 autobiography *Mr Manchester and the Factory Girl*, his ex-wife Lindsay Reade recalled him proclaiming, "Suddenly there was an album [*Horses*] that was fresh and didn't sound like all that other shite." (His enthusiasm would not last—"In '76 she was great because then she was a New York poetess playing at being a rock star. And by '77 she was a rock star playing at being a New York poetess"—but still it was his love for Patti that would help birth one of the great creative partnerships of the decade to come: Wilson later recalled first meeting artist Peter Saville at a Patti Smith concert. Together they would be responsible for that most iconic of post-punk British record labels, Factory.)

Others, however, were less convinced, debating and dissecting Patti in both the letters columns and the editorial pages of the weekly music papers *Melody Maker* and the *New Musical Express*. Both publications had, in recent months, been murmuring of changes afoot in the music scene, changes that would either launch the music ever upward toward new pinnacles of artistic expression and experimentation, or guide it back to the basic purity with which rock 'n' roll first came into the world. Emerson, Lake & Palmer or a pile of scratchy old Sun label singles—the choice, the warring voices were saying, was yours.

According to the *NME*, Patti fell firmly into the latter camp. Not in execution, of course, for *Horses* was as much a product of modern recording technology as any progressive rock marathon, but in attitude. It brought rock 'n' roll back from the abyss of overextended soloing with a basic four-piece band fronted by a lyricist with something to say. "First albums this good are pretty damn few and far between," wrote *NME*'s Charles Shaar Murray. "It's better than the first Roxy album, better than the first Beatles and Stones albums, better than Dylan's first album, as good as the first Doors and Who and Hendrix and Velvet Underground albums." And why? Because "it's strange, askew and flat-out weird. It's neurotic and unhealthy and dank, a message in a bottle sent from some place that you and I have only been to in the worst moments of self-doubting defeated psychosis." *Horses*, he concluded, "is what happens when the fuses blow and the light goes out."

But *Melody Maker* savaged it, complaining that *Horses* represented all that was "wrong with rock and roll right now. . . . There's no way that the completely contrived and affected 'amateurism' of *Horses* constitutes good rock and roll. That old 'so bad it's good' aesthetic has been played to death. *Horses* is just bad. Period."

How prescient those two opposing viewpoints were would become apparent in the months after *Horses'* release.

Jane Friedman lined up live shows to promote the album, and first the group returned to California for a clutch of gigs in Berkeley, San Francisco, and Los Angeles. In L.A., Don Snowden of the *Pasadena Guardian* pounced, complaining that at times "it was virtually impossible to decipher the lyrics over the roar of the band"—which was especially problematic, he pointed out, given Patti's reputation as a poet. But "even on a bad night, her best moments showed Patti Smith to be a unique and provocative artist well worth checking out."

It was in L.A., too, that Patti earned the enmity of a band that was, in the eyes of her fans, the diametric opposite of all that she represented. The all-teen, all-sexy Runaways had stepped out of impresario Kim Fowley's rehearsal studio and onto the stages of a world that wanted nothing more (or so Fowley hoped) than a taste of hard-rocking female jailbait.

Ivan Kral was first to witness the Runaways in action, watching them perform at the Starwood and then walking into the backstage area just as Kim Fowley emerged with Robert Plant by his side. The following night, onstage with Smith, he made a point of wearing his newly obtained Runaways T-shirt, and all the Runaways wanted was to return the favor, and say hello to Patti and her band.

So the quintet, led by singer Cherie Currie, wandered into Patti's dressing room at the Golden Bear in Huntington Beach, and they hadn't even opened their mouths when Patti, barely glancing up at the proffered handshakes, barked, "You girls. Out."

English journalist Chris Salewicz recorded the fallout in a 1976 interview with the Runaways. Currie set the ball rolling. "She was such a ... *LURRGHHHH*. I mean, she was so disgusting with those saggy ..."

"Tits," Jett said.

"Tits," Currie agreed.

Like Blondie's Debbie Harry, the Runaways theorized that they had fallen afoul of Patti's desire to become the first, and biggest, female rocker in the pool. The Dead Boys' Stiv Bators, a close friend of Joan Jett's, declared that Patti "couldn't stand competition. People talk about her as 'a patron of the arts,' with Jim Carroll and Tom Verlaine, but she blanked Richard Hell when she thought he was moving into her poetic territory, and she blanked Debbie and the Runaways because she wanted to be the only female rocker that anyone was talking about. She was merciless."

The band returned to the East Coast. Philly was next, and then it was back to New York City for three nights at the Bottom Line immediately after Christmas. It would be the faithful's first opportunity to catch the live set that had fallen into place in California. The new set would prove that, already, *Horses* was behind them, as new material began jockeying for position in their show.

It included the sinister dub of "Ain't It Strange" and the paradoxically pretty "Pumping (My Heart)," neither of which would see vinyl until the end of the following year. They performed a beautifully stylized version of "Privilege," former Manfred Mann front man Paul Jones's theme to the dystopian rock movie of the same name, which would remain unreleased until 1978. They had even taken to playing a medley of the Velvet Underground's "Pale Blue Eyes" and the old garage stomper "Louie Louie" that has never been officially released.

A handful of *Horses* favorites remained on board, of course, but both "Land" and "Birdland" were as likely to become the backdrop to new improvisations and verse as they were to adhere to their vinyl incarnations. "Remember when I used to do this in the old days?" Patti asked as she unwrapped a new verse, "Nigger Book," from her pocket. "Fresh off the acoustic typewriter?"

Around them, past poems such as "Seventh Heaven," "Snowball," "Space Monkey," "Seven Ways of Going," and "Mafia" might be reprised;

one night she pulled "Sally" out of her past, with a laughing "I can't believe I'm going to do this one." Some nights, Patti would drop into a few lines of Darlene Love's "The Boy I'm Going to Marry," or the almost painfully keening "Work Song," with its *I was working real hard* lament.

"It was important to us that we never stood still," Sohl explained. "Even when we were touring all the time and we had no time to rehearse or even think about what we were doing, we knew one another so well that we could just go off on these completely unrehearsed tangents, knowing that they would work."

The group would be on the road almost constantly for the next five months, a full American tour that touched down occasionally in what would become Patti's nests of strongest support—New York City and environs, Philadelphia, Boston, D.C., and Cleveland on the East Coast; the corridor from San Francisco to San Diego on the West—but ventured further afield too.

Their support act was John Cale, whose *Helen of Troy* album had been released the same week as *Horses*—although you got the impression that he'd have preferred if it hadn't been. Shortly before flying to New York City to work with Patti, he handed his label, Island, the demos for his new LP. From there, he headed over to Europe for a tour, then returned to London to find his demos on the release schedule. Furious and dismayed, he fled the UK, returned to New York City, and joined Patti in Jane Friedman's managerial stable.

Cale would appear onstage alone, with just his piano for company, performing a solo set of songs before Patti alone came out to join him. They would sing a couple of songs together, then as the full band appeared on stage, Cale would exit. But he would always return, running back onstage for the encore "My Generation," thundering his bass line through Patti's profanity-laced version of the old rocker and then, as Patti cried out her final incitement—*We created it, let's take it over!*—waiting for Lenny Kaye to hurl himself across the stage and catching the guitarist in his arms.

The first half of 1976 saw Patti and her band either hit their stride or reach their peak, depending upon one's personal point of view. Richard

Meltzer, writing in *Creem*, described their live show as "the best by a cunny since Billie Holiday and best by either gonad group since James Morrison's prime," and he was right. One of the most popular bootleg records of the year would be Patti's *Teenage Perversity & Ships in the Night*, recorded at the Roxy in Los Angeles on January 30, 1976. It captures the band literally seething, even overcoming the unexpected appearance of Iggy Pop onstage to describe how he had "just been worked over for a week by a Transylvanian masseuse in San Francisco."

Not everybody was a fan, however. An unannounced show at San Francisco's Boarding House in January prompted *San Francisco Chronicle* scribe John Wasserman to disguise his review as an open letter to Lily Tomlin, in which he asked outright, "Have you ever heard of Patti Smith? Well, she is a new comedienne. . . . I know that 'imitation is the sincerest form of flattery,' but I think this Patti Smith has gone too far. She is doing your act." Robert Weinter of *After Dark*, too, found her antics difficult to countenance: "The emergence of 'rock poetess' Patti Smith as a potential superstar is the greatest hoax perpetrated on the American public since Andy Warhol's soup cans and Patricia Hearst's kidnapping. Encouraging her to disseminate her minimal art is like encouraging the local garbage man to go onstage to clang garbage-can tops."

As she toured, Patti attracted more such castigations. But one couldn't help but feel that they were increasingly isolated voices in the wilderness. A lot of people might not have understood what Patti was doing. But those who got it really got it.

Arista, too, was following the group's progress. The label arranged for the show in Cleveland to be recorded in its entirety, then culled one track, the set-ending "My Generation." It became the B-side to the band's debut single, "Gloria," which had served as *Horses'* opening track. Arista expunged the expletives from "My Generation" with a high-pitched beep for the all-important UK release—all-important because the UK was already shaping up to be as fascinated with Patti as America, thanks to those first astonished reports filed in the *New Musical Express* and *Melody Maker*, and the occasional follow-ups since then.

Talking to the British press, Patti was infuriated by her first taste of record company censorship. "You tell the kids that I say not to buy it," she railed to Mick Gold in *Street Life*. "You tell them it's against my wishes. In the States we fought and fought for that recording not to be censored. Just like the American government wanted to censor Brancusi's sculpture *Bird in Space*. Brancusi had to fight to redefine sculpture and I'm fighting to redefine rock 'n' roll. . . . I would rather see somebody bootleg the American version and put it out the way it's supposed to be. It's not that I don't care about money, but this is blood money. We fought for that record to be released."

Her words fell on deaf ears at Arista. But on the streets of Britain, it was the imported French and American copies that sold the fastest, as dealers placed ads in the classified sections of the UK music papers announcing their stock of the unexpurgated version.

On March 9, 1976, the band arrived in Detroit, the evening's concert preceded by a reception at the Lafayette Coney Island, a landmark hot dog and chili joint. A handful of local musicians were there, and Patti pointed one out to Lenny Kaye.

"Who's that?"

"Fred Smith. Fred *'Sonic'* Smith," to differentiate him from their friend in Television.

Even his name sounded like poetry.

Born on September 13, 1949, Fred "Sonic" Smith was a native West Virginian, but he was Detroit through and through. It was there that he'd lived most of his life, and there in 1965 that he formed the MC5, joining forces with vocalist Rob Tyner, guitarist Wayne Kramer, bassist Michael Davis, and drummer Dennis Thompson in a band that was destined to become one of rock 'n' roll's most incendiary, as well as one of its most unappreciated.

A couple of early singles and a series of increasingly ferocious live shows kept the MC5 alive for the first few years, and then a meeting with countercultural activist John Sinclair twisted the quintet's none-too-developed view of the world outside their rehearsal room into a firestorm of politicized rhetoric. By the time Brother JC Crawford came aboard as an onstage poet/commentator, spieling Sinclair's revolutionary declarations over the cacophony of a rock band, the MC5 were an act of war, a declaration of hostilities.

They railed against the system, but unlike a lot of the era's other self-appointed rabble-rousers, they made it count. No weak-kneed trust-fund kids who'd just thrown their toys from the stroller; when the MC5 spoke, people listened. They deployed the American flag as a backdrop to their barrage, and swore that one day they would take it back from the governments and corporations that had co-opted it and return it to the people. They were, wrote Sinclair in his memoir *Guitar Army*, "challenging the biggest death machine in the history of the world," and the only flaw in their argument was that they didn't realize just how far that machine would go to preserve the status quo. The police routinely closed or busted their shows.

The MC5 released just one LP, the epochal *Kick Out the Jams*, before Sinclair was jailed and the group lost their way immediately. Two further albums came and went; Kramer followed Sinclair into prison. By the mid-1970s, with the MC5 just a memory, Fred Smith was playing in small clubs and friendly support spots with his Sonic's Rendezvous Band. Few people even glanced in his direction.

But Patti did. He was standing in front of a white radiator, she recalled to Lisa Robinson in 1988, "and the communication was instantaneous. It was more than that. It was mystical, really, something I never forgot."

She invited Smith to join her band onstage that same night, to add extra guitar to their "My Generation" encore, and she could tell by the way he played, she said, what kind of person he was—"better than me, stronger than me," she told Patricia Morrisroe.

He accompanied her back to her hotel after the show, and there the roots of a new song began to germinate, titled for the twenty-fifth floor of the hotel, where Patti's rooms were that night. The two Smiths spent the night together, and then remained in touch after Patti's tour moved on: late night phone calls, postcards, and letters that crossed America and then the ocean.

On April 17, Patti Smith made her network television debut, appearing on *Saturday Night Live* to perform "Gloria" and a carefully restructured "My Generation." The following night, the band made a special appearance back at Reno Sweeney. The tour was becoming a procession of highlights, but for the band, the most exciting ones were still to come.

On May 10, they played two shows in East Lansing, Michigan. They
then boarded a flight to London to commence their first European tour.
And if anybody doubted how excitedly the country was awaiting her,
the news announcement in the *New Musical Express*'s April 17 issue
wrapped up six months of anticipation into one single paragraph: "Patti
Smith, New York's queen of rock and arguably America's biggest female
cult phenomenon, is to make her British debut next month. Patti Smith
was recently hailed by *Rolling Stone* magazine as 'the best new solo artist since Bruce Springsteen.' . . . Another leading U.S. cult figure, Tom
Waits—sometimes described as 'the male Patti Smith,' is also in line for
a British visit."

Their first engagement was an appearance on the *Old Grey Whistle
Test*, the most important and most watched rock show on British television. More than anything else on the band's schedule, this appearance
was their chance to make a major impression. It would have been easiest,
then, for Patti to lead the band through a couple of the songs they had
been touring for the last six months, tight rockers that would catch the
audience's attention immediately. Instead, Kral recalled, she selected a
song that the band had never even rehearsed, much less played together:
"Hey Joe."

"When she said that was what we were going to play on *Old Grey
Whistle Test*, it was exciting. We were in London, we were on TV, and we
were walking a tightrope, playing an arrangement of a song we'd never
played. And, apparently, it caused a lot of fuss."

Jimi Hendrix had been dead for almost six years, but in British rock
circles, both his name and his legacy were sacrosanct. Artists who covered
his material did so at their own peril. When Rod Stewart scored a UK
hit with Hendrix's "Angel," there were reviews that condemned him for
blasphemy, and he performed the song with almost touching attention
to Hendrix's original. Nobody could say that about Patti's "Hey Joe."

The performance began with a passionate rampage through her own
"Land," with knowing nods to Oscar Wilde, Otis Redding, and, torn
from that week's newspaper headlines, the disgraced English politician
Jeremy Thorpe. The leader of the Liberal Party was embroiled in the
kind of sex scandal that only the truly righteous ever get mixed up in,

a dizzying panoply of hunky male models, murdered dogs, and fevered denials.

It was an astonishing performance, despite the cameramen simply not knowing what to focus on. According to the newspaper *Sounds'* man on the spot, writer Jonh Ingham, "The broadcast, as usual, misses the great moments. As the pulsating intro breaks into ['Land,'] she whips off her shades: missed. Suddenly she drops on her knees in front of Lenny, as though to eat his guitar: the cameramen leap wildly, but by the time they focus the exciting, mind-warp instant has passed. When they draw to a close there is an electric, tangible atmosphere—no-one moves or speaks. . . . Now that was television!"

But the cameras caught enough anyway: Patti an androgynous wire at the microphone, cooler than cool but kinda geeky as well, exuding indifference but seething inside, knowing that she had just ten minutes in which to show England what it had taken four years to introduce to New York City. And she succeeded. The following day, everybody who saw the broadcast had something to say about it, though it generally wasn't complimentary—all the more so since the show's own production staff promptly swung from Patti's live rendition of "Hey Joe" into archive footage of Hendrix performing it in 1968.

That first engagement over, the band flew to the continent: to Copenhagen on May 12, then after that Brussels, Amsterdam, and two nights in Paris, one of which is preserved on a cassette recording that remains precious to everyone who hears it.

It didn't seem too promising to begin with. Patti's voice was even more out of sorts than it normally felt, and as early as the second song of the night, "Kimberly," the musicians sounded ever so slightly perfunctory, with only Ivan Kral's lead guitar trying to hack anything fresh out of the rhythm and maybe push Patti into another dimension. Instead she made a hash of telling the audience a meandering joke, and things continued chaotic.

An error-strewn "Redondo Beach," a tentative "Free Money," and a lazy intro to "Privilege" were all punctuated by lengthy silences—and then suddenly everything fell into place as Patti pounced onto the brutal reiteration of the Twenty-Third Psalm that she had inserted into that song.

It was as if she had suddenly remembered who (and where) she was. And from then on, the performance was peerless. "Pissing in a River," one of the few new songs that had slipped into the set during the American tour, glistened with laconic longing, and the compulsive, hypnotic dub of "Ain't It Strange" swirled into a breathless rap through the lurching and only occasionally melodic jam that would one day become "Radio Ethiopia," which bled, in turn, into "Land" and "Gloria."

Live recordings from earlier in the year, as the band ground its way in triumph across the United States, are exhilarating, but they start to sound alike after a time, as the repetition of touring dulled the performers' instincts. No time at all separated the European shows from the American ones, but somehow the band had switched off the autopilot.

Then it was back to London, where the audience that awaited at the Chalk Farm Roundhouse was disparate and, thanks to *Whistle Test*, divided. Journalist Barry Miles (who "knew me when I was just a nobody," purred Patti) described the gathering as the "regular Sunday night Roundhouse crowd, stoned and shaking sack loads of dandruff over their Levi's, part Patti Smith cult fans, including a large number of women delighted to have someone female do for rock what David Bowie did for the males," plus "a few fungoids and weirdoes who have come to check her out."

Onstage, Patti's excitement was palpable. She dressed for the album cover, but she was giggling and laughing, applauding the audience that was applauding her before she'd even sung a note, bouncing up and down on the stage like a schoolgirl unwrapping her very own pony.

Somebody shouted for "Gloria," and Patti shouted it back at the audience. Someone laughed when she picked up her guitar; she laughed along and dedicated her next song to Keith Relf, the former lead vocalist with the Yardbirds who had died two days earlier, electrocuted by his own guitar. As "Radio Ethiopia" took form around her, Patti howled out feedback over her instrument's yowling, and then it was into the closing salvo. "Gloria" ended the set, "My Generation" opened the encore, and the entire room gave voice to its savage denouement.

Another rap ended the night, a few lines from her poem "Neo Boy": *everything*, she declared, *comes down so pasturized / everything comes down*

16 degrees / they say your amplifier is too loud . . . *Tic/toc tic/toc tic/toc /* *FUCK THE CLOCK!* Then it was bang into a triumphant "Time Is on My Side," and Patti knew, in that instant, that it was. Years later she would describe it as one of her favorite moments performing rock 'n' roll—the audience sang along, some weeping openly, and she reveled in the honest outpouring of emotion.

The band was back at the Roundhouse the following evening, but they also had time to explore London. Patti and Kaye caught the Rolling Stones at Earl's Court. Then somebody suggested they pile on down to the 100 Club on Oxford Street, to catch Malcolm McLaren's latest managerial enterprise, the Sex Pistols. Before she was halfway down the stairs, the band's front man, Johnny Rotten, recognized Patti and swung from whichever Pistols number he was caterwauling into a sneering chorus of *Horseshit! Horseshit! Horseshit!*

Patti loved it, but in an interview with Mary Harron of *Punk* magazine, Rotten professed himself less impressed. "I don't like Patti Smith. Just a bunch of bullshit going on about 'Oh, yeah, when I was in high school.' Two out of ten for effort." But that didn't stop him from hanging out around the hotel while the band was staying there; "the last night they had to carry her up the stairs. I liked her for that. She was such a physical wreck."

It was all a very long way from CBGB.

Patti and her parents, Grant and Beverly Smith. ROBERT MATHEU/RETNA

Patti, like so many of her generation, describes the French poet Rimbaud as her first hero.

The rare first edition of Patti's first poetry collection, *Seventh Heaven*.

Lenny Kaye. He and Patti met in a record store in 1971, and they are still performing together today. THERESA K., WWW.PUNKTURNS30.COM

Tom Verlaine of Television.

THERESA K., WWW.PUNKTURNS30.COM

Patti and Richard "DNV" Sohl, the keyboard-playing heart of the original Patti Smith Group. JORGEN ANGEL, WWW.ANGEL.DK

The 1977 reissue of Patti, Lenny Kaye, Richard Sohl, and a passing Tom Verlaine's first record.

AUTHOR'S COLLECTION

PATTI SMITH

HEY JOE
(VERSION)

PISS
FACTORY

The brilliant Czech guitarist Iván Kral.

The final piece of the jigsaw. Jay Dee Daugherty played his first gig with Patti the night she met Bob Dylan. THERESA K., WWW.PUNKTURNS30.COM

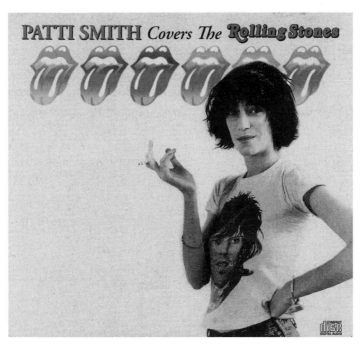

A classic Patti Smith bootleg, featuring the Keith Richards T-shirt Patti sometimes wore in performance. AUTHOR'S COLLECTION

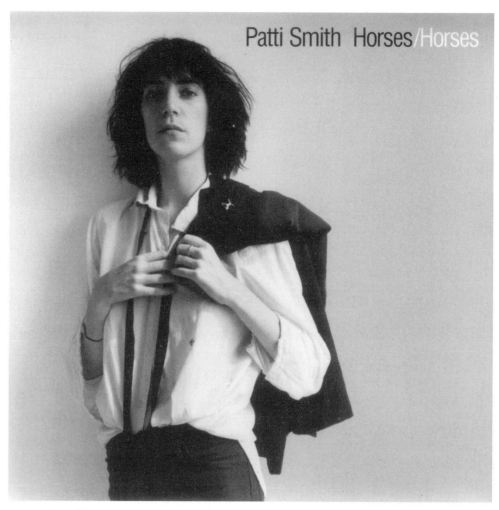

One of the most iconic images of the 1970s, Robert Mapplethorpe's photograph of Patti stares out from the anniversary rerelease of her debut LP. AUTHOR'S COLLECTION

One of the rarest of all Patti's books, her collaboration with Television's Tom Verlaine. AUTHOR'S COLLECTION

Patti—dancing in another dimension.

Patti in full flight,
Los Angeles, 1976.

Patti and Lenny Kaye in 1976—the
Mick and Keef of the new wave.

Patti starts a food fight at her infamous London press conference, 1976.

Ivan Kral and Patti in close harmony.

This is the sound of Radio Ethiopia.

Andi Ostrowe, roadie, friend, and confidante.

THERESA K., WWW.PUNKTURNS30.COM

Ivan grins behind his shades. Keyboard player Bruce Brody wonders why!

THERESA K., WWW.PUNKTURNS30.COM

Signing autographs—Ivan Kral, Patti, and the inevitable copy of *Horses*.

The fabulous picture sleeve adorning the French "Ask the Angels" single in 1977.

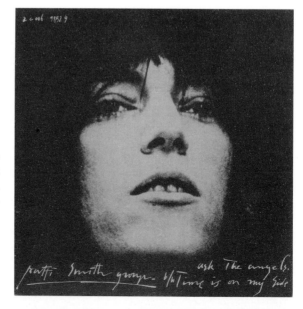

Patti's breakthrough album—in a sleeve, she said, designed to give her fans something they could masturbate to. AUTHOR'S COLLECTION

One of the most revealing of all Patti's late 1970s interviews appeared in this 1978 issue of Britain's best rock magazine.

AUTHOR'S COLLECTION

Patti Smith—the poetess who dared to rock.

THERESA K., WWW.PUNKTURNS30.COM

Patti and her longtime friend Jim Carroll share a stage in 1978.

Hand on heart, Patti in L.A., 1978.

I am an American artist. I have no guilt. Theresa K., www.punkturns30.com

MC5, the original rock 'n' roll niggers, outside of society and beyond the law. Guitarist Fred "Sonic" Smith (closest to the camera) never truly got over the band's reputation. Jorgen Angel, www.angel.dk

Patti's son Jackson, a regular presence alongside her onstage. THERESA K., WWW.PUNKTURNS30.COM

Patti's most recent book of poetry.
AUTHOR'S COLLECTION

Patti at the Chicago stop of the 2007 Lollapalooza tour.

10

BABELFIELD

B ACK IN NEW York City, the band began preparing to record
their second album. Live work was left to one side now; there
was a show to play in Milwaukee, and an afternoon in Central Park to
get through, but from then until a scheduled appearance in August at
the Orange Festival in Nimes, France (which, in any case, would be
canceled weeks later), they would all be able to sleep in their own beds
and hang out with their own friends.

On July 26, 1976, Patti dropped by the Ocean Club, the new venue
of former Max's Svengali Mickey Ruskin, where John Cale was playing
his own season of shows. There, a fortuitously rolling cassette captured
her stepping onstage as early as the second number, "Buffalo Ballet," to
add distinctive, and distinctively haunting, backing vocals to that most
plaintive of ballads, and then bouncing back just a couple of songs later
to keen behind "I'm Waiting for the Man" and attempt to snatch the
occasional verse. *Hey, white boy, what you doin' uptown?* she shrieks, then
extemporizes a line of her own, and suddenly the duet is a conversation,
Patti driving between the Lou Reed composition and her own "Rock n
Roll Nigger," while Lou Reed and Talking Head David Byrne, suddenly
onstage as well, strummed and rumbled behind them.

Even at the time, there was no doubt—either among the band or
elsewhere—that Patti Smith's second album was the acid test, all the
more so since *Horses* was received as something akin to a musical second

coming. Patti didn't just have to meet expectations; she had to exceed them.

So while outside observers were puzzling over whom she might select as a producer, floating names such as Lou Reed, David Bowie, and even Brian Eno (whose attempts to handle Television had ended in such ignominious failure), Patti was poring through the top forty in search of a producer who would take the band and its sound in the opposite direction entirely. She'd worked with a fellow artist and the world had heard the results. Now she wanted a technician. That's what she'd been seeking the first time around as well, but this time she was going to get one.

Even her bandmates raised their eyebrows when she first suggested Jack Douglas, but they also knew why she did it. Douglas was no inge-nue. He was assistant engineer on John Lennon's *Imagine* and engineer on the first New York Dolls album. He worked with Alice Cooper dur-ing that band's tenure under the aegis of producer Bob Ezrin, and when Ezrin turned down the opportunity to produce the second Aerosmith album, it was he who recommended Douglas to them. Since that time, Douglas and Aerosmith had carved three monster records out of their relationship, and if observers thought there was a hell of a gulf between Patti Smith and Aerosmith, then that only heightened Patti's excitement.

"I wanted to do a record that wasn't just a cerebral experience [but] more of a physical record," she later explained at a press conference in London covered by Allan Jones of *Melody Maker*. And from the moment the needle touched down on the opening "Ask the Angels," it was clear that she had accomplished it.

Recorded at New York City's Record Plant studios, the album would be dominated by the numbers that had been surfacing in Patti's live set over the past year. While "Radio Ethiopia" would be the title track and the centerpiece of the record, it was the songs at the fringes that allowed the album's heart to beat so loud. The miasmic dub of "Ain't It Strange" was in there; so was "Distant Fingers," which hadn't made it onto *Horses*. (This time around the hypnotic rag "Chiklets" would be left on the cutting room floor, a fate it certainly never deserved—it would remain unused until the album's mid-1990s rerelease.) The group tackled the ugly "Pumping (My Heart)" and then contrasted it with the impossibly beautiful "Pissing in a River," a passionate expression of devotion and love, set to an Ivan Kral melody that seemed almost heartbroken to be married to such a radio-unfriendly title.

Like the still-gestating "25th Floor" and "Godspeed," "Pissing in a River" was written for Fred Smith, the man whom Patti had so recently met and whom she already knew she was destined to spend her future loving. *Every move I made I move to you,* she sang. *And I came like a magnet for you, now.* Whereas the other two songs would look back at the night the pair first met ("Godspeed" even references the coat Fred was wearing that evening), "Pissing in a River" is the declaration of togetherness, forever-ness, that would develop from that initial encounter, squeezed through the prism of uncertainty, fear, and insecurity that so often accompanies the first months of a relationship.

Although Fred Smith was married at the time, he and his wife, Sigrid, were in the slow process of breaking up, and he was moving into a relationship with Kathy Asheton, whose brother Scott played with Smith in Sonic's Rendezvous Band. If a part of Patti's unconscious mind looked back at her time with Sam Shepard and wondered whether she was stepping back into that same sad circus, nobody would have been surprised. Which is perhaps why, in "Pissing in a River," she crafted lyrics that are a prayer to insecurity in its most painful guise.

She then turned the song over to Kral to beautify. Indeed, Kral was fast becoming Patti's most reliable writing partner. Across *Horses*, Lenny Kaye had been the only band member who received a straight cowriting credit, though Kral certainly added a dignified air to Patti and Allen Lanier's "Kimberly." Now he was stepping wholeheartedly into the spotlight. "Ask the Angels" and "Ain't It Strange" were both Smith/Kral compositions, and "Pumping (My Heart)" was a collaboration between them and Jay Dee Daugherty. The first record to be credited to the Patti Smith Group was clearly a group effort.

Even the dead had something to contribute—or so Patti later claimed. "I don't care what anybody says," she told *ZigZag* magazine's John Tobler in April 1978, "I don't care if they think I'm full of shit." Listen to "Poppies," she said, the song that merged with the most horrifying aspect of a new prose piece, "Babel," about a rape taking place under the influence of gas: *She lay there and the gas traveled fast / Through the dorsal spine and down and around the anal cavity.* "There's several voices, voice-overs like on *Horses.* There's one voice that came out of my mouth that scared me. I'm like a little one-hundred-pound girl, you know . . . but the voice in it sounds just like Hendrix, and I felt just like I was being taken over. It scared me. [And] I don't scare easy, believe me."

Yet even this spectral encounter would be overshadowed by the free-form chaos of the title track, "Radio Ethiopia."

Ethiopia was Rimbaud's last real home; it is also the home of Rastafarianism, the religion whose symbols and luminaries lie at the soul of Jamaican reggae music. Marijuana is the Rastafarian sacrament. Haile Selassie, who was the country's emperor between 1930 and his death in 1975, was Rastafari's God Incarnate, a messiah who would lead the African people back to the golden age that slavery had stolen from them. And his father, Ras Makonnen, had been one of Rimbaud's closest friends. Although Patti denied that she had embraced the religion itself, she did go through a period when "I was studying all aspects of Rastafarianism, including smoking a lot of pot while reading the Bible!"

Until now, she had eschewed drugs. "I regarded them as sacred and secret, something for jazz musicians or Hopi shamans," she told Simon Reynolds of the *Observer* in 2005. "I hated the suburbanization of drugs in the '60s." Now she felt free to explore, in the guise of the scholarship that would flavor, if not fixate, "Radio Ethiopia."

The song was further fueled by her friend Janet Hamill's recent return from that land. Tiring of New York City, Hamill had headed off to travel around the United States and Mexico and then caught a freighter across the Atlantic and journeyed through southern Europe and North Africa and down to Ethiopia. She'd returned in 1975 for the publication of her first collection of poems, and when she and Patti talked, their conversation frequently turned to Ethiopia—or Abyssinia, as it was known in Rimbaud's day.

Rimbaud spent two years in Harar dealing in coffee and weapons; it was his illness alone that forced him back to France, and he was desperate to return to Abyssinia as he lay dying in the French port town of Marseille. His final letter to his sister, written the day before he died, begs her to find him some stretcher bearers, to carry him to a freighter that he knew was about to leave for Harar. "I am unable to do what I must do," he wrote. "The first dog on the street can tell you that."

Patti's song, she told Stephen Foehr in the *Shambhala Sun*, "was exploring Rimbaud's state of mind at that moment when he experienced perhaps the last bit of excitement in his life—the hope of returning to Abyssinia—while realizing that he wasn't going anywhere except where God was going to take him."

Patti felt she shared that destiny.

As the band prepared to record the track, it was still without lyrics, a ten-minute flood of power, emotion, and raw spectral energy that, at sometimes twice that length, had been climaxing Patti's shows since her California sojourn the previous November. Live, it was a powerhouse; it often segued out of a reading of Jim Morrison's "American Prayer," while bass and guitar rumbled behind her, then wandered through snatches of old verse and impromptu stream of consciousness. In the studio, it became (and remains) one of Patti Smith's most astonishing performances, and one of the group's most pivotal: an apparently free-form but in reality deeply structured sequence of riff and melody that only slowly reveals its true nature to the listener.

Arguably, nothing that either Patti or her musicians would ever accomplish afterward could hope to surpass it, for what would be the point? "Radio Ethiopia" is a frozen moment in time, but it is a striking moment of both crisis and accomplishment. "Perhaps it was the repetition of performing, for the flow of language that seemed infinite, that poured through my hand onto sheets of paper onto the wall and into the air, seemed to dry up as we created *Radio Ethiopia*," she admitted in a note published in *Patti Smith Complete*. "How then to communicate? To reinvent words. Disassociate them. Redefine them."

She flew blind. "Fuck the slang scrawled across our practice room walls," the note continued. Words were not the be-all and end-all of poetry. Sound, too, could be words, and while Patti's note would credit Fred Smith as being the person who, "with few words, showed me the way to draw from my instrument another language," that realization was only a part of the alchemical equation that Patti first teased and then tortured from "Radio Ethiopia."

Few people in New York City at the time have forgotten the night that the song was recorded. It was August 9, 1976, and a storm was unfolding over the city, a hurricane that had some people contemplating evacuation, and others rushing to protect their homes and businesses from the elements. At Record Plant, Jack Douglas was plugging the gaps beneath the studio doors with towels and rags and strewing newspapers across the floor in readiness for the expected deluge. Patti alone may have been aware of the full moon "setting up for the night of the Lion. The emblem of Ethiopia. The Kingdom of Sheba," her note put it.

"Radio Ethiopia" would be recorded in a single take, one take that would last for as long as it needed to. It left nothing to chance, and everything.

"Nobody looked at each other, but we were ready," Patti wrote. The five musicians in a circle, Patti clutching the 1957 Fender Duo-Sonic that she'd just purchased from Manny's Guitars, and which might once have belonged to Jimi Hendrix. "Legend or not, it was mine." She paid $110 for it, but she had no intention of learning to play it. "I was interested in expressing ideas . . . within the realm of sound." And "Radio Ethiopia" flowed from there, the sound of a clothed naked woman, celebrating the storm but not feeling its impact, "just me on my knees laughing hysterically, thankful for the privilege of playing in a rock and roll band."

She revisited the moment in a new verse, "High on Rebellion": *what i feel when i'm playing guitar is completely cold and crazy, like i don't owe nobody nothing and it's a test just to see how far I can relax in to the cold wave of a note.*

Later, she declared that she would not be working with Jack Douglas again but admitted that he allowed the band to work at its own pace, jamming for as long as it took for them to find the rhythm they required, and that he threw aside his own instincts and not only recorded but also mixed "Radio Ethiopia" live in the studio. In fact, when Patti and the band mused on the possibility of overdubbing the track with the sounds of radios fading in and out, it was Douglas who told them to let it stand as it was, naked and unadorned.

"This is not an avant-garde project of mine," Patti had prophetically ad-libbed while performing the embryonic "Radio Ethiopia" in Paris earlier in the year. "I still want to be your valentine." And for anybody who values intention as an art form, and sees successful execution in the defiance of all expectations, she succeeded.

With the sessions at an end, the Patti Smith Group played a couple of New York state shows at Hamilton College in Clinton and Hofstra University in Hempstead, both shows effectively previewing everything that *Radio Ethiopia* had to offer. The band was gearing up for its next challenge: a swift return to the now-slavering Europe for two weeks worth of gigs.

The tour fell on the very eve of release for *Radio Ethiopia*, an album that was already getting a rough ride from critics. Much as Patti predicted, and certainly as she expected, reviewers who had waxed platitudinous over *Horses* simply failed to comprehend the new disc; they demanded to know what had happened to the poetry, slammed the heavy tracks as mutant metal, condemned the ballads for being too pretty.

"Patti Smith certainly has one hell of a lot to answer for," growled Marianne Partridge's review in *Melody Maker*. "Not only does she unashamedly use her band as a backcloth for her pretentious 'poetic' ramblings, but she simultaneously comes on as the savior of raw-power rock and roll as it struggles to survive the onslaught of esoteric rock. In other words, she's into the myth-making business. And in this, her second album, the myth is exposed . . . as cheap thrills."

That, perhaps, was only to be expected; *Melody Maker* had scarcely been supportive either of Patti or of the fast-collecting storm clouds of punk. But *Rolling Stone*'s Dave Marsh was also dismissive: "While Smith can be an inventive, sometimes inspired writer and performer, her band is basically just another loud punk-rock gang of primitives, riff-based and redundant. The rhythm is disjointed, the guitar chording trite and elementary. . . . Smith obviously would like to be just another rock singer, with a band that could reach a broad, tough teenage audience. Ceding control to a band that lacks her best qualities and encourages her worst . . . is hardly the way to go about it." Marsh also drew an utterly mystifying parallel between the "vulgar" "Pissing in a River" and the "transcendent quality" of "Piss Factory"—two songs that surely have nothing more in common than the very different meaning of a single term in their titles.

But he was not alone. When it rains misunderstanding, it pours, and gathering up the collected reviews, it felt as though only the ever-loyal *Creem* was still on Patti's side, as Richard Meltzer turned in a typically anarchic but never less than glowing riposte to the po-faced miseries elsewhere in the media. "It's really a bonafide certified *good'un*, y'know," he raved, and everyone else who both read that and loved the record thought, "Thank heavens *somebody* understands."

Patti probably felt the same way. She was in a defiant mood already, referring to herself as a military field marshal, comparing life in a band to the rigors of the army, and penning a beautiful new verse, "Babel Field," in which Marine Corps maneuvers and guerrilla training, instruments and weapons, guitar necks as bayonets, flash and crash through the chaos of war, which itself is reduced to *violent hieroglyphs of sound and motion*. A guitar weighs less than a machine gun, she wrote, but it packs as much punch, and when she steps up to the microphone, *I have no fear*. In performance, she would occasionally reinforce the punch by adding discordant guitar to the verse and retitling it "Bumblebee."

She would face down the media in the same way that she faced down hecklers: schooled in the politics of rock journalism herself, although she rarely adhered to their most brutal tenets, she was well aware of the ease with which the most devoted pack of critics can turn on the tip of a stylus, raising you up just to knock you down later. (Some people even suggested that she had purposefully constructed *Radio Ethiopia* to provoke such a brutal response so that she could get the critical firestorm out of the way and then regain equilibrium with the next release.)

For instance, when some critics noted that the band frequently drowned out Patti herself, they decided that this meant she had scaled back her poetic intentions. Patti mocked this off-target accusation mercilessly. "If everybody's hung up about poetry, there's a big fucking poem in the record," she would argue at her London press conference. "Tell them if they're hung up because there's no poem in the record . . . it's got the longest poem in the history of man. It took me four months. . . . The poem, I don't say it . . . everything you don't hear on the record because of the bass and drums . . . I've written the poem. In other words, it's like when you listen to *Madame Butterfly*."

She would elaborate to *Sounds'* Sandy Robertson in March 1978: "People think that because you write poetry that every word you say is supposed to be, like, gilded or something. I think that language is almost obsolete anyway. I write poetry because I was seduced by the word." The word, however, had been supplanted now. Language was dead. Sound was the new common denominator. Rock 'n' roll, she predicted, will be "the most universal language in the next ten years," and *Radio Ethiopia* was its first word.

"This album is, I think, much more feminine than the first album," she explained to another *Sounds* correspondent, Vivien Goldman, in November 1976. "The rhythm, it's more like ocean. . . . 'Radio Ethiopia' I think is very inspiring. I was listening to old Albert Ayler records, live, and they're not that much different to 'Radio Ethiopia.' All it is, is a commitment and a surrendering to a certain energy."

That may be so, or it may be bullshit. The live show, after all, had been driving deliriously toward those same peaks of dissonance, feedback, and pummeling riffery for half a year now. And rehearsals for the European tour suggested that the barrage was about to grow louder.

Crisis. Two days before they left for Europe, September 27, Richard Sohl was forced to pull out of the party. The pianist's doctors had diagnosed physical exhaustion. He'd always been the physically slightest member of the band, even when lined up alongside Patti's natural frailty, and the last year of almost nonstop travel, gigging, and recording had finally exacted the harshest toll. He couldn't have toured if he'd wanted to, and Patti had no intention of even suggesting he try.

A quick call rallied one of Lenny Kaye's friends, keyboard player Andy Paley, down from Boston. His band, the Paley Brothers, were on the rise at the time, and he was also the producer behind the recent revival of the Shangri-Las. The archetypal 1960s girl group had reformed that summer to record a new album with Paley at the helm—and with a sharp eye firmly focused on Blondie, whose own repertoire still included the Shangri-Las' "Out on the Street." The record was never completed, but the Shangri-Las would play CBGB one night, an impromptu performance with Paley and Kaye in their backing band.

"Andy is real crazy," Patti laughed to *New Musical Express* writer Charles Shaar Murray in October 1976. "He's amazing. Amazingly crazy. He was telling me what a good soldier he was gonna be . . . and he's so *spaced out.*"

The tour would consume the entire month of October, opening in Scandinavia, where the first night at Stockholm's Konserthuset was filmed for broadcast on local television. It's the only full visual record in circulation today of the band at the height of its musical and improvisational talents, as Patti stepped for the first time into her role as a rock performer first, a poet and artist second.

She dances awkwardly but beguilingly, turning her back on the audience more than once to sing directly to her bandmates instead. Or she flails unself-consciously, whirling through a breathtaking "Ain't It Strange," dropping on to her back and then raising herself crablike on all fours, strapping on a guitar as she raps a breathless prelude to "Radio Ethiopia": *Deep in the heart of your brain is a lever, in the heart of your brain is a switch, deep in the heart of your existence.* Today, of course, the improvised riffs and lyrics of "Radio Ethiopia" might border on the familiar, but it is easy to place yourself back in the crowd in Stockholm, with the song screaming out for the first time, endless and maybe even nameless, a catacomb of sound that only resolved itself into something approaching a song for the pleasure of snatching that solace away again.

After Scandinavia, the tour would swing down through one-night stands in Belgium, the Netherlands, Switzerland, West Germany, and Austria, before settling into Patti's beloved Paris. It was not an easy journey, and Andy Paley appeared to be the inadvertent root of much of the difficulty. "You know what he put us through?" Patti asked Charles Shaar Murray. The first night on the road, he was interviewed by a woman whose command of the English language was apparently limited to the word "champagne." So they ordered some up and proceeded to have a party. "Then," continued Patti, "he had a nervous breakdown and heart attack." In fact, it was only a *suspected* heart attack, while the group was flying to Hamburg, but still, an ambulance was waiting to pick him up when the plane landed and rush him to hospital. He was discharged in time for the next show—and returned promptly to his chosen on-the-road lifestyle.

New Musical Express journalist Murray joined the tour in Amsterdam, catching the show at the Paradiso and then meeting up with Patti as she toured the city the following morning, stopping by a flea market and watching as she pawed through a record stall and emerged triumphant with a handful of bootlegs, three of her own and one by Blue Öyster Cult. She was still showing off her finds, and recommending *Teenage Perversity & Ships in the Night* to anyone who cared, when the storeowner caught sight of her.

Assuming this strange woman was planning to steal the record, he grabbed for it. Patti stood her ground.

"Fuck you, asshole. I'm Patti Smith and this is *my record!* I ain't getting any money for this. I oughtta call the cops on ya."

Then she turned and walked imperiously away.

Eventually the tour arrived in Paris, for two shows, three days, and a bittersweet reunion. Nico, the impossible beauty whom Patti knew from her earliest days in New York, had relocated to the city. Now a suicidal smack-head, she'd been dropped by her last record company, Island, after they misconstrued as racist a remark she made about not liking Negroes. As a child, she said, she was raped by a black man; as an adult, she had lived with a Black Panthers death threat hanging over her head. Being in their presence, she said, made her nervous.

It was not the only way in which Nico had grown paranoid and frightened. One of her idols, Ulrike Meinhof (one-half of the so-called Baader-Meinhof Gang, a left-wing guerrilla organization that flourished in mid-1970s West Germany) was dead, having committed suicide in prison, and Nico's natural tendency to absorb the trials of her icons left her feeling as though she, too, was incarcerated on a spiritual death row. On top of all that, her harmonium, the instrument with which she had recorded three of the most remarkable records of the decade so far, was gone, either stolen or sold to pay off a drug debt. She was at rock bottom.

"I was without money and now I couldn't even earn a living playing without my organ. A friend of mine saw one with green bellows in
an obscure shop, the only one in Paris. Patti bought it for me. I was so
happy and ashamed. I said 'I'll give you back the money when I get it,'
but she insisted the organ was a present, and I should forget about the
money. I cried. I was ashamed she saw me without money."

She told Richard Witts, "I felt like she could be a sister, because she
was the double of Philippe Garrel [the movie director and, at that time,
Nico's lover], and I liked to be together with her."

Patti's generosity would help Nico place her career back on track,
and so would her example. When she visited London eighteen months
later, Nico would find herself feted by the same punk audience that Patti
had helped to kick-start; a former member of the Velvet Underground
could scarcely go wrong in a city so enraptured by the new music. And
when it *did* go wrong, as the assembled hordes of punk stood bemused
and outraged by the solitary woman making medieval noise on the spit-
drenched stage (so much for the egalitarianism with which punk had
first spread its wings), that, too, was a lesson that she could have learned
from Patti Smith. And she would turn it around.

Nico was not the only cherished icon with whom Patti reconnected
during her stay in Paris. On her second trip to the city in 1972, she had
stood at Jim Morrison's grave and dreamed that he would emerge to
share a duet with her. Now, four years later, she received the visitation
that she had been searching for.

She was onstage at the city's Pavillon de Paris, a theater built on
the site of an old slaughterhouse, and no matter how hard she tried to
suppress the impression, "I had a really weird feeling that Jim was there,
there with the people." They were just going into "Land" with its invocation of horses, she told John Tobler, "and, of course, I can't not think
of Jim when I'm in Paris. . . . I realized I was in the slaughterhouse for
horses, and I was gonna do 'Horses,' and then I remembered 'Horse Latitudes,' so I sort of went into a drift, going into the leather raft carrying
the to-be-slaughtered-horses of 'Horse Latitudes,' and then I got a really
weird feeling that I was being taken over, and I started crying, and my
voice has changed."

It was, she swore, Jim Morrison.

"I don't think he's alive like a human being, but I don't think he's dead in a completed high stage, like the other guys are. I don't think his work was done. . . . I think he had a book to write; he wanted to leave his greatness through poetry. Morrison had this obsession about poetry, and he never completed himself, and I feel him. I feel him bugging me."

11

HIGH ON REBELLION

PUNK ROCK HAD yet to become a mainstream concern when the Patti Smith Group touched down in London in October 1976. Little more than a month had elapsed since the Sex Pistols–headlined 100 Club Punk Festival first alerted the media at large to the emergence of a powerful new musical movement, but another month would need to pass before the Pistols appeared cussing and cursing on nationwide television and turned an underground cult into an overground sensation.

The requirements of the explosion-to-come were still being streamlined. Not only was the design of the uniform that would mark someone as a punk evolving, but the stylizing of the musical nuances, too, were moving away from the sonic free-for-all that hallmarked the nascent movement's first few months, toward the strict three-chord structure that today's world knows as punk rock. And somewhere along the line, some time during the summertime that divided Patti's first London shows from her second, she had been firmly placed on the outside looking in.

It was a development she surely had expected. A year and a half later, she would counsel British youth via Sandy Robertson of *Sounds*: "We're only here to provide inspiration, and be a temporary life raft until you're ready to do your own work. . . . I think that we must steal from masters, that we need teachers. Every great man has been an apprentice in his life, it's how you pay your dues. I feel like I paid my dues to the Rolling Stones, and now I don't need them. I still believe in them, though. I don't feel any desire to say, 'Fuck you' to the Stones; they gave me a lot."

But that, she discovered, was the difference between herself and many of her British fans. It would be an absurd generalization (although that has not stopped some commentators) to say that British youth rose up as one to say "fuck you" to the music of the previous decade and replace it with punk rock, to consign everything that had gone before to the dustbins of history. But a lot of them did, and in among all the discarded ELP, ELO, Rolling Stones, and Beatles albums with which the nation's used record stores were now overflowing, there was a lot of more recent fare as well. Bruce Springsteen, Nils Lofgren, Graham Parker, Dr. Feelgood . . . so many names had risen up in the past year or so, haunted the headlines for a few glorious months, and then been cast aside as suddenly irrelevant.

Radio Ethiopia would not suffer that same fate, but not because Patti was immune to the culling. It would be overlooked altogether, left unsold on British record shelves as the full weight of the music press's diatribes sank into the impressionable skulls of prospective buyers and the notion that poetry had a part to play in punk rock was abandoned.

Ticket sales for the UK leg of the tour were sluggish. Two shows at London's three-thousand-plus-capacity Hammersmith Odeon suddenly seemed oddly ambitious, while scheduled gigs in Birmingham, Manchester, and Edinburgh were beginning to resemble implausible conceits. There was even talk that the latter two concerts might be canceled due to poor ticket sales.

Upon her landing in London, at the same press conference where Patti defended her poetic intentions, a questioner asked whether she had any idea why the gigs weren't selling out. She could have answered this question, too, if she'd chosen. Instead, she bellowed "fuck you" at the masses and pelted them with food. By the end of the rapidly curtailed conference, she was reiterating her status as the field marshal of rock 'n' roll, and warning a room full of journalists, "I'm declaring war."

"For a two-year-old," wrote cub journalist and avowed Patti fan Julie Burchill, "it would have been a very impressive performance. From the Queen of Rock and Roll, it was like watching God jerk off."

But the London shows were imperious regardless. "We're Gonna Have a Real Good Time Together" opened, of course, though Patti's first words to the audience were a reminder of the city's other live attraction that evening: "I'd like to thank you all for not going to see Peter Frampton tonight." A slinky "Kimberly" and a funky "Redondo Beach" kept the roars of recognition going, before a haunting piano passage fooled everyone into expecting a new song. Instead, they got an elegiac "Free Money."

The show was almost halfway over before "Ask the Angels" ushered in the material from the new album, bookended between "Louie Louie" and a triumphant "Time Is on My Side." But "Pumping (My Heart)" was dense and unfamiliar, and an epic "Ain't It Strange" wrapped itself into twelve minutes of concentric circles around that most lazily compulsive of almost-reggae rhythms, before—depending upon where your musical tastes were sitting—Patti either thrilled or baffled the crowd by introducing reggae icon Tapper Zukie to the mix.

Possibly the finest Jamaican toaster of the mid-1970s, Tapper Zukie was a magical wordsmith whose sense of timing has seldom been equaled. The first Jamaican DJ to take up residence in the UK, he was a firm favorite on British-based sound systems of the time. His album *MPLA* would be one the biggest-selling British reggae releases of 1976, and with the now-historic merging of roots reggae and the early punk scene already under way, Zukie found himself as popular with white rockers as with the Jamaican community. When Patti invited him onto her stage, she believed she was introducing Zukie to her audience and conferring her stamp of approval on him. For many of the evening's witnesses, it was as likely the other way around.

Zukie told writer Peter I, "I was on tour . . . and this guy Don Letts was runnin' a record shop down in the West End, and he talk to this lady when she came into the shop and say she want to come in contact with me. . . . And he call my friend Militant Barry and hook up with me and say Patti Smith want us to come down to Hammersmith Odeon, so we went. . . . And she just bowed down in front of me and said 'Man, when I see you, man, it's like seeing James Brown.' . . .

"She said she learned to play 'pon record from my album *Man Ah Warrior*. So she walk me out on the stage in front of about five thousand people and bow down in front of me and tell them that she learnt to play music from my album."

Ivan Kral, who never traveled without his Super 8 camera, set up one of the roadies at the side of the stage with instructions to film everything that looked worthwhile. He was rewarded with a stellar sequence of Zukie, proud and prancing on the lip of the stage, while even Patti relegated herself to a supporting role behind him.

A handful of hecklers arose from the stalls. Early on, reacting to the Odeon's all-seated policy, one voice demanded, "Next time, make it the Roundhouse." But as they grew more virulent, Patti responded with the staccato signals of "Radio Ethiopia," an eternity of feedback, riffing, and caterwauling that only slowly resolved itself back into anything the audience might recognize—a motorvatin' guitar and harp riff—and then snatched it away again with a furious "Rock n Roll Nigger." And then they were into the home stretch: everyone hailed a swaggering "Gloria," and you may never have heard "Land" reduced to an audience clap-along before, but it didn't seem to phase Patti any. Shame that the cassette tape that preserved the evening for posterity should run out before the song did, but it was still a great rendition.

The following week's reviews passed sneering commentary on Patti's attempts to smash her guitar at the end of the performance, raising it above her head and bringing it down on the ground repeatedly. She failed, and the guitar remained resolutely intact. But Kral revealed a secret: She didn't really fail. She didn't intend to break it, and by the time it was finally granted retirement, that little old guitar was still in one piece.

As they had back in May, the Patti Smith Group also fanned out to sightsee, shop, and take in some other concerts around London. For Kral, the highlight was getting a ticket to see his childhood idol Cliff Richard. For Patti, it was the chance to hightail it down to the ICA to catch the Clash, another of the bands rising up on punk's first wave, and join them onstage for a knockabout thrash through their own "I'm So Bored with the USA."

Suddenly, it seemed, Andy Paley was recalled to America by other commitments two shows from the end of the tour. As feared, the Manchester and Edinburgh shows were canceled.

Home by the end of the month, Patti took in Bruce Springsteen's latest New York City performance, at the Palladium on October 30. She joined him on stage too, for a head-spinning collision of his "Rosalita" and her "Land." She had danced onstage with him in the past, but tonight's collaboration between the king and queen of the New York City streets, as tired journalists had already dubbed them, was something special, so special that when the Patti Smith Group returned to the city after a short jaunt to California, Springsteen would appear both in the audience and on the stage. So would John Cale, whose recent bandmate Bruce Brody had replaced Andy Paley on keyboards.

The band was playing a full week of shows at the Bottom Line, dynamic evenings in which absolutely nothing could be accused of conforming to a script. One night, when Kaye leaped into the audience during "Ain't It Strange," Patti followed him, and the pair embarked on a crazy game of chase, leaping onto tables before she dragged him back to the stage. "It was just a lot of this adolescent energy and anarchy," Kaye recalled to Patricia Morrisroe, "and there was something very liberating about it because we were pushing the edge of the envelope."

The repertoire matched the mayhem. Back on home turf, Patti slipped guilelessly between rock and verse, often opening the shows with a succession of rapid-fire verbiage even before "We're Gonna Have a Real Good Time Together" brought the band into view. Old British Invasion covers flew out of the memory banks; improvisations wrapped around the most familiar album tracks; Dolly Parton's country classic "Jolene" rubbed shoulders with "Ballad of a Bad Boy." Patti was in her element, and when Springsteen leaped onstage on the fifth night, turning up at both the early and late shows, a raucous "Land" became a hypnotic "Not Fade Away," "Radio Ethiopia" merged with "Rock n Roll Nigger," and if anybody ever questioned whether a year on the road had reduced the Patti Smith Group to a regimented pile driver—another of the accusations that were spit out by the UK press—this was their response: a series of shows so loose and unstructured that the only thing that could ever have kept them together was the instinctive connection Patti and her musicians had shared since their earliest days as a band.

The anarchy continued. The day after the Bottom Line residency ended, on November 29, Patti was scheduled to speak at a twenty-four-hour "Hungerthon" being arranged by WNEW radio and hosted by the genteel singer-songwriter Harry Chapin. It was Chapin who was charged with the task of asking Patti to moderate her language, as there was no time delay, and he who received her withering on-air response. WNEW prided itself as being an alternative to traditional rock radio, but how alternative was it really, Patti demanded to know, if "the first thing that happens when I walk in is that you tell me you don't have a bleep machine and to watch what I say?"

Her tirade went on, and while it echoed in part the disaffected cries of the punk rock generation, it also spoke for every concern Patti had ever voiced through her own work. "Rock 'n' roll is being taken over by the people again. By young kids who don't want to hear about your digital delay. They don't want to hear about any of this stuff. They don't want to hear that they can't do an Eric Clapton solo. They just want to get out there and just get down on a rhythm. They want to crawl like a dog or they want to rise up. They just want to feel something."

She weaved in a message to match the fundraiser's own aims. Demanding that the rich West use its power to feed the hungry of the world rather than worry about "what color they are, or . . . what they're listening to on their radios"—or, as the undercurrent of her conversation made clear, any of the other questions or conditions that the West seemed to employ whenever a Third World nation went cap in hand for aid. But neither Chapin nor Metromedia, WNEW's owners, were amused. Plans for the station to broadcast the Patti Smith Group's New Year's Eve show at the New York Palladium were abandoned.

In March 1977, the *Yipster Times* would publish Patti's page-long defense of her actions and denouncement of her critics: "We believe in the total freedom of communication and we will not be compromised. . . . They are trying to silence us, but they cannot succeed." And, paraphrasing Jim Morrison, "We Want The Radio And We Want It Now." The article was accompanied by French photographer, artist, and singer Lizzy "Lyzzy" Mercier Descloux's famous photograph of Patti seated on a sidewalk in Paris, cigarette in hand, beneath a single graffiti-scrawled slogan, *Vive l'anarchie*.

Other broadcasters were less squeamish. On December 7, the Patti Smith Group recorded two songs, "Ask the Angels" and "Free Money," for the *Mike Douglas Show.*

They then set out on one of the most oddly mismatched tours of their entire career. Nobody seems certain what genius it was who thought the Patti Smith Group could ever share an audience, or anything else for that matter, with Sparks, the hyper-ironic California siblings who had spent the last two years as superstars in Europe but whose American profile seemed doomed forever to languish against a wall of humor-free apathy.

Hilly Michaels, Sparks' New Yorker drummer, was astonished by the pairing. "Sparks and Patti Smith on the same bill for a good dozen shows? Fellini couldn't have thought up something that weird. It was like a grandiose traveling musical oddities tour for a while, and there was a lot of friction between the Patti Smith Group and us." Some nights, Sparks were not even granted a sound check before the doors opened.

Only Ivan Kral offered Michaels any respite from the hostility. Michaels had been playing alongside Mick Ronson when Kral auditioned for the guitarist's band just before he joined Patti, and Michaels recalled, "He was a super-nice guy and my only warm relief with a friendly 'hi' to me when we all toured together."

One concession was made to the distinctly different audiences that the two bands could expect to attract: an agreement to alternate the headline slot. Michaels continued, "Depending on the city, either she or we would open first. We had our pockets of places where we were stronger, where the crowd went absolutely wild when we took the stage, and Patti had hers."

In Montreal, Canada, a solidly Sparks-loving crowd was making so much noise before the show started that Patti, having agreed to open that evening, was too nervous to even come out of her dressing room. At the Masonic Auditorium in Detroit on December 12, on the other hand, a fanatically devoted Patti audience greeted Sparks on stage with a hail of abuse that swiftly graduated to flying bottles.

Another night, Michaels confessed, brought one of the scariest experiences of his entire onstage life. Again Sparks faced a loyal Patti Smith crowd, and as they ran out onto the stage, the entire venue erupted into a chorus of catcalls. "There was this thunderous '*boooooooo*' resonating from three-thousand-plus people, just as we were getting ready to start. We were all a bit paralyzed by that! It was an uphill struggle from the get-go, and we had to perform our asses off for every single show."

It was with some relief that the two bands finally parted company following a show at Seneca College in Toronto, Canada, on December 19. The Patti Smith Group headed back to New York City, to wrap up a tumultuous year with a tumultuous performance: their New Year's Eve gig at the Palladium.

Robert Christgau reported on the show for the *Village Voice*, marveling at an audience that rushed the stage "like KISS fans," and then celebrating the performance's climax by describing it as "the true 'My Generation.'" The song began with Patti wrestling a guitar away from her female roadie, Andi Ostrowe, "and ended with [her]—joined eventually by Ivan Kral—performing the legendary guitar-smashing ritual that the Who gave up in the sixties."

Patti, too, would soon be giving up that sort of ritual. But whereas the Who, and all the other acts who had set themselves up in opposition to the status quo of the day, eventually retired from the battlefield, mission unfulfilled—because how could it be fulfilled with *Tommy* around your neck?—when Patti retired, it was because her job was done.

Six weeks after her last London show, the Sex Pistols appeared on British television and cursed their way into tabloid immortality. Punk rock was confirmed as *the* musical fashion of the next two years and was set to become the father of most of the others that followed. Even today, more than thirty years after punk came to life, it remains an underground current, one that has survived every effort to tame, blame, or merely contain its energies.

Its birth was not painless, and there were moments when it felt as though the infant might never live to adulthood. But Patti kept a close eye on her child all the same, and today when you ask her what punk rock means, her answer is unhesitating. "I think it doesn't necessarily have to take any specific form of music, because it's really a spirit," she told Gerri Lim of the Singapore magazine *Big O* in 1995. "And what the spirit is, I think, it removes itself or tries to repurify things when things get too convoluted or when they get too commercial. There's this resurgent spirit that people call punk that purifies everything again. . . .

"It's the new guard coming in to purify, to let things renew and begin again."

12

THE SALVATION OF ROCK

THE STAGE WAS as dark as a well-lit stage could be. Shadowed by amplifiers, blocked by her bandmates, and surrounded by the accoutrements that the headlining act deemed essential to their well-being, Patti was performing in near-total blackness.

Or so it seemed to her as she whirled around the tiny space she had been able to claim for her own, as she spun deliriously to the music that her bandmates were making, as she reached for the microphone in mid-twist, then tumbled, tripping over a monitor, black in the blackness at the lip of the stage.

And she fell.

The Patti Smith Group's berth as opening act on the latest Bob Seger tour had begun in Chapel Hill, North Carolina, on January 21, 1977, and moved down to the Hollywood Sportatorium in Broward County, Florida, the following day. Tampa was next, and then onward. Beyond the current tour, the group was scheduled to appear at the Nassau Coliseum outside New York City with the Ramones and the Blue Öyster Cult before moving on to West Germany and France in March. But then came Patti's accident and everything was canceled.

They were onstage at Tampa's Curtis-Hixon Hall, six songs into a set that had already bedazzled the Seger crowd with "Land," "Ask the Angels," "Redondo Beach," "Free Money," and "Pumping (My Heart)." Now they were pulsing through an extravagantly protracted "Ain't

It Strange," Patti spinning around the stage—forgetting, perhaps, that their allotted space in Seger's domain was considerably less than she was accustomed to using. With the stage in darkness, she had either forgotten or not even noticed the monitor that lurked between her feet and the microphone. They were six, maybe seven minutes into the song and suddenly she tumbled, backward over the monitor, to the concrete floor fifteen feet below.

For a moment the band played on; from behind the drum riser, Jay Dee Daugherty thought, "She's either dead or she's gonna jump back up onstage," he remembered in *Please Kill Me*. He was wrong on both counts. The musicians slowed, and then halted; from the audience, there were a few cries of alarm, and even more of puzzlement. "Did she fall?"

It felt as though she were in a Bugs Bunny cartoon, she said later, those frozen moments as a character steps out over a cliff and keeps walking in midair until he suddenly realizes there is nothing holding him up. But she could afford to joke. Although she had not, as some reports were quick to claim, broken her neck in strict medical terms, she had suffered two cracked vertebrae and a handful of breaks in the bones of her face.

She was bleeding from wounds that would require twenty-two stitches, and as she was maneuvered out of the venue by a team of paramedics from Tampa General Hospital, her bandmates simply stared in mute horror at one another. The gig was over, that was for certain, and maybe the tour as well. But what else was going to fall victim to Patti's crash?

"I felt myself going and I said—GET BACK HERE! I gripped my consciousness by the throat . . . the biggest battle was in my head, and I won."

She'd just written a poem for Tapper Zukie, she told *Sounds'* Vivien Goldman soon after. "It's called 'Tapper the Extractor' [and] it's the best poem I've written for a real long time. Tapper's poem kept me from losing consciousness; it's all about 'the thread of return.' . . . Yeah, the thread of return kept me here."

One does not hold the key, she told herself; *he extends it.*

Lying in the hospital, she could already hear the whispers; convalescing, she heard them louder. There were rumors circulating that she had been drunk or stoned. That she had jumped, even. She would refute them all. If she was in any kind of state, it was a spiritual one—the music and the moment woven into one, driving her to a delirium in which her surroundings ceased to exist. Until the moment they demanded her attention.

She was still daydreaming as she was rushed into surgery. The nature of her injuries demanded that she not be placed under anesthetic immediately, so the first hours of her treatment were a wall of pain. But as the surgeons sewed up the gashes, Patti simply closed her eyes and imagined herself to be wounded on some Civil War battlefield. "I pretended I was Robert E. Lee."

The cracked vertebrae were not her only serious injury. Her eyesight, too, had been compromised by nerve damage, and for a short time there were genuine fears that her legs might be paralyzed. Spinal surgery was suggested, together with a punishing regimen of physical therapy, but for the moment the best thing that she could do was wait out the immediate injuries with bed rest and sufficient drugs to make her feel normal again.

That's why the first reports from her sick chamber appeared so positive. Lying there in a cast, a brace, and traction, she answered every inquiry with a smile and a nod: "I'm feeling great. Oh, yeah, I'll be back." She continued giving interviews, informing the world that she was fine. "I'm so *lucky*," she constantly repeated on the phone with Vivien Goldman. "The doctors can't *believe* it!"

Even the West German promoter of her next European tour put the telephone down convinced that the group's scheduled gigs were still on, after a few minutes of conversation with Patti.

Months later, in her April 1978 interview with John Tobler, she had a clearer perspective. "I couldn't move and I was saying, 'Yeah, everything's cool, I'll be in Germany in a couple of weeks.' I got my agents and everybody in a lot of trouble 'cos I was feeling great; meanwhile I couldn't even get out of bed. Also I'd never been injured before, so I didn't understand. To me it was like having the chicken pox."

But she could not truly rest, of course. Four years had passed since the publication of her last full book of poetry, *Witt*. Since then just one further collection had appeared, *The Night*, teaming eleven of Patti's poems with eleven by Tom Verlaine. It was originally intended to be followed by a second collaborative effort, *Independence Day*, but that never materialized; Patti's only new publications since then were the Gotham Book Mart's editions of her poems "A Useless Death" and "Ha! Ha! Houdini," the former a three-page chapbook, the latter eight pages bound together with a tiny padlock.

Now, however, she had time to think, and to consider a proposal from publisher G. P. Putnam's Sons that she curate a retrospective edition of her verse. It would be titled *Babel*.

Roadie Andi Ostrowe took dictation at Patti's bedside, while entertaining the invalid with recollections of her past life in the Peace Corps. The two women's friendship dated back to the day Ostrowe turned up at one of Patti's *Radio Ethiopia* recording sessions and handed her a letter franked with some Ethiopian stamps. Now she sat and talked of her own experiences in Ethiopia, while Patti volleyed rapid-fire questions back at her. Such distractions, Patti said later, proved essential.

All the same, Patti laughed, *Babel* was born under the influence of the pain pills that she was constantly in need of and that plunged her into "a very subliminal landscape." *i have been lying here for a long time in stillness*, she wrote in "Penicillin." *sick, immobile. i can't get a grip or feel.*

Even so, she was rightfully proud of all that she was able to accomplish: sixty-two titled pieces tracing Patti's evolution as a writer and poet, harking back as far as "k.o.d.a.k.," "Georgia O'Keefe" [*sic*], "Edie Sedgwick," and "Marianne Faithfull"; hovering in the present day with "Ain't It Strange" and "Babel Field"; and, although she was not yet aware of the fact, looking forward to her recovery and return to action, with "Easter," destined to become one of her best-loved songs.

She also drove into the heart of her own increasingly carefully constructed mythology. The opening piece, "Notice," outlines the requirements of a heroine: *the artist. the premier mistress writhing . . . the freedom to be intense . . . to defy social order and break the slow kill monotony of censorship.* Little that Patti has written before or since has better encapsulated her own vision of her place in the arts.

Friends dropped by, and occasionally she wrote with them. Richard Hell sat by her bedside and they passed the typewriter back and forth, reading what each other had written and then hammering down the next thoughts of their own. Tom Verlaine was there, fresh from recording Television's debut album, and so was Jane Friedman, her manager.

Both of those relationships would be severed before Patti's convalescence was through—Verlaine by Patti's love for Fred Smith, Friedman because it seemed that much of her time was now being dedicated to John Cale, as he set up his Spy record label. Lawyer Ina Meibach would handle Patti's affairs from now on, but only as far as anyone could do that. Patti was her own boss and she always had been, and you stepped on her toes at your own peril. You could ask her doctors about that. Or her bandmates. Apparently the first thing she told them when they came to see her was not to join Linda Ronstadt's backing band.

With Lenny Kaye she hatched the reemergence of Mer, the label they had birthed with their debut single "Hey Joe." It had flickered only once since then, with the American release of Tapper Zukie's *Man Ah Warrior*, but they would fund new operations by leasing the reissue rights for "Hey Joe" to Seymour Stein's Sire label. Patti was already outlining her intentions for Mer: a home for performers she and Kaye believed had promise that needed to be nurtured. There would be no long-term contracts or long-time aims. Mer was interested only in an artist's first work, or special projects that perhaps no other label would touch; Patti spoke of producing, and playing guitar on, an album of extracts from the novel *The Wild Boys* by its author, William Burroughs.

That wouldn't happen, and the Mer project itself was stillborn. But Patti had still more ways of keeping herself occupied. She was arranging for gallery showings of her drawings across New York City and then in West Germany, and she threw herself into physical therapy as though she were Muhammad Ali preparing for a title bout or Mr. America getting ready to take on the world. In fact, those were the examples she named when anyone asked if she should really be pushing so hard. And, when she told her doctors that she had targeted Easter Sunday as the day she would return to performing, even the skeptics among them knew that she would probably succeed.

That, she said later, was why that one new poem, "Easter," was so important to her. It was the day that she would rise from the dead.

Patti's return was a week behind schedule. Easter Sunday fell on April 10, and nine days later she was recording a performance for the *Mike Douglas Show*, stepping back to the poems "Work Song" and "Prayer," the latter of which she had reworked as "Keith Richards Blues." The Rolling Stone was still awaiting the outcome of a Toronto drug bust two months previous, and there were very real fears that he would be jailed.

Patti's onstage resurrection would not take place on schedule either, but the lines outside CBGB still snaked around the block when she returned to action on May 4, 1977. The occasion was a benefit for *Punk* magazine, the stylishly anarchic chronicle of New York City's underground culture.

Returning to CBGB was the best thing she could have done. She remembered how she had to be carried on stage at the beginning of the residency, so weak was she from months in bed and a body full of medication. "I had them put a chair on the stage," she told William Burroughs in an interview published in *Spin* magazine. And then, she told *ZigZag* in the aftermath of that memorable show, "I got on the stage, plugged in my amp, grabbed my guitar, and immediately raped my guitar, immediately kicked in my amplifier, immediately was jumping out."

Although Patti's set was short that night, it was impressive regardless. She sang "Kimberly" and "Pissing in a River," pulled out the old Spencer Davis Group garage classic "Gimme Some Lovin'," Sam Cooke's "Working on the Chain Gang," and the Ramones' "I Wanna Be Your Boyfriend." Then she turned to the Velvet Underground's "I'm Waiting for the Man," and Lou Reed leaped onstage alongside her, to duet with a triumphant Patti. The night, she insisted to Burroughs, was "the best therapy that I had," so good that she promptly arranged an entire season of further shows, to commence at the end of the month.

She took some precautions, of course. Large swaths of the set were gifted to either Kaye or Kral, who rehearsed the band through some favorite oldies and then took lead vocals on them as well.

But the precautions proved unnecessary. "I didn't do everything good at first, but every night I got stronger," she told *ZigZag*. "I feel crazier now than ever. The strength I now have compensates for the mania I've developed. I didn't learn my lesson." By the end of that residency, she wasn't only back on her feet; she had even taken off her neck brace, rejuvenated by the power of CBGB.

"Easter" moved into the set, and as spring turned into summer 1977, far from bemoaning her absence from what was elsewhere proving to be one of the most exciting years in recent New York City musical history, Patti reveled in her freedom to simply kick back and enjoy it.

All of the bands that had strained behind her in the early days of CBGB were driving hard now. The Ramones, having delivered their debut album in summer 1976, were already looking toward the release of their third. Both the Talking Heads and Blondie had issued their first LPs; Richard Hell was working toward his maiden set, and Television were now celebrating the release of theirs, that epic maelstrom of icicles and angles called *Marquee Moon*.

Looking back on the unity that once bound together these groups and so many others, Patti could grow nostalgic for an age that would never return. But that was also the nature of art—and the thing that she loved about it. Performers were united for however long they needed to be, and then the greatest moved on to new pastures.

It made her laugh to think of Blondie and Television now treading the same boards at London's Hammersmith Odeon that she had visited six months before. Doubtless, she laughed even harder when she recalled the November 1975 issue of the *New Musical Express* in which English journalist Charles Shaar Murray had deconstructed Blondie as "a garage-type band" fronted by "this cute little bundle of platinum hair with a voice like a squeaky bath toy." But the very fact that a bunch of kids and early-twenties from a club at the lowest end of New York City's spectrum were now headlining a theater at the top of London's—that justified everything they had all fought for in the years when they were nobodies.

Patti was still convalescing, but she was of course already considering her next move. A new album—that went without saying. But even before she breathed a word about it, she knew that it would swerve as dramatically away from her last LP, the miasmic glory of *Radio Ethiopia*, as that album had swung away from the skeletal beauty of *Horses*.

The album would take shape around "Easter," her prayer of rebirth and rejuvenation. It would nod to the past by clearing up some of the most deserving old soldiers in the group's live repertoire: "Rock n Roll Nigger" (her original choice for the new LP's title), "Space Monkey," and, at long last, "Privilege."

And it would speak publicly of her long-distance romance with Fred. They scarcely ever got to see one another, and they had the long-distance phone bills to prove it. But "25th Floor" and "Godspeed" spoke of the love that was growing between them, and the mood of the music would broadcast that sentimentality even further. (Meanwhile, a new poem in *Babel*, "Thread," would speak to the domesticity that Patti felt when the pair were together: *i was sitting by the window holding your button. i wanted to sew it on your coat.*)

But *Easter* would also be constructed around an awareness that after two albums that were already being spoken of as "cult" favorites, fans and Patti's label alike expected her to finally step out into the commercial daylight. The pressure was exacerbated by, of all people, her old rivals Blondie. Signed to the small Private Stock Records label at the end of 1976, the group had transferred to the major Chrysalis in early 1977, and with their first, eponymous album picking up excellent results and fair sales, all indications were that the group would be breaking through—in Europe, if not the United States—with their second album, *Plastic Letters*.

That set was being recorded around the same time that the Patti Smith Group went into the studio themselves, on November 7, 1977, to begin work on *Easter*. Producer Jimmy Iovine would oversee the sessions; Patti selected him because she liked what he'd been doing with Bruce Springsteen. Iovine had been engineer on Springsteen's 1975 album *Born to Run* and had just wrapped up work in the same capacity on the long-awaited follow-up *Darkness on the Edge of Town*.

The *Easter* job was a big deal for Iovine. Although he'd known Patti for over a year now, since they met at the Record Plant studios in 1976, he also knew that she could have worked with any producer she wanted. Instead, she called in a guy who had just one major-label credit to his name: Flame, a band he formed with singer Marge Raymond that was backed up by sundry members of Springsteen's E Street Band.

Iovine realized that the Patti Smith Group would require careful handling. Not in terms of personality; he got along famously with all of them. But he needed to point out that he was a producer, not a miracle worker, and listening to the group's outlines of the album, some people had already started wondering if a miracle was what they actually required.

The gigs that the Patti Smith Group had played since her return from injury were a very different beast from those that preceded it. Patti herself acknowledged that the songs had become a lot shorter and faster. There was still room for improvisation, such as that magnificent in-concert moment when the hard-riffing (and, to be truthful, somewhat pedestrian) "25th Floor" lurched into "High on Rebellion," the self-defining snatch of *Babel* that answered so many of her musical critics while at the same time it offered them further ammunition to use against her: *here I am struggling and filled with dread*. But even "Privilege," for so long a touchstone for lyrical flights of fancy, could be accused of having settled down, although the blasphemies that were so much a part of it, the cries of *goddamn* that rang through the coda, would soon be outraging radio all the same.

It was the clutch of new songs that would be accompanying the band into the studio that really documented how far the band had shifted from its earlier improvisational roots. They simply didn't pack the manic edge that was once the hallmark of Smith's writing. Some of them had not even seen a live stage yet, and as the new album unfolded across the winter, any analysis of its progress could not help but acknowledge how unfulfilled those songs felt. "Till Victory," "We Three," even the chanted mystique of the fan favorite "Ghost Dance"—all could have benefited immeasurably from a few months of road work, and the possibility that Patti was leaning hard toward her record label's desire for a solid commercial success, rather than another album of cult appeal, had never seemed so probable.

Lenny Kaye tried to play down the commercial sheen, by looking toward the future. The band had just flipped its modus operandi, that's all, recording songs before they performed them live. A few months on the road would soon roughen them up. And when journalist Sandy

Robertson repeated the suggestion that they were chasing a hit record, Kaye was adamant: "There was no conscious drive to sell records, that was like our last thought."

Or was it? Even Patti may not have thought it through yet, but a hit record does more than elevate its makers into the echelons of pop stardom. It can also be a nest egg for the future, for a time when an artist cannot (through injury—a bad fall, for example) or will not (for personal reasons—a new love affair) continue performing.

Patti had already acknowledged that there might come a time when she would no longer be working, and the songwriting credits on the new record were designed to offset that shock for her bandmates, at least in financial terms. On *Radio Ethiopia*, Ivan Kral had been her most frequent songwriting partner. This time, he shared only as many writing credits as Jay Dee Daugherty—that is to say, one. Patti explained that the decision to spread the credits around was made in the name of democracy. But democracy now? Or democracy for the future?

Despite Patti's and Kaye's protestations, Jimmy Iovine was under no illusions as to what was expected of him. The album was moving along nicely, but Iovine had yet to hear a solitary song that struck him as a potential hit single, and that was what Arista was calling for.

Iovine had already pulled two live recordings onto the disc: the medley of "25th Floor" and "High on Rebellion" and a reading of the poem "Babelogue." The latter would segue dramatically into the seething "Rock n Roll Nigger," a song that the label was already eyeing with considerable trepidation. The notion that the most explosive word in racism could be reclaimed as a label for all outsiders was not a new one; John and Yoko Ono had planted the same seed five years ago with "Woman Is the Nigger of the World." And one only needed to read Patti's lyrics to understand that she was making a similar point. But the analogy remained an obscure one, and Arista knew that anytime anyone heard that word, they were immediately going to bristle.

Not for the first time, Patti's guarantee of complete artistic control, which was one of the hooks that had pulled her onto Arista in the first place, struck the bosses as one freedom too far. But the suggestion that the lyrics be altered was not one that anybody would broach, either

openly or surreptitiously. That meant there was no way that the strongest and most commercial song on the LP so far could ever be released
as a radio-friendly 45.

Which was why Iovine called up Bruce Springsteen one day to ask
whether he had any plans for a demo that had been gathering dust on
the shelf following their most recent album sessions. Springsteen had
completed only the chorus, but Iovine thought it might be just what the
Patti Smith album needed.

Still, when Iovine passed the demo on to Patti, she accepted the gift
with something less than wild enthusiasm. She had no compunction
about allowing other writers to share in her songwriting credits, but
only because they supplied the musical palette that she was unable to
create. The idea of, essentially, collaborating on her lyrics, too, was not
one that she had ever considered, nor one that she welcomed now. For
a time, the song sat more or less unplayed.

But one evening, waiting for Fred Smith's now all-but-nightly call, she
popped the cassette into the player, listened once, and then listened again
and again. Iovine had told her that he loved the idea of a woman singing
from a man's point of view; Springsteen added that the song was written
in her key. Now she realized that both were correct. "Bruce . . . gave me
the music, and it had some mumbling on it," she told John Tobler in
October 1978, "and Bruce is a genius mumbler, like the sexiest mumbler
I ever heard. I just listened to it, and the words just tumbled out of me."
Long before the phone finally rang, she had drafted the lyrics that would
soon become an anthem.

"[Bruce] wrote the tag, *Because the night belongs to lovers*," she added,
"which was in between the mumbling; he'd say that every once in a
while. He said I didn't have to keep that bit, but I thought it was really
nice—I always write the lyrics to my own songs, unless they're covers,
but I respected his lyrics, and I thought it was a very nice sentiment,
so I built the rest of the lyrics, which are obviously mine, around his
sentiment."

"Because the Night" was recorded and slotted into the near-
complete album just days after Patti finished writing it. She was already
convinced that she had her hit single. To make room for the newcomer,

Patti dropped "Godspeed" from the track list, and set it up to be her next B-side instead.

It was time to consider the album cover. Patti wanted something sexy, something sensual—something that she could jerk off to, she laughed. "I thought if I could do it as an experiment, then fifteen-year-old boys could do it," she told *Rolling Stone*'s Charles M. Young, "and that would make me very happy." Photographer Lynn Goldsmith delivered. Patti dismissed the inevitable criticism: "People say to me, 'aren't you afraid of becoming a sex object?' Especially a lot of writers are obsessed with making you feel guilty or upset because you might become a sex object. Well, I find that very exciting. I think sex is one of the five highest sensations one can experience. A very high orgasm is a way of communication with our Creator."

Easter was complete. It was scheduled for release in March 1978—just in time for Easter. The single "Because the Night" would follow close behind.

Patti remained busy. Her art exhibitions in New York City, including one at the Gotham Book Mart, were both huge successes; so was another at the Galerie Veith Turske in Cologne, West Germany. She flew to that city to give a reading in October 1977; then, back home just days later, the full band performed a phenomenal set at a benefit for the Hayden Planetarium.

Deliberately, though, they kept the new album's contents under wraps. Not until the first night of their year-end three-day run at CBGB, on December 29, would the Patti Smith Group offer up any hint as to what *Easter* portended, as half the album's contents were drip-fed into the set list. It would be twenty-four hours more before she finally premiered "Because the Night," with coauthor Springsteen joining her on stage to help the song along.

The new year started slowly, though, and it was the beginning of February 1978 before the Patti Smith Group finally convened for anything more than rehearsals, flying out to Ann Arbor—Fred "Sonic" Smith's home turf—to play four shows at the Second Chance. A six-hundred-capacity club at 516 East Liberty Street that opened in 1974 as a student hangout, the Second Chance was now a magnet, in the words of the *Ann Arbor Observer*, for "younger audiences from Detroit's western suburbs," a "seedy" clientele in the eyes of some observers, and a more "unruly" one as well. But also a more excitable one. When the Ramones played the Second Chance in February 1977, with Sonic's Rendezvous Band opening for them, the show passed into history as one of the most gloriously volatile the Ramones ever played outside of New York City—so much so that they were back there for a repeat showing in June.

The venue was certainly a second home for Sonic's Rendezvous Band, and their supporters were out in force as Fred Smith's group lined up to open Patti's four shows. Especially as it went without saying that Sonic himself would join the headliners on stage for much of their set as well.

What nobody expected, though, was the surprise that Fred and Patti were waiting to deliver. That Patti was leaving New York City, to live with Fred in Detroit. The couple had already taken rooms in the Book Cadillac Hotel; they would get started with the house hunting as soon as they could.

Leaving New York City was "a very tough thing"; she would never tire of saying that. But it was "a great joy" as well, the adventure of a lifetime. "You know, like a pioneer. It's like you have to 'Go West!' I've always been a very East Coast girl," she told William Burroughs. "[But] when I was a teenager I thought that the coolest city wasn't New York, it was Detroit"—because Detroit had Motown.

More than that, though, there was the knowledge that she really didn't care where she lived, so long as she was with Smith. "I have met the person in my life that I've been waiting to meet since I was a little girl. . . . For the first time, I'm not pursuing—the person has opened up to me another way to express myself truly." As Patti prepared for the release of her album of rebirth, she was preparing for a new birth as well, counting down the days until she and Fred could be together without rock 'n' roll getting in the way.

And right now there seemed to be a lot of days to get through. There were a couple of American shows to perform, in Redondo Beach, California, and Buffalo, New York. Soon the band would be off on its third tour of Europe—but first she'd been asked to appear at Arista's 1978 sales conference, an event whose entire focus, it seems, was aimed toward the Patti Smith Group.

The day of the conference, February 28, 1978, would have been the late Rolling Stone Brian Jones's thirty-fifth birthday; Patti had always noted anniversaries like that, even if she wasn't sure what they portended. Tonight, though, despite all the awful connotations that the term "sales conference" usually bears, the mood inside the room was electric, as though everyone was celebrating something momentous. A birthday, a new day.

Even more excitingly, Arista was taping Patti's performance, a selection of readings from *Babel*, with an eye toward releasing a full Patti Smith poetry album. There was even talk of it being released in the Savoy Jazz series, Patti crowed to John Tobler. "Be in there with Albert Ayler and all those guys."

Unfortunately, events would move too fast. Just one excerpt from the performance, a truly stirring "Babel Field," ever saw the light of day (it would appear as a UK B-side later in the year), as the label heads begin to reconsider what was happening with Patti's career.

A veteran Arista staffer laid out their dilemma a few years later: "On the one hand we had 'Because the Night,' which the entire label was behind, and *Easter*, which we knew was going to be huge, but on the other, we had Patti Smith's reputation as a poetess and an artist, which really never sat well with the label, because how do you sell that?

"I think when Clive [Davis] first signed her, that was the direction he saw her moving in, but things had changed since then—punk rock was now huge and Patti Smith was a part of that movement whether she liked it or not, and she was also the first person from that movement to be signed. So there was a sense at the label, both in London and in New York City, that if anybody needed a hit record, it was the woman who started it all, which placed the people who believed in her at the start under a lot of pressure, and meant that projects they had maybe hoped to see through had to be put back; the poetry album, for instance. And I think it put Patti under a lot of pressure as well, which is why things turned out as they did."

Patti never released that poetry album. Instead, she would turn to John Giorno's Poetry Systems, the poet's now decade-old mission to spotlight the harshest and most beautiful contemporary verse and writers that New York City (and beyond) had to offer. Patti's epic "The Histories of the Universe" would appear on his 1978 spoken-word collection *Big Ego*, alongside contributions from Philip Glass, Laurie Anderson, and Jackie Curtis, among others.

Later in the year, she would also perform at Giorno's Nova Convention, a festival honoring William Burroughs. Patti gifted her "Poem for Jim Morrison" and "Bumblebee" to the souvenir live album, and offered her tribute to the guest of honor: "If all the stuff that we say about music being the most universal communication . . . Mr. Burroughs and Mr. Gysin and all these people, the thing they've given me is the foresight and the freedom to communicate with the future through sound."

She also looked back to her first reading at St. Mark's Poetry Project, all those years before. "They didn't mind me but they were very shocked at Lenny . . . poor Lenny, with his little Champ amp. Heavy metal had come into St. Mark's. But times have changed," she chuckled. "Look how big Lenny's amp is now."

Her art, it seemed, was becoming very separate from her commerce.

As before, the Patti Smith Group launched their European tour in Scandinavia, wound their way south through West Germany, the Netherlands and Belgium, and France, then hopped the water to London at the end of March 1978. They appeared on British television's top-rated arts magazine program, *The South Bank Show*, where they performed, perhaps surprisingly, "Rock n Roll Nigger." They also returned to the *Old Grey Whistle Test* to thrash "25th Floor" and "Because the Night," and finally there were three nights at the Rainbow Theatre, a two-thousand-seater in North London's Finsbury Park, and a reunion with Tapper Zukie, support act at all three shows.

Easter entered the UK chart that same week, buoyed by a clutch of reviews that may not have been wholeheartedly supportive but were at least more positive than those that had greeted its predecessor. Advance orders were pouring in for "Because the Night" as well, sufficient to see it on the UK singles chart before the end of the month.

It would ultimately peak at #5, held out of the #1 slot by the combined powers of German disco band Boney M., a 1950s revival act called the Darts (extolling, ironically, the virtues of a "Boy from New York City"), and the two latest releases from the Bee Gees' factory of hits; history tends to overlook them today, but there was a moment in the late 1970s when the brothers Gibb were even bigger than punk rock, and this was it.

Lower on the listings, Blondie's "(I'm Always Touched by Your) Presence, Dear" was serving up that band's second UK hit, following the #2 smash "Denis" earlier in the year. For now, though, the Patti Smith Group was the biggest name in punk, American or British, and the only negative aspect was Patti's own seemingly growing detachment from it all.

"I'd like to see this album sell a billion copies and Patti become a superstar," Lester Bangs wrote in *Phonograph Record Magazine*, "even though I know that eventuality will turn her into even more of a monster than she's already become. Better her than Styx, or that guy who wants to hold you till the fear in him subsides." How Patti must have shuddered when she read those words; she didn't want to be a superstar or a monster. She wanted to stop.

In concert, she seemed tired. *Melody Maker*'s Chris Brazier caught one of the Rainbow shows and said it outright: "She has none of the bounding excess of energy, the sheer childlike exuberance that used to crackle through her performance." She barely spoke to the audience; she rarely budged from her perch in front of the microphone. To crowds who may never have caught her in the past, her performance was probably everything they hoped for, and there were definitely moments of high drama: Her arrival onstage at the start, a tatty little figure in an outsized bowler hat, clutching a crook and a little toy sheep and declaring, "The Lord is my shepherd." The segue from a somber "We Three" to a breathless "Time Is on My Side." Kral throwing a hint of "Whole Lotta Love" into a fiery "Radio Ethiopia." All of these were moments to cherish. But to fans who had caught any of her previous London shows, or seen her anywhere else for that matter, this was not the Patti Smith they remembered.

In fact, Patti was feeling unwell at the London shows. In West Germany, Paul Morley of the *New Musical Express* reported, she had been "mesmerising . . . honouring the vibrant spirits of destiny, anarchy, surrealism." But next she sat down to talk with the British media, and that, too, seemed an oddly disheartened performance.

Easter, of course, dominated her thoughts—but not only the album. Christian mythology, too, was paramount in her mind as she discussed her own relationship with Christ—something, she said, she was still learning to reevaluate.

She was not on the verge of a full-fledged religious conversion; she would not undergo the kind of transformation that, coincidentally, was awaiting Bob Dylan before the year was out. But when she spoke of Christianity, she did so with a fervor that she had once reserved for her personal heroes and theories alone. And those heroes themselves had a new member in their ranks. "To me, Christ, Jimi Hendrix, Brian Jones, Jim Morrison, they're all the same," she informed Chris Brazier. "To me, the greatest thing about Christ is not necessarily Christ himself but the belief of the people that have kept him alive through the centuries."

She still stuck by the lyric that, to many people, best encapsulates her early, ragged beauty, the line from "Oath" (and, later, "Gloria"), that insists *Jesus died for somebody's sins but not mine*. But now she was willing to explain it. "I wasn't saying that I didn't like Christ or didn't believe in him, just that I wanted to take the responsibility for the things I do. . . . I believe that crime goes hand in hand with art, and I didn't want some unknown entity taking the blame or credit for anything I do."

She also believed that she needed to accept "a more New Testament kind of communication." In the Old Testament, she explained, man communicated directly with God; in the New, he required a go-between, Jesus. "Well, I'm a one-to-one girl and I have always sought to communicate with God through myself." Now she wasn't so sure. "I feel that was one of the reasons I fell offstage. . . . I'm reevaluating my state of being." Maybe, she was thinking, we need that middleman to help us understand what God is really saying, rather than trusting to our own instincts to translate his words correctly.

But who are we, and who is God? Replace the concept of a supreme being with that of true love (which isn't as much of a stretch, though the right wing might argue), replace the concept of an emissary with that of the object of true love, and perhaps one gets at what Patti was truly saying. Though she bound it up in so much mystique and mystery that a lot of people stop reading halfway through the first paragraph, what she had realized was that she didn't need to go it alone anymore. That there was someone else ready to stand beside her.

She had not found God. She had found Fred.

Back in the United States, radio flooded behind "Because the Night," and as both single and LP soared upwards (they came to rest, ultimately, at #13 and #20, respectively), Patti celebrated: "The whole point of doing work is to communicate ecstasy or joy. . . . We're communicating to a lot more people.

"I think it's great that I have a hit single," she told Charles Young in *Rolling Stone*. "Because what it means is that it's possible to have integrity and be successful again. I mean, I believe that in their hearts, all the great '60s guys had great integrity and they all did great work. They all had a sort of political consciousness and some spiritual consciousness. And they were successful. The way I look at it, I haven't changed none. I haven't changed since I was seven years old. And I've gotten more corrupt in certain ways."

It was not lost on her, of course, that many of the people who were drawn to the song came to it from the Springsteen angle. After a three-year silence on the recording front as he fought with a former manager, Springsteen was preparing to stir again with *Darkness on the Edge of Town*, and fans who had been driven to fever pitch by the live shows that filled that gap were snatching at every little bit of Boss that they could lay their paws on.

Nor could Patti overlook the fact that the bulk of *Easter* was being widely regarded a mere sideshow to the main event of "Because the Night." She expected AM radio stations to play only the single, but it was "pretty gutless," she complained to Steve Simels in *Stereo Review*, for the once-wide-open vistas of FM radio to have constricted so much that they were doing the same. Even so, she admitted to Young that a lot of the LP was scarcely suitable for radio play. "The album includes on it *fuck*, *piss*, *shit*, *seed*, *nigger*—it's got everything but *shitlicker* on it. Ya know, it's much more daring, much more perverse, and, ah, much more corrupt than *Radio Ethiopia*." Which only confirmed Jimmy Iovine's earlier fears for *Easter*—that it was a good album without any radio-friendly pop fodder to speak of.

It became a major issue when the time came to choose a follow-up single. Arista's American office evaded the issue altogether by not even releasing one. In the UK, the label plumped for "Privilege," hoping to juxtapose the old song's familiarity and the inevitable media-whipped storm about the *goddamns*. Arista provided further incentive for purchasers by including a new live recording of "25th Floor" and the sales conference rendition of "Babel Field"—by now known as "Babelfield"—on the twelve-inch single. But "Privilege" faltered at #72 that summer; British radio steadfastly avoided it precisely because of the blasphemies.

Still, Patti respected Arista's decision to release "Privilege," all the more so since it contrasted so sharply with their treatment of "My Generation" two years earlier. Advance research had already made it clear that the single would receive no airplay, but what Patti would describe to John Tobler as "a new regime at Arista . . . who really fight for me" was not deterred. At the time, singles weren't only released to become hits; sometimes they were there to make a point about the artist, and anybody coming to Patti Smith for the first time via that bumper twelve-inch package would have learned a lot.

The Patti Smith Group toured the United States through the spring and early summer of 1978. They hopped back to the UK at the end of August, for a week of shows that commenced with a headlining performance at the annual Reading Festival. Next they hit the continent, and then they were back touring America into December. It was an exhausting workload, one that was only exacerbated by the sheer weight of promotional work Patti had piled onto her shoulders as well.

But it was not without its highlights. In June 1978, nearly thirteen years after she first saw the Rolling Stones live in Philadelphia, Patti opened for them in Atlanta, as the old warhorse toured its *Some Girls* LP. And in July she hit the cover of *Rolling Stone* magazine; Charles Young's article inside unequivocally proclaimed her "at the age of thirty-one, a star."

She added in a handful of UK interviews to promote the belated publication of *Babel* in that country. In fact, the collection was in for a rough ride, at least from the media. There were some horrifically cruel reviews in the British press, including *New Musical Express* writer Ian Penman's insistence that "most of us were writing better than this in the lower Sixth [eleventh grade], with or without expensive drugs, friends or book deals. . . . This is self-conceit, and it should have been burnt out or burnt years ago. This is semi-literature, and I hate it even more when I realise that it's probably the only book of 'poetry' a lot of impressionable young people will buy this or any other year."

His final observation was probably correct; thirty-plus years later, if you can find a copy of *Babel* in a used bookstore, much of it will be either marked up or underlined. It may not have been destined to land with the cultural impact of a Kerouac or Ginsberg volume, but to a generation that was coming of literary age in the late 1970s, *Babel* was as valuable a work as any of Patti's predecessors' might have been—and as relevant as well. Ginsberg himself acknowledged this when he remarked to Victor Bockris, "I was surprised by Patti Smith's rise. . . . I wonder how she'll do. I was reading Rimbaud's last letters, [written] when he was dying, about how miserable life was and 'all I am is a motionless stump' and I'm wondering how she's going to deal with that aspect of heroism."

How indeed?

13

BURNING ROSES

PATTI HAD BEEN working her way up the ladder for close to a decade—longer than that if one wanted to consider the years she spent seeking her identity in the first place. In that time, she had lived as enthusiastically as she could have wished, never pausing for breath or even thinking of doing so. But now she was in her early thirties, in a field that still viewed an artist leaving his or her twenties with uneasy suspicion. The past was behind her. All that mattered was the future, a future that she was building around a change in style, a change in direction, a change in life.

Her late-night telephone conversations with Fred had never been less than passionate. But in the past, it was a passion built around the impracticalities of their present and the dreams they could only glimpse of what might be to come. Not any longer. Now those dreams were in reach, waiting for her at the end of the next record, the next tour.

So why did she still feel ill?

Not ill as in "Get me to the doctor; I think there's something wrong." She had passed through those fires the previous year, and only the occasional pain and a drug regimen remained. This sickness was internal.

In part, it may have stemmed from the events of December 9, 1978, when her brother, Todd, was injured in an altercation at Max's Kansas City. Sid Vicious, the former Sex Pistols bassist, had only recently made bail after being charged with the murder of his American girlfriend

179

Nancy Spungen in October. He propositioned Todd's girlfriend, and when Todd reacted, Vicious attacked. He smashed a glass in Todd's face, and as Vicious was arrested again, Patti rushed to the hospital, where doctors fought not only to repair the damage but also to save Todd's eyesight. His recuperation was long and painful, and nobody could have blamed Patti if her thoughts sometimes seemed to be miles away with her brother. Todd's scars would clearly mark her work over the next year.

But Patti's ill mood was about more than that. It was discontent and unhappiness; it was frustration and rage. The commercial success that had enfolded her in the wake of "Because the Night" should not have shaken her as much as it did. But it did, and she wasn't certain why. Hindsight, ladled liberally onto her career by sundry historians and critics, has attributed Patti's withdrawal from her original identity first, the entire machine soon after, either to her accident in early 1977, to her move thirteen months later away from the city that shaped her, to the love that drew her from the city, or to the realization that her "career" really did not mean as much to her as she once believed.

In fact, it was all of these things. And it was the knowledge that she had a job to do and an audience to please, and she could not return home until it was finished.

So maybe it was time to finish.

The Patti Smith Group wrapped up 1978 with their now-traditional end-of-year residency at CBGB, three shows that took them up to New Year's Eve. Just twenty-four hours earlier, John Cale had emerged from over a year's worth of silence to play the same venue. With a scratch band built around Ritchie Fliegler and Bruce Brody (both veterans of his last live setup), Judy Nylon, and guests Ivan Kral and Jay Dee Daugherty, Cale turned in a short but cataclysmic set that seemed, and might even have been, part improvisation, part sheer brutality, and part mad genius. Nylon's "Dance of the Seven Veils" might have acknowledged Patti's influence in its collision of rock and poetics, but it was a savage invocation regardless, while Nylon's duet with Cale through "Even Cowgirls Get the Blues" was all spectral howls and sibilant whispers.

Ivan Kral was at his best that night—he needed to be. And he was at his best again the following night, when Patti took the same stage. So why did he, and the rest of the band, feel so uneasy?

Maybe it was the speed with which Patti insisted on recording their next LP, knowing full well that they really didn't have much of anything to record.

Joining the band at Bearsville Studios in upstate New York was keyboard player Richard Sohl, back in his rightful place after a year out of action while he fought illness and exhaustion. Patti also reunited with her former paramour Todd Rundgren, who would produce the new album. His involvement had already been described as the ideal way of recreating the successes of *Easter*.

It wasn't.

"I thought that it would be nice to work with a friend," Patti told the British magazine *Uncut* in 2004. What's more, "I knew that he would contribute to the musical sense of the record. He was very good with using keyboards; he was a pianist himself and a lot of those songs evolved around that." But "it was not an easy record to make."

The Patti Smith Group arrived at Bearsville in almost total disarray. Not only had they not had the opportunity to rehearse any new material together before the sessions began, but they had scarcely even written any. "They didn't have material," Rundgren lamented in John Tobler and Stuart Grundy's book *The Record Producers*.

"But they were committed to doing an album, and they showed up wanting to do one, but not really ready for it. . . . They left me with the responsibility of trying to turn it into something, and I really didn't know what to do most of the time. I certainly can't tell Patti how to make music, but at the same time, it wasn't as if there was any there ready to be worked with." If he hadn't been working with an old friend, he said, the entire situation could have become "very nasty" indeed.

To Patti, the album "was a difficult record to make because we were out of the city, in the middle of winter in Bearsville, pretty much snowed in," she told *Uncut*. But she already knew, or at least suspected, that it might be the last album she would ever make. "I felt that I had really expressed everything that I knew how to express. So there I had a lot of thoughts doing that record."

Joyful thoughts and relieved thoughts. The end was in sight.

She handed over a couple of things she had written. "Frederick" was destined to become one of the album's best-known songs, even before the sessions were complete. But the album's other jewel, "Dancing Barefoot," didn't even exist until the recording was almost over and Rundgren demanded more songs. Kral produced a cassette tape of song ideas that he carried around with him. Rundgren listened and then came back to say which one he wanted them to work up.

And so it was that the last song Kral wrote for the Patti Smith Group was one of the first he had ever written; the riff for "Dancing Barefoot" was one he composed back in Prague when he was thirteen or fourteen years old. Later, Rundgren would single out "Dancing Barefoot" as the song that came together most successfully.

Kral's gift for melody was visible, too, on two other songs, the hefty "Revenge," with its Beatles-ish intro, and the punishing semiautobiography of "Citizen Ship": *There were tanks all over my city.* They weren't bad songs, either. Or, at least, they were the closest to what might have eased out of the band in earlier years.

The scrabble for material continued. The poem "Seven Ways of Going" was reprised from so many years before. Later, listeners could extrapolate some kind of warning from its weary prose, Patti *undulating in the lewd impostered night,* before turning *my neck toward home.* But the portentous accompaniment that Rundgren layered around the distinctly straining vocal was a poor match for one of Patti's most questioning works.

She recorded a cover of the old Byrds' chest-beater "So You Want to Be (a Rock 'n' Roll Star)." She'd first heard it from the artist Ed Hanson back in 1968, and at the time, she'd rebelled against the cynicism that permeates the lyrics, the notion that no matter how high one climbs, the ride is still a painful one. She knew better now.

It would be left to the title track, like that of *Easter,* to truly place the new album in perspective. "Wave" was a hesitant conversation between Patti and a silent interlocutor, while cello, piano, bass, and organ washed around her voice. Haunting and almost hurting, it would become the final track on the LP—and listening to it, one could also take it to be the final song of her career.

Wave to the children / Wave goodbye.

Outside her music, it was not a sentiment she expressed publicly, nor did she confide in her bandmates. But to Rundgren she confessed it: she'd decided to retire once *Wave* had been waved off. "Patti wanted to record with me for a couple of reasons," Rundgren told Tobler and Grundy. "One was that she knew at the time that she wasn't going to be making any more records in the immediate future, and because we've been friends for a long time, she just wanted an opportunity for us to work together before she stopped making records.

"The other reason was also because I was a friend—and this isn't necessarily a good thing—they wanted me to pull together something that wasn't there, to bridge a gap that was almost unbridgeable, because Patti was already halfway out of the business."

Rundgren had sworn not to tell Kral, Kaye, Daugherty, and Sohl what Patti had planned, well aware that if they found out, they would have one eye on their futures before a note had even been taped. But they figured it out anyway. They'd all been working with Patti long enough that even if they didn't know exactly *what* she was thinking, they could still see the track that her thought train was taking. And, of course, she had provided one warning sign: when she'd up and left New York City.

Prior to her departure, the Patti Smith Group had functioned around the principles of twenty-four-hour collaboration. That's not to say that the musicians had spent twenty-four hours a day every day in one another's company, but it did mean that if one should have an idea that required the input of his or her bandmates, the entire group could be brought together in one room in no time at all. That was no longer possible. On the road or in the studio, of course, they were still in the same close proximity as they'd always been. But the rest of the time, almost five hundred miles yawned between the musicians and their vocalist. Soon *Wave* would offer the listening public a grandstand view of the group's creative dislocation.

Even more so than *Easter*, which itself had disappointed as much as it exhilarated, *Wave* was the work of five players brought together to write as they recorded. There was no doubt that with the same opportunity for organic growth as the songs that marked out *Horses* and *Radio Ethiopia*, numbers like "Revenge" and "Broken Flag" could have developed into something truly memorable. Instead, they simply existed, neither statements of power nor explosions of energy; neither spiraling balls of sound and imagery nor tantalizing glimpses into some deep emotional labyrinth.

Too much of the album was rushed and rapid, as if the band knew that its time was limited and just wanted to get one last album out of its system before pushing on with the rest of the musicians' lives. None of the four band members doubted that they would continue on in their chosen careers once Patti admitted what they suspected she had decided, but of course they did not know what form those careers would take.

The uncertainty, perhaps even bordering on mistrust, was agonizing. Almost a year's worth of touring had been arranged for the album's aftermath, back and forth between the United States and Europe until the fall. But would they actually play all the dates? Most of them? Some of them?

Nobody doubted Patti's professionalism. If she could fulfill her scheduled obligations, she would. But she was still under doctor's orders as a consequence of the accident—still undergoing chiropractic treatment, still on medication. Add that to her barely disguised loss of interest in the things that had once intrigued her, and the increasingly resigned tone that she took when discussing music itself, and if a block of shows should be canceled, or even an entire season of them, nobody would be too surprised.

As it was, they would march on for a little longer.

It was in March 1979, with the album complete and the first dates of the Patti Smith Group's next American tour on the horizon, that Patti gave the interview to William Burroughs that was later published in *Spin* magazine. In it, she laid out her own interpretation of the changes that had affected her over the past couple of years.

"When I entered into rock 'n' roll," she told her old friend, "I entered into it in a political sort of way. . . . I felt that rock 'n' roll, after the death of a lot of the '60s people, and after the disillusionment of a lot of people after the '60s and early '70s, people really just wanted to be left alone for a little while. . . . But when '73 came around, and early '74, it was just getting worse and worse, and there was no indication of anything new, of anyone regathering their strength and coming back to do anything. I felt that it was important for some of us that had a lot of strength to initiate some new energy."

She hadn't aspired to be a star. If anything, as she had said so often in the past, she simply wanted to inspire other people to get up and do something, anything, that would rid their culture of the malaise of inactivity. "I feel that when I was a teenager, I was very lucky. I grew up out of the John F. Kennedy, Bob Dylan, Rolling Stones era, and there was a lot of food for thought in those times. . . . my mind was constantly fertile. And I felt that in the early–middle '70s, there wasn't much happening at all to stimulate the minds of the new generations."

There still wasn't. Writer Nik Cohn once warned that "this year's anarchists are next year's boring old farts," and too few of the performers who rose up on either the musical or the cultural tides of punk had lasted the pace with their vision intact. Among her own peers, Television had broken up under the pressure of, among other things, releasing a second album, *Adventure*, that could not compare with their first. The Ramones had developed into something that even Joey Ramone privately admitted exhausted most of its energy avoiding tumbling into cliche ("and we didn't always succeed"). Richard Hell had all but turned his back on rock music altogether. Besides her own band, only Blondie and Talking Heads had truly survived, and Blondie's future was debatable, as the boys in the band battled to be heard above the media pack's demand for more and more Debbie.

Patti had no intention of being caught in the same trap. "I didn't start doing what I was doing to build myself a career. And I find myself at a time in my life when, if I'm not careful, that's exactly what's gonna be built for me." It was 1979, she said, "and I'm still involved in this thing. But it's come to a point in my life [where] I have to stop and say, 'What am I doing?'"

Once again, the Patti Smith Group's itinerary commenced with a clutch of shows at the Second Chance in Ann Arbor, what was now Patti's home territory. The opening portents were good. Three nights saw the band members reacquaint themselves with one another and with the new material, and it was sounding good. Ticket sales—and, apparently, record sales—were not harmed by the distinctly underwhelmed response that *Wave* prompted from the critics. (Even long-time supporter Robert Christgau, while remaining positive, could only describe *Wave* as being "quirkier than the more generally satisfying *Easter*.")

But the tour schedule was exhausting—some forty-two shows in half a dozen countries—and the longer it went on, the more it became apparent that Patti just wasn't enjoying herself. With the stage dominated by the same giant American flag that had once ruled the MC5's stage, and the live show dominated by the songs that seemingly demanded the least from the performers, there were times when it felt as though the band was almost courting the audience's hostility simply to try to enliven the proceedings.

And, as too many reviewers reported, concertgoers were often left bemused by the number of oldies that had made their way into the group's show. What to make of the Who's "The Kids Are Alright," Manfred Mann's "5-4-3-2-1," Presley's "Jailhouse Rock," John Lennon's "It's So Hard" and "Cold Turkey," Dylan's "All Along the Watchtower," or the Yardbirds' "For Your Love"? Only one oldie, Patti's increasingly bitter cover of the Byrds' "So You Want to Be (a Rock 'n' Roll Star)," seemed to belong, because it was the one that most seemed to reflect her mood. Scarring the melody with her thrashed and discordant guitar interludes, scything through the sentiment with world-weary vocals and claustrophobic sarcasm, she would spit the song out nightly. *Ah, the promise of the night just swirls around you.* So you wanna be a rock 'n' roll star? Well, have fun with that.

As always, there were moments of high passion—"Privilege" seldom failed to draw the old shaman out of the shadows—and high camp—whatever were they thinking as Lenny Kaye took over lead vocals for "Pumping (My Heart)" while Patti worked out with a skipping rope? There was high drama, too, the "Star Spangled Banner" feeding back out of the amps as Patti launched into her familiar rant: *I am an American artist. I have no guilt. I have no truth but the truth inside you. All together we can know all there is to know*. She paused and the band ripped into a scathing "Rock n Roll Nigger."

There was the April night that she broadcast live across West Germany, Patti reminding the *Rockpalast* audience that it was an honor for her to be speaking to so many millions of people at once "because we've been banned live in America." The same night that the warrior queen became unexpected peacemaker, quelling a fight in the front row. "Settle the fuck down. Stop acting like assholes and settle the fuck down, man." So there were high points as the tour wandered on. But they relied on chance rather than intention.

Several times across the crippling itinerary, Patti would accept bookings for poetry readings, no matter how far out of her way they took her. A short gap in between American shows in June saw her fly to West Germany and Switzerland for a couple of readings; a day off in September, bookended by shows in Amsterdam and Paris, would be spent flying to Italy to present a reading after a screening of the movie *More American Graffiti*. Why make such an effort? Because it was different, it broke the chain, it made a change.

In August, Fred Smith was alongside her as she played a pair of benefit concerts to raise money for the Detroit Symphony Orchestra. That month in San Francisco, the band made an unannounced and unexpected return to the Boarding House, the same small club where she'd played unannounced back in the *Horses* era. This time, she joked and laughed her way through "The Boy I'm Going to Marry" and Debbie Boone's "You Light Up My Life," a ghastly hit ballad Patti took a liking to the previous year. With Daugherty and Sohl on joint keyboards, the performance felt much like her earliest shows all those years before, when fame still seemed as implausible as it was inessential, and audiences were drawn largely by the promise of the unexpected.

But the feeling didn't last. In London in September, journalist Chris Bohn came away from the band's Wembley Arena show mourning, "This is not meant to be a crucifixion. I hoped for a resurrection and saw only a willful martyr." His words would prove truer than he could have imagined: as Patti moved on to Italy for the final two shows of the tour, she offered herself up in the middle of a political riot.

The first Italian gig took place in Bologna, in the same kind of soul-lessly vast and infinitely echoing football stadium into which so many of the tour's performances had been cast. The local Communist Party assumed for itself a role similar to the one the Hell's Angels had been assigned at Altamont a decade earlier, prevailing upon the venue's pro-moter to allow it to provide security for the show. This arrangement essentially transformed the venue into a free-for-all, with admission fees waived by the simple expedient of removing the fences. Backstage secu-rity was placed in the hands of whoever wanted to stand around in the bowels of the stadium looking threatening, and the audience was raised to such a pitch of excitement that even the local police seemed content to simply watch from afar.

The band was exhausted before they hit the stage, worn out from trying to impose even a little sanity onto the proceedings. By the time the show got under way, all five musicians would have been happy to throw in the towel. Somehow they got through the performance; some-how, an eighty-thousand-strong audience seemed to be enjoying what it heard. But the stage was under constant siege from would-be dancers and hangers-on, and Patti's road crew, too, was worn down by the events of the day. The show, everybody angrily agreed, was a farce.

Add to that the pressure of an Italian media that insisted on dog-ging Patti's footsteps everywhere she went, and the crowds of teenaged girls who hung on every corner, all clad identically in the outfits they borrowed from *Horses'* front cover, and it was touch and go whether the following night's concert, at the Stadio Comunale in Florence on September 10, would even take place. It did, but it would be the last one.

She had predicted the moment in *Babel*. In a prose piece titled simply "Italy (the Round)," and dedicated to Pasolini, she envisioned *the fluid muscle of the crowd. the hot lights. action as a blade that cuts another slice. . . . nostalgic ruins in/ruin.*

the films are disintegrating . . . the heroine removes herself from the fading aura.

Again the American flag flew proudly, at a time when the United States' relations with the borderline-Communist Italy were at a postwar low. Again the crowd rioted, unrestrained by either the venue's security or any sense of personal responsibility, whipped to a frenzy not by the band's performance (which, as so often on the tour, was merely adequate) but by the mere presence of the band on stage. And tonight, as the band swung into the last phase of the set, the roiling hysteria exploded. Part of the audience invaded the stage; the remainder seemed intent on destroying the venue.

The band returned to the hotel, shaken and still shaking, and all eyes were on Patti as the group commenced the inevitable postmortem. But Patti's announcement rendered it moot. After keeping her own counsel all tour long, after dodging any suggestion that she might be considering some kind of break in the aftermath of *Wave*, Patti finally told the band what had been on her mind for so long.

She recalled the conversation years later, talking with the *Australian*'s Richard Jinman. "We were on the edge of success, particularly in Europe. I could smell it. We were getting into the area where people accept anything you do and it was time to reassess myself as a human being and an artist."

Onstage that night, as she sang "Gloria" for the final time, she had made one lyric change. Most people didn't even notice it, but it meant something to her. *Jesus died for somebody's sins—why not mine?*

"I didn't even think of it as retiring," she told Ramsay Pennybacker of the *Philadelphia Weekly*. "It's a very stable thing, which I tried to explain to people, but sometimes they found it unacceptable. I mean, I've read everything—that I burned out, that I was on drugs—which was totally untrue. I was actually at the top of my game. In Europe, the last show we did was without an opening act. We played before seventy thousand people in Florence. And we were very successful in Europe. And that was the last job I did—for seventy thousand people and it was just our show.

"But the reason I left was because I had met a man who I deeply loved. Who had been through all of that. Who wanted a quiet life, to raise a family."

The Patti Smith Group was finished. Patti was off to Detroit to raise a family with Fred, and though they weren't quite the last words she ever shouted from a stage, the last words of "My Generation" still hung unanswerable in the air, just begging for somebody to paraphrase them.

She created it. Let somebody else take it over.

14

THREAD

FROM ITALY, PATTI flew directly to Detroit. It was her home now—she had no doubts about that. But it takes time to get used to a strange place. It takes even longer before you start feeling comfortable there, and for the locals to treat you like one of their own.

It takes time before they will say hello.

"I did miss the light of [New York City] and how good it had been to me and my friends," Patti mourned to Lisa Robinson in 1988. "But I never for a moment had any regrets, or thought that 'I could have been a contender,' or any of that stuff. That doesn't mean that certain aspects of adjusting weren't difficult, but for me the most important things are the people that I care about and my work."

Fred "Sonic" Smith, too, was difficult to get to know. Although nobody would question his contribution to the history of American rock 'n' roll, he remained unheralded for much of his lifetime, and throughout the brightest years of his career, he was at best an underdog and at worst a victim.

He was one of that select band of musicians whom the authorities, for whatever reason, single out as deserving of the harshest treatment that can be meted out to them. The MC5 were pariahs in their own time, regular victims of police harassment and worse. In his *Guitar Army* memoir, band manager John Sinclair recalls how he and Smith "were brutally assaulted, beaten, MACEd, and arrested by members of the National Security Police, the Oakland County Sheriff's Department, and the Michigan State Police while performing at a teen-club in Oakland" one night—and that was just one incident among many.

If their treatment at the hands of law enforcement engendered a persecution complex in the band, the behavior of the music industry in general only furthered the sense of martyrdom. No matter that the band was signed, during its lifetime, to two of the most influential record labels in the country, Elektra and Atlantic. Wayne Kramer told author Nina Antonia, "[The record industry] despised us because of an anarchistic behavior and militant political stance. We came out of Detroit with our big Marshall amplifiers and spangly clothes, and we leaped around like some unholy version of James Brown on acid, playing free jazz and screaming 'Kick Out the Jams, Motherfuckers' at a time when they were just learning to market three days of peace and love. The last thing anybody wanted was a gun-toting, high-volume rock band from Detroit."

If Fred or his bandmates came out of that experience with a chip on their shoulder, nobody could blame them—even if they had remained bitter for years to come. Because the MC5's reputation did not fade with the passing years. If anything, it became exaggerated, and with that came a sense that the band's members could never be forgiven for the sins of their youth. Detroit radio not only ignored the MC5; it also seemed to have disowned them.

Fred pretended not to care, disguised his hurt beneath a gruff exterior. In 1978, Sonic's Rendezvous Band had visited the UK as the backing group for Iggy Pop. As his bandmates happily entertained all comers in their London dressing room, Smith alone had glowered in the corner, the very air around him defying fans and autograph hunters to disturb him.

"Fred was the artist in the band," MC5 front man Rob Tyner explained. "He was the one who was always pushing us to make a musical statement as loud as the political statements." And whereas the rest of the 5 reveled in their outlaw status, Smith was the one who always asked why people didn't just listen to their music. "He was like a hermit," Tyner continued. "Not physically, because he could party like the rest of us, but intellectually. He wanted to be taken seriously as an artist and he cut a lot of himself off from a lot of people because he didn't think they would understand him."

Patti understood him—understood, too, that eight years after the death of the MC5, her boyfriend was still hurt by the group's failure. Even their eventual adoption as one of the unquestioned pioneers of the punk movement meant nothing to Fred, for he had seen the band in the tradition of Sun Ra, Albert Ayler, and the great modern jazzers. As Kramer told *Addicted to Noise*, "when he started writing his own songs and guitar breaks, he had his own whole musical vocabulary."

It was that vocabulary he intended to teach to Patti. He had long given up hope of resuming a musical career of his own. Sonic's Rendezvous Band issued just one solitary 45 during their lifetime, "City Slang"; no record label would touch them, and he had abandoned hope that any ever would. Without ever thinking of Patti as some kind of mouthpiece for his own work—for who could ever see his soulmate as such?—Fred was nevertheless aware on some level that if the world was to hear what he had to say, it would be through the art of another great artist.

Six months after Patti's return from Europe, on March 1, 1980, she and Fred Smith were married.

Her calendar for the months that followed was clear. There was just one final show for the Patti Smith Group to play, another benefit for the Detroit Symphony Orchestra, but even that performance was fragmented. Patti opened the show alone, reading her poetry. Sohl joined her for a gentle "Hymn," before Fred took his place for an abstract sound painting, accompanying a movie of Jackson Pollock at work. Patti played clarinet, Fred played sax, and an unmanned guitar squawked feedback throughout. Only when that was over did the full band appear, to roar through an improvised jam, and then it was over.

Briefly back in New York City a few weeks later, Patti called her bandmates together at their accountant's office and told them they should find themselves a new band.

Because she had.

For much of the next fifteen years, Patti would remain out of the public view. She would still write, and she and her husband would make music together. But they would not perform, they would not speak to the press, and with just one exception, they would not release any of the songs and sounds they created.

That was not always their intention. Indeed, their first attempt to step out of their silence took place within a year of Patti taking leave of the stage, as they laid down the first steps toward a new Patti Smith album.

It promised to be a departure from her past. Under Fred's tutelage, she was becoming a proficient clarinet player, and the pair would be up late into the night improvising. Or he would talk to her about her singing, encouraging her to make more use of her voice than she ever had in the past, composing songs that he knew would help her reveal her finest qualities.

But with just five songs complete, Patti discovered that she was pregnant with the couple's first child, Jackson Frederick, and all work halted. A couple of years later, she and Fred cut another couple of songs, and then they stopped again. And when they resumed once more in 1986, that too looked like another false dawn.

"We began to rehearse and things with friends," she recalled for Mary Anne Cassata of the *Music Paper*. "We felt we had something worthwhile to share, so we went ahead and started working on the album. Right in the middle of recording I found out I was going to have another baby. That was a surprise. We did as much as we could. We recorded until it was too strenuous for me."

But there may have been another reason for the cessation of these sessions. The faintest of rumors circulated at the time, insisting that no less a figure than Clive Davis had intervened to ask whether Patti needed to work so closely with her husband. Could she not instead reconvene the old band or build a new one to accompany her? It was just a rumor; nothing that has been said or written in the years since then has offered even a hint of substance to it. But if a whisper of it had reached Fred's ears, the bitterness and, perhaps, insecurity that he had already amassed could only have been set ablaze afresh.

The sessions halted, then, not only until the baby was born but through daughter Jesse Paris's first months too, because "there's no job harder than being a wife and a mother," she told Neil Strauss of the *New York Times* in 1995. "It's a position that should be respected and honored, not looked upon as some sappy alternative. It's much more demanding, and required much more nobility than the other work I did."

In her youth, she recalled to Richard Jinman, she'd lived as an artist, bordering upon a vagabond, sleeping wherever she could find a quiet spot ("subways and graveyards"), and forever wondering where her next square meal might come from. Now she was learning the other side of life, cooking and cleaning, changing diapers, "an endless, difficult, but honorable task" that forced her, she said, to work harder than she ever had in her life.

"I don't mind being called a housewife," she insisted in her *New York Times* interview. "Though I didn't disappear to be a housewife. I disappeared to be by the side of the man that I loved. . . . I think nothing greater could have happened to me at that time. I learned a lot of things in that process: humility, respect for others. . . . I developed my skills and hopefully developed into the clean human being that I was as a child."

She read, immersing herself in authors that her rock 'n' roll stardom had forced her to abandon or never even investigate. She got hooked on the cable network USA's *Kung Fu Theatre*, and rewatched *Route 66*. She started painting again, and lost herself in the world of sixteenth-century Japanese literature. She returned to her poetry, and broached another discipline, writing novels.

They were not for the eyes of her public, however. She wrote to amuse herself, to satisfy her urge to create, to place her thoughts and imagination into some kind of permanent form. And she wrote for Fred.

It was strange, her friends admitted later, to see the woman who had once been so vivaciously self-reliant suddenly turn around and allow herself to become so subsumed in another person's personality. Fred became her sounding board, not only for her writing but for her desires as well. In other lives, other relationships, he could even have been seen as manipulative and controlling. But Patti saw only beauty. In 1996, she told Lisa Robinson, "Fred's philosophy was that you create art in the world, but we could also create art just for ourselves. I suppose that's somewhat selfish, but I can assure you it was beautiful."

"He was the suggester in the family," she declared to Ben Edmonds of *Mojo* magazine in 1996. "He was clearly the boss, although he liked to pretend that he wasn't."

It was a portrait of Fred that at least one of his old MC5 associates, Rob Tyner, recognized immediately. "Fred was very controlling, or he could be, but the way he did it, you didn't realize. Toward the end of the MC5, with all of us trying to make our voices heard, he was the quiet one; he'd say his piece and then leave the rest of us to rant and rage about something, then when we were exhausted he'd say his piece again and we'd agree with him. He didn't wear us down with his opinions, he let us wear ourselves down with our own. I can see him doing the same thing with Patti. So it's not even control, it's very gentle persuasion, and you don't realize what he's done until you've already agreed with him."

Patti's life as an artist had turned upside down. In place of the selfish routine she had previously relied upon, she learned to work around the demands of her family. Children "immediately take you out of yourself," she reminded Lisa Robinson in 1988. "Overnight, you cease to be self-involved. All the million little things you were concerned with in terms of life or work—you know, I had to work a special way, I needed silence, I needed this kind of music—all that's gone immediately. You have to relearn everything you do. If I wanted to write, I had to learn to write in the morning, whereas I used to write all night and sleep all day."

Now she would work in the mornings, while the children were feeding or sleeping, sipping her morning coffee and learning how to write with the sun, not the moon, as her muse. "I spent the whole '80s learning how to write by myself, from a quarter of a page a day to pages and pages a day," she told Robinson in her 1996 interview.

To the public, however, she had completely disappeared.

Patti was not the only star of the New York City scene to have apparently vanished. Richard Hell, too, saw the dawn of the new decade as a sign to end his involvement in the music, proclaiming, "I was sick of having to sell my entire life in return for [making records]. If that is the price of recording, I'd rather not do it.

"I outgrew pretty quickly the thrill of being a public figure. As far as it went for me, that was enough. The benefits are nowhere near worth the price."

Patti agreed with him. She replaced adulation with love, a career with a life. For Hell, "as long as I can stagger on doing the kind of work I want to do and can pay my rent, I'll be happy." For Patti, "Because the Night" meant she probably wouldn't even need to worry about the rent for a while.

The recordings that Patti, Fred, and a visiting Richard Sohl had intended to inaugurate in mid-1986 lay dormant for close to twelve months. And even when the musicians resumed work, it was in the knowledge that they were completely in the dark. In New York in 1976, Patti had had her finger on the pulse of the music that needed to be made, because she was in a large part responsible for that pulse even existing. Ten years later in Detroit, however, she really had no idea of what the music of the day sounded like.

She listened to the radio a lot, but it told her nothing. She heard the urban angst of hip-hop, the cold distance of electronica, the mindless repetition of dance. There was no single stream of musical conscious-ness to which she could reach out, nothing that she could draw from or improve upon. Once, music had spoken with the voice of millions. Now it seemed to simply listen to the accountants and to the disparate themes of so many different cliques that vied like rival grocery stores for a share of the global marketplace.

She turned inwards, then, ignoring the concerns that the outside world might have, and concentrating instead on those that she and her husband entertained. She still listened to the radio, but it was movies from which she drew the most: the Japanese director Akira Kurosawa, whose *Ran* was alluring enough that the Smiths went out in a blizzard to catch it; Godard and Bertolucci; Paul Schrader's *Mishima*; Woody Allen's *The Purple Rose of Cairo*.

And slowly, with Fred as her musical director, Jay Dee Daugherty join-ing Sohl in the band, and Jimmy Iovine returning as producer, an album took shape: *Dream of Life*, Patti Smith's fifth and her first in almost a decade. "Jimmy is wonderful to work with," she enthused to the *Music Paper*. "Fred and him really collaborated well on this project. The important thing is that all the musicians were properly represented. It was a real collaboration on everyone's part. Everyone really did their part, from Richard Sohl to the assistant engineer. Everyone put so much into this production."

If there was a theme to the album, she added, it was the need for open and unsullied communication. "Songs like 'Where Duty Calls' and 'Up There Down There' shake a few fingers. The underlying principle is the communication between man and woman, between parent and child, between one and their creator. Planetary communication. It's positiveness behind hope, and also awareness of these kinds of difficult situations."

The album would also reveal that despite her withdrawal from the public eye, Patti had not lived, or written, in complete isolation. The outside world impinged upon her, inspiring her to write about the things about which she felt the strongest. When 241 US military personnel were killed by a terrorist bomb at the First Battalion, Eighth Marine Headquarters in Beirut, on October 23, 1983, she was moved to compose "Where Duty Calls": *May the blanket of kings cover them.* When Samuel J. Wagstaff, Robert Mapplethorpe's photographic mentor, passed away midway through the album sessions, on January 14, 1987, she scribbled down "Paths That Cross."

In Patti and her husband's minds, however, the key to the album was "People Have the Power," a 1980s successor to John Lennon's "Power to the People" that she referred to in the *Music Paper* as "a network of communication." It would not only become the album's first single but develop into the most universal song she ever performed—a clarion call to enlightenment, to unlocking the potential that exists in each and every person but is buried so deeply beneath social and cultural conditioning that only a rare handful ever realize it.

Fred came up with the title. Patti was washing the dishes, she recalled in *Patti Smith Complete*, when he walked into the kitchen and demanded, simply, "People have the power. Write it."

The next few weeks were spent listening to the recorded speeches of the Reverend Jesse Jackson, absorbing the Bible with sister Linda, and contemplating an end to the bloody war going on in Afghanistan at the time, between the native populace and the invading Russians. (Patti would not be alone in later pondering the irony in the fact that no sooner did the ongoing condemnation of the Western world finally convince the Soviets to leave the country, than the Taliban moved in, setting the stage for an American invasion little more than a decade later.)

"This song became our anthem for *Dream of Life*," she wrote, the keystone of an album that the Smiths viewed as a joint manifesto for the unlocking of the human spirit—*joint* because although it was released and marketed as a Patti Smith album, in her mind it was nothing less than a total collaboration that should have been credited to both Patti and Fred, had such an appellation not reeked just a little too much of John and Yoko—or, worse, Paul and Linda.

"It's the only real document we have of Fred's range," she told Ben Edmonds. "He wrote all the music, arranged everything; a lot of the song titles, the album title, the concept of the songs . . . were all Fred's. I told him we should call it by both our names but he wouldn't. But he had promised me that on [our next] album he would sing on it and we'd put both our names on it."

To the *Music Paper*, Patti described *Dream of Life* as just the first in a series of upcoming projects. She and Fred had a lot of other ideas and songs, she explained, that they hadn't even touched upon. Many, many songs. "We're looking into the future with some other works."

Dream of Life was released in June 1988, destined for a chart peak in the mid-60s. Listeners and critics were cautious. Those who hoped that Patti would simply pick up where *Wave* left off (or maybe even look further back to *Horses* and *Radio Ethiopia*) were certainly disappointed; those who merely expected to be entertained were left unfulfilled and perhaps even baffled.

Listened to in the context of either Patti or Fred's past work, it did not fit in, nor did it blend with the music that was being made elsewhere in the mid-to-late 1980s. A true picture of the Smiths' life together it may have been, but it was a cultural orphan all the same, and while reviews certainly *tried* to affect interest and enthusiasm, the album did not offer them any encouragement.

Indeed, even "People Have the Power"—soon to become so powerful and stirring an anthem—seemed like little more than a piece of pointless polemic. The most perceptive contemporary reviews were those that essentially suggested *Dream of Life* was an album that you needed to live with for a time, in the hope that its beauty was simply better disguised than most.

Still, it is a tragedy that Patti and Fred would record just one further piece of music for release, for the soundtrack to Wim Wenders's 1991 movie *Until the End of the World*. "It Takes Time," cut with percussionist Hearn Gadbois and bassist Kasim Sulton, was a moody piece that not only exemplified the closeness with which the two Smiths worked but also the nature of their working relationship. Not only did Fred write the music and parts of the poetry, she told Ben Edmonds, "he actually dictated how he wanted me to read my parts."

Again, people who remembered the Patti of old were astonished to read that. Nobody dictated to Patti Smith. But for Patti, Fred's presence in her life was the reason why she never stopped thinking about her music. Because living with Fred, she declared, her life *was* music, whether they were recording it or playing it, writing it or merely talking about it. She did not need the roar of the crowd, because she had Fred's applause. She did not need the words of the critics, because she had Fred's opinion. And she did not need the constant reassurance that her audience still loved her, because she had Fred's love.

It sounded so simple. But it was also true.

And then everything was snatched away from her.

The string of tragedies began on March 9, 1989, the thirteenth anniversary of Patti meeting Fred Smith. She was watching an early-morning broadcast of *Tosca* on A&E when she received a call from Robert Mapplethorpe's brother. Robert had died during the night of AIDS-related complications.

Just before he died, Mapplethorpe had asked Patti to write a memoir of their friendship, and she had sworn that she would. But she did not yet feel ready to assume that responsibility. Still, she knew that Robert would have wanted her to remember him with a new piece of work rather than further tears. She took out her notebook and began composing a new collection of poetry. "I started writing this piece," she recalled to Lisa Robinson in 1996, "and then I just wrote in a fever for days. . . .

"And I finished it, then I just put it away."

It was, after all, just one of several poetic volumes that she wrote during the 1980s and early 1990s and that she intended would see publication at some point. There was also a mass of prose work that she was, and is still, in the process of sorting out: one, a lengthy character study that she described as Hesse-ian; another about a traveler who never traveled; and a third about a trumpet player who experienced a mystical awakening in Katmandu. The problem was, she laughed to Jeff Baker of OregonLive.com, "I'm a real messy writer. I'll write one narrative in seven notebooks, interspersed with poems and diaries and observations." It would take her a year simply to disentangle everything. It was a condition that Mapplethorpe would have recognized instantly and for which he would frequently chide her.

As Patti continued to toil largely in private, her husband was making plans for her return to the stage. Back in 1988, a newborn baby on hand had ensured there would be no tour to promote the newly released *Dream of Life*. By 1990, however, Fred was talking of convening a new band, with Richard Sohl on keyboards and a percussionist to be decided, and just going out on the road. It would not be a conventional rock outing; as he laid out his vision to Patti, he envisaged something leaning closer toward what he called spoken art, Patti's poetry accompanied by interpretative improvisation from the two musicians.

But on June 3, 1990, the world awoke to learn that Richard Sohl had passed away just days after his thirty-seventh birthday, killed by the weak heart that had always restricted him, and Fred abandoned that dream.

Patti did emerge briefly in 1992 to release a new volume of poetry, *Woolgathering*. And the next year she took the stage in Central Park at the family-friendly SummerStage celebration, flying into New York City with Fred by her side and then flying out again straight after. There was no pressure, no thought of a comeback, and perhaps Patti proved her lack of preparation by forgetting some of the words to "People Have the Power." Nevertheless, she would later tell Evelyn McDonnell of the *Village Voice*, that afternoon "was one of the happiest nights of my life. I couldn't believe how great these people were. The whole atmosphere—not just the audience, but I had my brother there, and Fred was there, and so I have really happy memories of it."

Memories made all the more meaningful by the heartbreak that swiftly followed. On November 9, 1994, Fred Smith suffered a fatal heart attack. When Mapplethorpe died, Patti had thrown herself into her work to deal with his passing. But now, with her husband gone, she would barely write a word for an entire month. Her brother, Todd, was the first to rally to her side, the one who was always trying to pull her back together. Slowly, tremulously, she started writing again—and then Todd passed away as well.

Two coronaries in two months.

Both men were forty-five.

Whereas Fred's death had forced her to halt, Todd's convinced her to move. He had been beside her throughout the first weeks of her widowhood, constantly encouraging her to work again. Now that he, too, was gone, she did not want his last passions to have been in vain.

At St. Mark's Church on January 1, 1995, two days after her forty-eighth birthday and fifty-three days after the death of her husband, Patti took the stage to read her verse and sing a single song. It was the same thing she'd done nearly a quarter-century earlier, at her first-ever public performance. Back in 1971, the song was "Mack the Knife"—a song of defiance. This time, she had chosen to perform "Ghost Dance," a hymn of birth, from the album *Easter*, which was dedicated to the eternity of the human spirit. In that simple decision, there was a single defining statement. *We shall live again.*

Patti was performing at the church because she had promised she would, months before, while Fred was still alive. She'd been working on a new book of poetry at the time, "a book of poems and stories and things that pretty much surrounded a lot of people that I had lost," including Mapplethorpe and Sohl. "And also people that I admired," she explained to Gerri Lim of *Big O*. She'd written a poem for the ballet dancer Rudolf Nureyev, one for the playwright Jean Genet, one for Audrey Hepburn. "Just different people that I really liked that influenced me." And as she wrote, she felt the need to perform, because when she performed, she knew, it encouraged her to write. She might not even have discussed the invitation with Fred before she agreed to fly to New York for the show. That's how important it was to her.

In the aftermath of two more loved ones' deaths, she had forced herself to keep her commitment. And there she was, back on stage. But she wasn't really there, because she flew straight back to Detroit once the performance was over, and she pulled the shutters down again. It was too early. It was too soon.

Then one day in February 1995, the telephone rang. It was Allen Ginsberg. Modern America's greatest living poet was almost seventy now, but he was still as active as he ever was, still writing and reading. He was in Ann Arbor, or on his way there, for a reading for Jewel Heart, a spiritual, cultural, and humanitarian organization dedicated to propagating Tibetan Buddhist wisdom to the world.

Tibet, of which Patti had dreamed since she was twelve.

The Jewel House reading was already sold out. Four thousand people had paid to hear Ginsberg. Perhaps, Ginsberg ventured, they would like to hear Patti as well? She was touched by the offer, touched by his words, which she would often recall. "Let go of the spirit of the departed," he told her, "and continue your life's celebration." She agreed to perform.

Ginsberg opened the show and held the stage through to the intermission. Then he delivered the promise that much of the audience was already anticipating, speaking quietly and gently of a poet "who took poetry from lofts, bookshops, and gallery performances to the rock 'n' roll world stage. We're really pleased and happy that"—pause—"Patti Smith." The rest of his sentence was lost beneath the roar of applause that rose up from the stalls, just as the intermission was drowned out beneath the hum of expectation.

Patti started slowly, with a poem she wrote after reading the Dalai Lama's autobiography, *Freedom in Exile*, in 1991. (She would meet the man in September 1995, at the World Peace Conference in Berlin.) She dipped in and out of her other writings, reducing the audience alternately to laughter and tears but always holding them in the palm of her hand. She asked herself, was performing always this easy? Did it always come this naturally to her? New York City the previous month had been hard, and when her memory swept back to the last time she toured, in 1979, with the stage at the end of an enormous sports stadium, those shows were even harder.

"I traveled the world with a rock 'n' roll band in the '70s," she reminded the crowd, and paused while it bellowed its applause. "The last job we ever played was in Italy in a big soccer arena." The show had ended in chaos, a riot and a revelation. Now she read "Florence," titled for the scene of that final concert but tonight dedicated to her brother Todd, her road manager throughout so much of her career. Instinctively, her eyes flickered to the side of the stage, almost as if she expected to see him standing there as he always had. But there is only shadow and strangers, and *never again,* she said in a shaky voice, would she ever *experience such selfless devotion, such singular care.*

She counted Ginsberg's backing band of viola, bass, and guitar into a haunting cover of "The Twelfth of Never," the tear-stained ballad that everyone from Johnny Mathis to Donny Osmond had made their own, then finished with "Cowboy Truths," from *Woolgathering.* The first she dedicated to Fred; the second could be offered up to the world. And offstage, backstage, she dedicated herself to the future.

Rolling Stone would later declare her return to be the "comeback of the year," and excitable fans would call it a resurrection, too. But 1995 was not the resumption of an old career—it was the beginning of a new one, one that might have been enflamed by the fires of the past but was going to stand on its own feet regardless, because that was all that Patti Smith knew how to do.

Later, once people become accustomed to having her back, a few voices—old voices, past voices—would complain that she wasn't the same woman, the same talent, the same power that she'd been twenty years before. And she would look at them and shake her head sadly.

"No I'm not," she'd reply. "Are you?"

15

SCREAM OF THE BUTTERFLY

PATTI NEVER FELT the need to inform the world which came first—her decision to return to performing, or her relationship with Oliver Ray, the twenty-something guitarist and photographer whom she met for the first time at Ginsberg's Jewel Heart benefit. It did not matter, to her or to him, that more than a quarter of a century separated their birth dates, that when Ray was born in 1973, Patti was already two years into the five-year plan that would culminate in superstardom, or that by the time he started middle school, she had already retired. Slowly but effortlessly, Ray slipped into that role of coconspirator, partner, and muse that only a very select handful of others had occupied.

In fact, the two life choices probably informed each other. Jewel Heart had reminded Patti how much she loved performing; Oliver reminded her to keep on reminding herself.

It was difficult, of course. The tiniest thing could remind her of her late husband—the most innocent remark, the least question or suggestion. Even being asked about her future. After Richard Sohl's death had scuttled Fred's plans for a new tour, he had begun to formulate another vision to revive his wife's career. Looking around at a musical environment that suddenly seemed to be swamped by tough, independent female vocalists, from Courtney Love to PJ Harvey, Fred saw Patti's influence everywhere. He wanted her to take her rightful place among them.

Now other people were echoing Fred's insistence, and Patti responded with the same amazement she'd had when Fred first broached the idea. She told Andrew Masterson of the *Age*, "I find it hard to believe that I could have so much impact. It's an extreme honor. I wouldn't look at it as a burden. It is an honor and a responsibility and I'm still examining it."

And she knew that the best way to examine anything is out in the field.

On April 8, 1995, Patti appeared at a tribute concert for the war-ravaged nation of Bosnia at a Methodist church in Ann Arbor, not far from the aching, empty wound of the family home. Lenny Kaye was her sole accompanist. Later that same evening, she played two sets at a second benefit, this one organized in her late husband's memory across town at the Ark.

The latter performance was less a concert and more of a free-for-all. Patti opened the proceedings with harsh recitals of "Piss Factory," "Dog Dream," and "Sohl," then ceded the stage to a succession of other performers: her sister Kimberly Smith, roadie Andi Ostrowe, and local performers Scott Morgan, Gary Rasmussen, and poetess Carolyn Striho. Patti waited in the darkness on the edge of the stage and interspersed their music with further snatches of verse.

Lenny Kaye delivered a sharp take on the Left Banke's "Walk Away Renee," and there was high drama as Carolyn Striho returned to accompany Patti through Nirvana's "On a Plain." Exactly one year before, the shotgun-shelled body of the Seattle band's lead singer, Kurt Cobain, had been discovered in a room above the family garage, and Patti, aware as she always was of the strength of anniversaries, was anxious to pay tribute to the fallen warrior, a performer whose obituaries had already raised him to the same echelon as John Lennon and Jim Morrison. Later in the evening, she would perform Cobain's "Come as You Are" as well, and then follow it with a new poem, "About a Boy," dedicated to Cobain, but to a part of Fred as well.

Perhaps sounding rather more grandmotherly than her older fans would be comfortable acknowledging, Patti mourned to *Mojo*'s Ben Edmonds, "When Kurt Cobain took his life, Fred and I were extremely disturbed about that. Both of us liked his work. We thought it was good for young people. . . . He had a future. As parents, we were deeply disturbed to see this young boy take his own life. The waste, and the emotional debris he left for others to clean up.

"I was also concerned how it would affect young people who looked up to him, or looked to him for answers. I guess that's the danger of looking to anyone else for answers, but I perceived that he had a responsibility. To himself, to the origin of his gifts, to his family, to the younger generation."

She wrote the song for two reasons, then. One was to wish Cobain well as his soul continued its journey. The other was to chastise him for leaving the world to get along without him. The question of whether or not a rock star, living or dead, should have such responsibility thrust upon him was one that she was unwilling to consider.

In Patti's youth, and that of her early fans, premature death had offered an immortality—and, of course, a tragic romance—that had nothing whatsoever in common with any "example" the deceased might have been setting by his or her demise. But in Patti's middle age, the two had become inextricably linked, a consequence, perhaps, of the very culture of cheap modern celebrity that she found so distasteful elsewhere.

Once, a pop star had been just that, a pop star. Now he or she was expected to be a role model as well. And maybe that was how things ought to be. It just sounded strange hearing Patti—who, after all, had scarcely suffered from the deaths of her first musical idols (all of whom at least materially contributed to their own deaths, even if they did not physically pull a trigger)—voicing that same opinion.

The Ark applause was still ringing in her ears as Patti accepted an invitation to record a song for an upcoming women's charity compilation, *Ain't Nuthin' but a She Thing*, an exquisite collection of songs that already boasted offerings from Annie Lennox, Sinead O'Connor, Luscious Jackson, and hip-hop divas Salt-N-Pepa. Patti, possibly to the organizers' surprise, agreed immediately, but rather than offer up a new song, or the kind of cover for which she was once renowned, she instead turned in a slow, sultry purr through the torch classic "Don't Smoke in Bed."

For anybody who had not heard her sing since *Dream of Life* (or cared to since *Wave* or *Easter*), it was a revelatory performance. More than that, though, it was a heroic performance, not because Patti had the gall to take on a classic of the American songbook, but because she delivered a version that owed nothing to Nina Simone, who had recorded the best-known version. It was so solidly her own that a decade later she would still be performing it; in a review of her February 2008 appearance in the Lincoln Center's American Songbook series, *New York Times* critic Stephen Holden would write that her performance of "Don't Smoke in Bed" was "dark, dramatic" and "held its own beside [any other] interpretations."

"Don't Smoke in Bed" was a charitable contribution. Elsewhere, however, Patti did not disguise the fact that a lot of the career decisions she made now were financially motivated. Although her catalog was still selling, and was about to receive a fresh boost as Arista compiled her five existing albums into a remastered box set, *The Patti Smith Masters*, she was well aware that her responsibilities as a mother did not end with merely raising her two children, thirteen-year-old Jackson and eight-year-old Jesse. Their education, too, needed to be paid for, and she and Fred had talked long into the night, in the year before his death, of a return to the studio, to ensure that the kids would be taken care of. "I'm a single parent," she told A. D. Amorosi in the *Philadelphia City Paper*. "I have to provide a living for my family. I am alone without my companion after eighteen years."

But that was not the only reason why she was inching back into the spotlight. There was also the need to reconnect with a world beyond grief.

At the end of April 1995, Patti offered herself to a second local Tibet benefit; in mid-May, she played a couple of nights at a small club in nearby Ferndale, Michigan; and in early June, having spent the previous few weeks rehearsing with Carolyn Striho's band, the Detroit Energy Asylum, she was onstage in Pontiac, Michigan. These were low-key shows, tentative steps to determine whether people really did care as much about her return as her friends and fans were convinced they did. But any doubts that she might still have entertained regarding her place in the modern world were firmly dismissed by the response to her next gig, at the Phoenix Concert Hall in Toronto on July 5.

There, in a performance that began with the same one-two poetic punch of "Piss Factory" and "Dog Dream" that had ignited the Fred Smith tribute in April, the Detroit Energy crew eschewed what could have been considered Patti Smith's greatest hits to present instead the portrait that Neil Strauss would encapsulate in the *New York Times* later in the year. "Ms. Smith," he wrote, "appears to be taking on a new image in the 90's, that of an extremely empathetic and compassionate woman pushed back into the public eye by the hand of death."

The selections included "Don't Smoke in Bed," "Because the Night," "People Have the Power," "Paths That Cross," "The Jackson Song," "Poppies," "Ghost Dance," and "Land," interspersed with verse—"Babelfield" and "Hey Joe" both made defiant appearances. "Farewell Reel" was a new song, but an old one as well, combining a melody she wrote after her husband taught her to play guitar with lyrics that he commenced about a month before he died and Patti completed soon after.

The *Village Voice*, a supporter from the dawn of her performing days, was there in the person of Evelyn McDonnell. "Fronting a band for the first time in 16 years, the woman who brought a shamanistic force to punk's tattered style is in an expressive trance. She seems unconscious of her elegant, long-boned fingers as they flutter before her, or as she crosses her arms over her chest and rests her hand on her shoulders, anchoring body to earth."

She was performing "Dancing Barefoot," and quite unintentionally, it seemed, transforming it from a song of love to a declaration of purpose. "Chanting the line 'Oh God I fell for you,'" marveled McDonnell, "she suddenly changes it to 'Oh God I'm back again' and looked dazedly out at the club—her face mirroring the crowd's disbelief and joy." And when her eyes met Oliver Ray's, and she saw that same light glowing on his face, she knew she had made the correct decision.

Ray, Patti told the world, was a poet, a guitarist, an artist in his own right, and the inspiration behind a lot of what she was preparing to do. He'd been there for her as she rode the shock waves of the past few months, and he would be there for her now as she started writing songs again—beginning with "Fireflies," which blossomed out of a piece of music he was writing one day when she stopped to listen. Two additional songs were written with Ray by her side—"Walkin' Blind," which she would give to the *Dead Man Walking* movie soundtrack album, and "Wander I Go," which she'd share with Jeff Buckley—and it was these songs that gave her the strength to write more.

On July 27, Patti returned to SummerStage in New York City for a performance that spliced verse and song in a way that Patti had not attempted since the early 1970s. Her 1993 appearance had been one of her happiest moments; tonight her happiness would be tinged with bittersweetness, but the performance would prove no less triumphant. Two years ago, she had simply been interrupting her silence. Now she was breaking it.

The forty-minute set ranged back and forth across her career: "Land," dedicated to Robert Mapplethorpe, and "Y," which was taken from a poem about him; "Ballad of a Bad Boy," which she wrote for Sam Shepard. A piece from the late 1970s called "Wing," and then out came the band, Lenny Kaye and her sister Kimberly, both bearing acoustic guitars, to sing and chant through "Ghost Dance," "Paths That Cross," and "People Have the Power."

It was a lighthearted set awash in good vibes and strummed acoustics. The following day, however, offered up the return that even Patti's oldest supporters had been waiting for, as she hooked up again with Kaye and with drummer Jay Dee Daugherty, added a friend of Lenny's, Tony Shanahan, on bass, and mounted a one-off surprise show at Lollapalooza.

Lollapalooza was in its fifth consecutive year now, a leviathan festival of alternative rock that was originally conceived as a vehicle for Jane's Addiction's farewell tour but then altered the face of live music for the decade. At a time when the United States in general, and the music industry in particular, swore that it was paralyzed by a ghastly recession, Lollapalooza proved that people were still willing to go out and have a good time—provided that a good time was guaranteed. In other words, recession wasn't to blame for the country's malaise. People were just sick of being sold the same old shit.

By July 1995, the latest incarnation of the traveling show had lumbered as far as Randall's Island, New York, with a bill that included Kurt Cobain's widow Courtney Love and her band Hole, Sonic Youth, Beck,

Moby, Cypress Hill, and more. Enlisted at the last minute, Patti was granted a thirty-minute spot on the festival's second stage. She wound up performing for an hour, in front of an audience that probably included every single musician on the afternoon's bill, few of whom were even old enough to have seen her perform before.

She won them all over, with a fiery performance that was both magical and, to some, messianic, as she not only unleashed a seething "People Have the Power" but also made it apparent that she was determined to ensure that they kept it.

Time and again as she eased herself back into the world of interviews, Patti acknowledged that it was not the performances themselves that she missed during the years she spent in Detroit so much as the people she performed to—and now they were with her everywhere. Hours after Lollapalooza, she was signing books at Barnes & Noble on Astor Place in Manhattan. A new anthology, *Early Work, 1970–1979*, had just been published; it contained exactly what the cover would suggest. The purpose of the collection, she explained to Gerri Lim of *Big O*, was to relieve her fans of the ballooning costs that were now attached to her out-of-print writings. "It came to my attention that some people were selling copies of my old books to kids for a lot of money, so I agreed to have them compiled." As for the signing, "It was exhausting. Hundreds of people showed up."

Patti knew that her fans were still fascinated by her past—although her eyes were now focused on her future.

She had been friends with Rosemary Carroll, poet Jim's ex-wife, ever since Rosemary first appeared in Jim's life in the mid-1970s. Now they were business associates as well. Casting around for somebody to manage her career as she built toward her rock 'n' roll return, Patti knew that Rosemary would do the job well. Plus, she wanted somebody who could keep everyone else's demands in check, because she still wasn't certain whether she'd be able to do it herself.

She need not have worried on that account.

"She's polite but firm about the scope of our interview," the *Village Voice*'s Evelyn McDonnell recalled of becoming the first journalist to sit down in earnest with Patti in 1995. "This is a transitional time for her, as she eases herself back into the spotlight, and we have a transitional talk: Nothing about the deaths, the family . . . or even her new material. We talk exactly the allotted hour."

That hour raced past, though. Patti was wild with enthusiasm, talking of recording and live work. "I always liked performing while we were recording, because I like to keep in contact with the people. Somehow that energy you receive gets funneled into the record. I mean, you're doing a record for everybody, and I like to go into the studio having a sense of those people—some symbol of them."

Her old record deal with Arista was still in place, though she was adamant that even after all these years, the label still didn't truly understand what she did. They let her get on with it, though; that was the main thing. Also still in place, it seemed, was a large part of her old band, the Patti Smith Group that rose with her to such heights in the late 1970s. After recent appearances alongside her already, both Lenny Kaye and Jay Dee Daugherty were lined up to return, and to *Big O* she spoke of featuring "other guitar players on this record—my old guitar player Ivan Kral and perhaps Tom Verlaine and certain other people might be guest-playing."

In fact, Kral would never return, held back by his own career in the modern Czech Republic and by private disagreements with Patti herself. And, of course, Richard Sohl was dead. But Luis Resto, borrowed from the Detroit Energy Asylum, "plays very similar to Richard"; Tony Shanahan was back on bass, and Electric Lady studios, down in the Village, had just been booked for July.

The choice of venue was not arbitrary. The first time Patti had visited the studio was the day she met Jimi Hendrix. The second time she'd been there was to record her first-ever single, "Hey Joe," in 1974. And the third, a year later, had been to cut *Horses.* As she returned to the Electric Lady for her first visit since her debut album, she immersed herself in the memories the place still held.

Patti stood in the hallway looking at the murals and gold discs with which the studio was decorated. Suddenly she remembered standing in that same spot in 1975, with Robert Mapplethorpe taking pictures of her and John Cale. And at that moment, Lenny Kaye walked over, stood beside her and said, "Amazing, isn't it?"

"It was like he could feel what I was feeling," she told Ben Edmonds. "The first time we were back in the studio, just hearing those Lenny guitar tones and Jay on the drums, it . . . triggered so many memories."

Chronologically, the new album was ignited by two songs drawn from Patti's years with Fred. She had collected a stash of cassettes of her late husband's songwriting ideas, but at first she found them too painful to listen to. It was Lenny who played through them and selected "Summer Cannibals," a composition that Fred had had lying around since the early 1970s, and the punchy "Gone Again," a song that would have been the title track to the couple's next joint album, had Fred lived. "Gone Again" was also the last piece of music Fred had composed for the record, and now Patti needed to marshal all her resources to write the lyrics.

Some songs remained too personal. Patti had written "She Walked Home" in spring 1994, following the death of Jackie Kennedy; she read in a magazine that when the former First Lady heard she was dying, she took one final walk alone through Central Park. "She Walked Home" captured that image, and later in the year as Fred lay dying, he would often ask Patti to play it to him while he sang along. The song, she said, became Fred's own. She would never record it.

Oliver Ray's magnificent "Fireflies" was on board, and with it a liquid guitar from Patti's old friend Tom Verlaine. Verlaine also appeared on "Wander I Go," recorded at the same sessions but absent from the finished disc. A spectral throb, it added the visiting Jeff Buckley's acoustic to Verlaine's electric guitar. Buckley would become a constant presence in the studio, and Patti was delighted. As young lovers, she and Robert Mapplethorpe would "neck like high school kids" to his father Tim Buckley's *Goodbye and Hello* album, Patti confessed in *Mojo*, and the son would make an equally indelible impression on *Gone Again*. Jeff harmonized high through "Beneath the Southern Cross" and asked for the session for "Fireflies" to be delayed so he could run home to grab his essrage, an Egyptian instrument that he knew the piece was crying out for.

Luis Resto was Patti's collaborator on the sweet "My Madrigal"; Lenny Kaye resparked their old songwriting partnership on the fluttering "Beneath the Southern Cross." But it was the songs that Patti alone composed that were destined to become the heart of *Gone Again*. Contrary to those reviewers who would later pick out the Fred-led rockers as the album's highlights, tracks like "About a Boy,""Dead to the World,""Wing," and "Ravens" gave *Gone Again* its most memorable flavor; over the drifting soundscapes, Patti's lyrics resonated like the poems they might once have been, beautiful visions poised just on the musical side of improvisation, and built not around tune but around imagery.

"*Gone Again* is more personal than Fred and I ever wanted to do an album," Patti would later admit to Jon Pareles of the *New York Times*. "I know that it's a pretty personal piece of work to inflict on people." But she didn't care. She made it for herself.

Few of the album's songs had been through the crucible of live performance; only "About a Boy," "Farewell Reel," and her super-stylized take on Bob Dylan's "Wicked Messenger" had a firm place in her live set. Two decades earlier, her later work with the Patti Smith Group had suffered from a lack of live exposure, as had *Dream of Life* in 1988. This time, however, it was not a significant shortcoming, since Patti's method of songwriting had changed. No more jamming for hours with her bandmates; no more extemporizing lyrics and rhythms onstage. "I practiced really hard and learned to write these little songs." (She admitted, however, "I never learned to play anything but waltz time." Consequently, Jon Pareles observed, "*Gone Again* is full of waltzes.")

Patti's first album in eight years would not be released until mid-1996. In the meantime, summer 1995 gave way to fall, and studio sessions were replaced with a slow dance of occasional concerts, one-off appearances, and benefits, most of which saw Patti still more confident reading than singing, and apparently stepping willingly into the role of spiritual guide to a growing array of musical admirers.

As her husband had insisted, Patti's influence was inescapable. Though new revolutions had arisen during Patti's years away, their figureheads were her devotees. Thurston Moore of New York's Sonic Youth and Michael Stipe of Athens, Georgia–based college favorites REM both spoke glowingly of Patti as both an influence and an inspiration—and they would be rewarded with her friendship and collaboration.

"I didn't know her," Moore wrote in *Bomb* magazine. "I could only embrace the identity I perceived. I was impressionable and she came on like an alien. . . . I wanted to meet her and take her to a movie, but she was so unobtainable and fantastic. I could only entrust my faith to the future. The future would allow me to have a date with Patti Smith or at least hang out with her."

He achieved that ambition in October 1995, when Patti and Lenny Kaye attended a celebration of Jack Kerouac in his hometown of Lowell, Massachusetts. Moore joined them and was asked to play guitar on three songs. They played shows in "cool churches" in Lowell and Boston, spent a day sightseeing around Kerouac's Lowell and another taking photographs—framed shots of Moore's hand—for an exhibition Patti was planning. "I was friends," he wrote, "with someone I had dreamed of being friends with for nearly twenty years."

Next, Patti visited San Francisco, for two shows that she recalled as the two extremes of her new approach. She described the first show to the *Philadelphia Weekly*'s Ramsay Pennybacker as "conservatively structured. It was upbeat but more of a typical poetry reading with some music. And the second show, just an hour later, was kind of wild. The people were more energetic and more interactive, and the show sort of lost its structure and it's like we were having a little party together with poetry and music."

Over two nights at the end of November, the twenty-fourth and twenty-fifth, Patti and her band took over Philadelphia's Theatre of Living Arts for three shows designed to showcase her new material for the first time, but also to get Patti used to the idea of being on the road again. Weeks earlier, a surprise call from Bob Dylan had ended with her agreeing to tour for the first time since 1979.

The last time Patti had spoken privately with Dylan was on that day in 1975 when they bumped into each other on Fourth Street in New York City. He'd shown her the photo of the two of them on the cover of the *Village Voice* and asked her if she knew who those two people were. At the time she laughed and said no. Now she knew. They were two people who, twenty years later, would be talking on the telephone, one hedging about her hopes for a renewed career; the other insisting that the world needed her presence.

Lenny Kaye, Jay Dee Daugherty, Tony Shanahan, and Tom Verlaine lined up as Patti's band. She knew that they were scarcely prepared to undertake any kind of tour, but she didn't care. No matter that they could cram in no more than five hours of rehearsal time. The musicians knew one another; they knew the material. They would get by.

Michael Stipe, after years as a fan, joined the tour as their official photographer. Oliver Ray was along as well, not only in his role as Patti's boyfriend but also to add his guitar to one song each evening. His appearances were brief, then, but they were scarcely unimportant. For the first time since Fred's death, Patti was seen to be happy in public.

It would be only a short outing, ten dates in six cities, shoehorned into what Dylan fans were already calling his Never Ending Tour, and few observers doubted that Dylan arranged the gigs more for Patti's benefit than his own. He rarely hit the road after Thanksgiving any longer, and he'd already thundered through over one hundred shows that year. But, as Patti would reflect to Neil Strauss in the *New York Times* once the tour was over, "I thought the audience was basically Bob's people, but they seemed real happy to see us because they know that I'm one of Bob's people, too."

The tour commenced on December 7, 1995, at the O'Neill Center in Danbury, Connecticut, with a set that was guaranteed both to please and to ease Patti back into the rigors of a full rock 'n' roll tour. To give the old fans something to cling to, Patti offered "Dancing Barefoot," "Because the Night," "Ghost Dance," "Rock n Roll Nigger," and, offering proof of its growing status as an anthem of sorts, "People Have the Power." Heralding the new era were "Wicked Messenger," "Walkin' Blind," the Rolling Stones' "Not Fade Away," and the epic "Beneath the Southern Cross." You could see Patti enjoying herself, reacquainting herself with all that she had once loved about performing, and reveling in Dylan's obvious concern and care.

The first night, she confessed to Ben Edmonds, was "pretty shaky." But only the first night. By the second, she was "back in familiar territory." And besides, she insisted that her sole intention on the tour was to set the stage for Dylan, to thank him for his faith in her by confirming his audience's faith in him. "I think we did a pretty good job and I know that he was happy."

And so was she. "I'm playing with one of my major influences, as a performer, writer," she told the *Philadelphia City Paper*. "From a very early time, talking about Philadelphia, one of my big things was taking the bus to Sam Goody's waiting for *Blonde on Blonde* to come out. Playing with him now brings a beautiful humor to the picture. It makes me think if I could just tap that girl, the dejected one on the bus, and tell her she'd be working with Dylan one day . . . It's just wonderful."

The tour was onto its third night, at the Orpheum Theater in Boston, when Dylan made the move he'd been waiting to make. One of Patti's favorite songs of his was "Dark Eyes," from his 1985 album *Empire Burlesque*. He'd rarely performed it since that time, and not once in the eight years of the Never Ending Tour. But tonight he did, sliding it in after "Mama, You've Been on My Mind"; Patti danced out on the stage to sing alongside him. "A lot of girls have come along since Patti started," Dylan told the audience afterward. "But Patti is still the best, you know."

They reprised the duet every night for the remainder of the tour, and on the final night of a three-gig stand at Philadelphia's Electric Factory, she reappeared during the encores to join him on "Blowin' in the Wind" as well. "Singing with him was just like being in heaven," she told *Mojo*. "I was so happy."

But as much as she loved celebrating and being celebrated by one of her idols, Patti didn't necessarily relish being placed on a pedestal by society at large. "Our culture has shifted the purpose and the goal of music and all of the arts," she later complained to *Observer* journalist Sean O'Hagan. "That's why I don't like MTV. Music television is all about the media-oriented version of what it is to be a rock star, it's not about what Bob Dylan or Jimi Hendrix were about—which included great images, sure, but they had spiritual and political and revolutionary content, too. I believe their early goal was to do something utterly and truly great, or nothing at all. All of them insisted on the primacy of the work—the art, not the artist. This emphasis on style that we have today—the image, the video, the stylist, the game plan—that's not rock 'n' roll at all. That's careerism."

She looked around at her peers on the comeback trail, patting their own self-satisfied backs with appearances on *MTV Unplugged* and *VH1 Storytellers*, "picking up their lifetime achievement awards." But what, she asked, were they *really* doing? Nothing. She snarled at the very existence of a hall of fame for rock music, seeing it as just another way to make money, not simply commercializing art but bastardizing it as well, reducing passion to a plaque on a wall. She shared, too, her late husband's loathing of any establishment operation that claimed, way too late in many cases, to be honoring the very same people it had done its best to ostracize in years gone by.

Rock 'n' roll did not need a museum. The fact that it existed was enough.

And yet there she was in January 1996, standing on stage at the Waldorf-Astoria Hotel in New York City, inducting the Velvet Underground into the Rock and Roll Hall of Fame. The same band whose first LP she had reviewed for *Creem* in 1974, knowing that even among the readers who had heard *of* the group, the number who had actually *heard* them was infinitesimally tiny.

That was how much things had changed since she'd been gone. Not that the Velvets were inducted, but that there was even a Rock and Roll Hall of Fame for them to be inducted into. The antisocial little monster called rock 'n' roll that she'd spent her teens and twenties defending, convinced that it was the one thing left to youth that had the power to make things different or better—that little monster was now a responsible member of society, a rebel no longer. And she despised that.

Lou Reed, John Cale, Sterling Morrison, Maureen Tucker, and Nico. The Velvet Underground, she told the assembled suits, "opened wounds worth opening, with a brutal innocence, without apology, cutting across the grain, gritty, urbanic. And in their search for the kingdom, for laughter, for salvation, they explored the darkest areas of the psyche." The Velvets were a triumph of the musician over the establishment, and the fact that people remembered their names proved that their victory was lasting. Could a Velvet Underground even form today, much less exist, much less make a difference?

Patti would change her tune about the Hall of Fame soon enough. Until then, she tried to remain optimistic. "I think things are a lot more open than they were in the '70s," she had told Gerrie Lim a few months earlier. "The field is quite wide and I'm really proud of a lot of the things that the new guard has done, all these groups from My Bloody Valentine to Nirvana. My son likes Green Day. There's a lot of energy in music right now." She herself would be content to play the outsider, the returning revolutionary—perhaps even (in the eyes of a prospective audience growing more and more excited about her return) the woman who would turn around the opening oath of her old take on "Gloria": to suggest that if Jesus wasn't up for the job, then maybe she would die for rock 'n' roll's sins.

At the Hall of Fame, however, she celebrated the past and then left the building at the first chance she was given, in tears of such vehemence that it was easier to fly home, which was still Detroit for a few months more, than spend another minute in its company.

Gone again.

16

A FIRE OF UNKNOWN ORIGIN

JUST AS PATTI was reintroducing herself to the world in mid-1995, one of her oldest friends was also garnering renewed public attention—albeit posthumously. Six years after the death of Robert Mapplethorpe, Massachusetts-born, Manhattan-based author and editor Patricia Morrisroe published her biography of the artist. It was a doorstop of a book, the fruits of some sixteen interviews between author and subject, and many more between Morrisroe and Mapplethorpe's associates, and it reexamined his life in painstaking, and often painful, detail.

Patti had been happy to be interviewed for the starkly titled *Mapplethorpe*. She was not so happy with what she read in it.

"I gave [Morrisroe] what I thought was a good sense of what it was like to be an artist," Patti complained to Hilton Als of *The New Yorker*. "I saw Robert go from an extremely shy misfit to an extremely accomplished person." But that process was "represented in the book as one hustle after another." When *she* remembered those days, she said, she recalled the joyfulness with which they approached every project, and the "youthful fervor" with which they completed it. They weren't plotting to be famous, she swore. It was just that they had "a million ideas and lots of energy." It was innocence, not calculation, that led them to lead the lives that they lived.

Just a year after the publication of *Mapplethorpe*, Patti released her own book in an attempt to eulogize her former partner. *The Coral Sea* was the piece Patti had begun writing on the day Mapplethorpe died. Its title was taken from one of his photographs, of the aircraft carrier USS *Coral Sea*, but its imagery was pure legend—the legend of everlasting friendship, two kids growing together and staying together, no matter how much turmoil life had forced them to endure. *The Coral Sea*, she said, had taken on a life of its own; it had called upon her to draw from all that she knew about Mapplethorpe both as an artist and as a human being. The writing had been easy, too, developing swiftly into a set of sixteen interwoven prose poems whose very energy, she felt, echoed that with which they had lived their lives.

But for the first time since she embarked on her comeback, Patti found the critics were less than enthralled. Her romantic, allegorical, and sometimes almost biblical tribute to her friend was seen as naive at best, self-serving in places, and no match for the vision of Mapplethorpe that was conjured in the pages of Morrisroe's biography. For the moment, *Mapplethorpe* was the account by which he was to be judged, rightly or wrongly.

It had been a long time since Patti had last faced up to public criticism, and longer still since it had hit her so hard. Respect was devilishly hard to come by, and shaken by the reception of *The Coral Sea*, Patti could be excused if she wondered whether her now-imminent comeback album, *Gone Again*, would suffer likewise—a victim not of outright dislike but of unfavorable comparison with a more imposing edifice. And whereas *The Coral Sea* was oft compared, absurdly, to *Mapplethorpe*, *Gone Again* was up against Patti's own past work.

It would not be an entirely fair comparison. If one listened to music purely for its tunes, for the choruses that could be easily sung along with, one would be hard pressed to distinguish the best of *Gone Again* from that of either *Easter* or *Wave*; Patti herself acknowledged that. Her music remained as clear and uncluttered as ever. But those were not the records she was competing with. Instead, her new album would be judged against the two discs that preceded them—in particular, the one that announced her to the world in the first place, the twenty-one-year-old *Horses*, just as each of the records that followed it had been. The fact that so many years separated the two records would not make an iota of difference in the eyes and ears of the critics.

It would have been so easy for reviewers to dismiss the record. What, they could have asked, did a returning Patti Smith have to offer that she had not already dispensed in the past? The same question, in other words, that is asked of every returning hero, from the latest vintage reunion (and the 1990s overflowed with such events) to the periodic returns to action of bands that had never really gone away (the Rolling Stones, for example).

But *Gone Again* received a far easier ride than anybody might have expected, borne aloft on a wave of generosity that bordered upon gratitude: *thank you* for returning, *thank you* for recording, *thank you* for remembering us. The fact that it deserved such largesse is of course immaterial; browsing today through the reviews that awaited *Gone Again*, one is still struck by the sheer love and affection with which Patti was received back into the arms of the critical establishment. When *Rolling Stone* featured *Gone Again* in its "essential recordings of the 1990s" poll in 1999, nobody would even think to question its inclusion.

Patti had continued teasing her audience with live shows through early 1996, as guest appearances and benefits again consumed far more of her time than full-on concerts. But when she did break cover with the band, the results were spectacular. Two nights at San Francisco's Warfield Theatre, opening a weeklong Californian sojourn, brought the audience to its knees with both shocking revivals, as "Gloria" returned from her grave to round out both nights, and new surprises, such as Lenny Kaye's renditions of "Love of the Common People" and Deep Purple's "Smoke on the Water," with the latter's signature riff performed by Jackson Smith, Patti's thirteen-year-old son.

Appearances on the FOX variety show *Saturday Night Special* in Los Angeles in May and *Later . . . with Jools Holland* in London in June brought out a driving "Gone Again" and a spoken "People Have the Power." Then, back in New York City for two nights at the Irving Plaza, she gave *The Late Show with David Letterman* a triumphant "Summer Cannibals."

She had much to celebrate. Not only had she made her musical comeback, but she had made a personal return as well, uprooting her life and family once again and coming home to New York City, to a brownstone in Greenwich Village. And now that she was there, it felt as though she had never left.

Yet she did not have long in which to unpack, and certainly no time to put everything away. In fact, she acknowledged, she might never do so. Thirty years before, sharing an apartment with Robert Mapplethorpe, she had driven him to distraction by leaving her art, her writings, her every thought scattered on the floor, as though the very act of dropping it was the only thing she created it for. Even now, she was still most comfortable amid the clutter of her creativity, in a tumbleweed tangle of manuscripts, photographs, paintings, and notebooks. Plastic toys and Polaroids. Favorite books and pop culture iconography. Newspaper cuttings and political tracts. And tour itineraries.

Her latest tour, so relaxed earlier in the year, was about to become far more grueling. She prepared for a return to Europe for the first time since 1979, with a schedule that seemed to pick up exactly where she left off in Florence. The reborn Patti Smith Group kicked things off at the Roskilde Festival in Denmark on June 30, and then it was on to the Paris Olympia and the Royal Albert Hall in London, and more shows all over the continent through July and August 1996. Next it would be America's turn, with gigs through to the end of the year, and then, almost without a break, the band headed to Japan and Australia for Patti's first-ever tours of those countries.

Patti had been driven to exhaustion by her schedule in the late 1970s, but now she was working as hard as she ever had. The difference was, she was doing it on her own terms. She was no longer competing for the attention of the marketplace, no longer driven by the need to keep up with the hit-makers of the day.

Through 1996, Patti's live repertoire had, in the words of Neil Strauss in the *New York Times*, essentially been an autobiography: "Patti Smith opened her sold-out concert on Friday night at Irving Plaza with a 1974 poem about a 16-year-old escaping a dead-end job to come to New York City and 'be somebody.' She ended the two-hour show with 'Farewell Reel,' from her first album in eight years, a song about a 49-year-old woman recovering from the death of her husband and preparing to re-enter the world. In between these autobiographical sketches, an entire life unfurled."

Now it was time to move ahead.

Peace and Noise, the album that Patti and the band began scheming shortly after returning from their Australian tour in January 1997, was the final fruition of the work that she and Fred Smith had been planning to pursue at the time of his death. After the release of *Dream of Life*, she told writer Margit Detweiler of the *Philadelphia City Paper*, "Fred and I had set about to do a more socially conscious record. . . . When he passed away I really didn't have the heart to do that particular record. I focused on *Gone Again* as a remembrance of Fred, but as I strengthened, I decided to continue the work we'd anticipated for ourselves." An issue-based album, she admitted to Jim Sullivan of the *Boston Globe*, "is not popular right now, but I don't really care about that stuff."

For all his influence over the proceedings, Fred Smith would receive no writing credits on the finished record. But the moods and topics were indeed those he would have prompted Patti to address, domestic issues that would range from the recent (March 1997) mass suicide of the Heaven's Gate cult to the drowning death that same spring of Jeff Buckley, the so-talented and promising singer-songwriter who'd made such an indelible impression on *Gone Again*.

But the album was recorded beneath the shadow of an even more personal loss for Patti: the April death of Allen Ginsberg.

Like Dylan at the bedside of Woody Guthrie, as Ginsberg lay dying in a New York City hospital, Patti barely stirred from his side as he faded; she owed him so much, and she owed him *that* much. Less than two years had elapsed since Ginsberg pulled Patti out of her own trough of despair with the reminder that she needed to go on living so as to honor those she had lost. Now she needed to draw upon those same reservoirs of strength and purpose once more. "It was a peaceful passing," she would tell the audience at the 1998 Tibet House benefit at Carnegie Hall. "Off he went." Gone again.

But while *Gone Again* had matched *Horses* in intensity and strength, the album that she was now assembling was intended to push deeper. Her live performances, so tentative at the beginning, had developed an incandescence of their own; the very act of stepping out on stage, she said, helped propel her toward new extremes of performance. Returning to the studio could only amplify that feeling. And if, as several outside observers were suggesting, *Gone Again* had returned Patti to her poetic beginnings, then *Peace and Noise* would surely follow in the footsteps of *Horses'* own successor, the once-reviled but now wholly rehabilitated *Radio Ethiopia.*

"The whole record is band oriented—everything is done by the band, except on 'Last Call' where Michael Stipe sings in the background," she promised the *Philadelphia City Paper.* "Everything is also pretty much live; one cut is totally improvised."

The album's potential became apparent in April 1997 when, just hours after a moving appearance at Allen Ginsberg's memorial at St. Mark's, Patti was onstage alongside Tom Clark, a member of the High Action Boys, at Brownies in the East Village, in a gig that also featured Marshall Crenshaw and Jim Carroll.

It was a benefit for Clark himself, and the guest of honor played seething guitar from a wheelchair. He had been home in DeKalb, Illinois, to attend his father's funeral; while attempting to move some furniture, he slipped and broke two bones in his leg. Clark was laid up for a month before Lenny Kaye drove out and brought him back to New York City. Now, as the guitarist faced medical bills, a rapacious landlord, and another five months before he could expect to stand again, Kaye and Dictators front man Handsome Dick Manitoba pooled their resources to lend him some support. The evening brought in some $5,000 for the beleaguered Clark.

Impressive as that sum was, onlookers were equally astonished to hear Patti pull "Radio Ethiopia" out of mothballs for the first time in two decades, segue it into a stylized version of "I'm So Lonesome I Could Cry" (the song she had performed at Ginsberg's memorial), and unleash, too, Bo Diddley's "Who Do You Love."

In its naked form, "Who Do You Love" is a primeval rocker whose bayou-dark visions of rattlesnakes and human skulls might easily have been written with Patti in mind. Its spirit would soon infuse "Memento Mori," the one song intended for the gestating new album that allowed the Patti of today to merge with the Patti of the now-mythic past. In a frenzied, soul-shattered resurrection, Johnny, the main character of "Land," graduated from the locker room to the beaches of some far-away war. The full-band composition opened with a spectral recollection of the Doors' "The End" echoing over the soundtrack to Francis Ford Coppola's *Apocalypse Now* (then and now the most effective use of a rock song in a movie ever). From there it lurched into the riff from "Who Do You Love," Lenny Kaye and Oliver Ray—now a full member of the band, following the departure of Tom Verlaine—dueling like snipers over the hypnotic rhythm.

The track was taken note for note from eleven minutes of improvisation in the studio, Patti enthused to the *Philadelphia City Paper*. "We recorded in an old propeller factory/studio where there were these huge overhead fans that look like propellers. They reminded me of the tops of helicopters, like blades. I improvised on that. The piece is a remembrance of a boyhood friend of my late husband who was killed in Vietnam in a helicopter crash."

Just as compelling were Patti's personal recollections of a childhood spent far from the nightmares of modern life but locked within nightmares of another sort, a theme that ran through the track "1959."

In 1959, she explained to Jeff Apter of NYROCK.com, she was a kid growing up in an eventful time. And thanks to the twenty-twenty vision with which we all look back on our childhoods, she claimed to remember it all—even the elements that she would not have experienced at the time. She may have danced to Eddie Cochran's "Somethin' Else" and thrilled to the Chevy Impala, "this amazing thing with huuuuuge fins and all," but she would not have recognized a Jackson Pollock or known then that it was the year Kerouac published *On the Road*. But no matter; the events of that year were all a part of her past now: Castro taking over Cuba, Buddy Holly perishing in an Iowa field, the Russians landing the first unmanned craft on the moon, and the forty-eight states becoming fifty. It was also the year of the failed Tibetan uprising against the Chinese occupation. "Looking back, I wondered how it was that we could survive World War II yet do nothing about helping Tibet."

The song would earn Patti her first-ever Grammy nomination. Unfortunately, it would prove to be one of the few bright spots on *Peace and Noise*, an album that, for all its promise, lacked the magic Patti had been conjuring so effortlessly in concert. (The only song that came close was "Spell," which borrowed affectionately from sundry Ginsbergian beat raps and his poem "Footnote to Howl.") To many ears, the record was less a collection of songs than a succession of panegyrics and homilies, Patti making Patti noises, bereft of either substance or strength. Even the songs that touched upon her own life appeared less than convinced or convincing, an accusation that she scarcely seemed interested in rebutting.

Onstage at Irving Plaza the previous year, Patti had told the crowd, "I am so well-loved lately that I am turning into a walking Hallmark card." Patti was fast ascending, and she knew it, to a position perched benignly somewhere between Earth Mother and Mother Superior: a gentle, almost grandmotherly figure whose life had been so touched by tragedy that audiences were prepared to be more forgiving of her frailties, more accepting of her lapses—and more open to her pronouncements. Too many people, in fact, looked to Patti to dictate their own feelings on a given subject; her recent performance schedules often read like a what's what of worthwhile causes. And now, too much of *Peace and Noise* seemed to rejoice in that status.

Reviews were certainly harsh. Ben Ratliff of the *New York Times* deemed it "monochromatic . . . tame, unadventurous stuff." Reviewers that praised the album's electric punch, the fact that it was more "rock 'n' roll" than its predecessor, missed the point of course; if one musical truth rang through Patti's entire songwriting career, it was that the songs that rocked the hardest were often the laziest, that she was at her strongest and most compulsive when all the rules were set aside and the musicians played to the beat of their own hearts. Patti herself was not satisfied with *Peace and Noise*—or, at least, she knew that it could have been better, and that the band that created it could have done better.

The band had gone back on the road, prefacing *Peace and Noise*'s November 1997 release with four shows at CBGB before hitting the rest of the country. It was not, technically, a tour, Patti informed the *Boston Globe*: "I can't really tour; I have two kids. I'm visiting certain places, being very choosy about where I go and basically playing places that have been supportive or I like for a particular reason. Boston has always been supportive and I'm going to Rhode Island because it's kind of obscure. It's one of the original thirteen colonies, isn't it? I like supporting the original thirteen colonies."

In fact, the serious business of touring would not begin until summer 1998, when Patti launched into a series of dates that catapulted her from the Bowery Ballroom in New York City at the end of July; across to Austria, Hungary, and Belgium; back to the United States; around the globe to Australia and New Zealand; back on the road in America until Christmas; and finally to two more shows at the Bowery Ballroom. In all, she made more than fifty public appearances in 1998, including tributes to Ginsberg and Kerouac, benefits for Tibet, and a guest spot with REM when they performed in New York City, in which she duetted that band's "E-Bow the Letter" with cowriter Michael Stipe.

But once again, she was already looking forward to her next album. "I'm always writing," she told New Zealand journalist Graham Reid when the outing touched down there, "but after we finish this tour we are going back to do an album, maybe a double album, with the same group of people . . . that created *Peace and Noise*. Oliver Ray and I wrote most of the songs on *Peace and Noise* and we're still continuing to do a lot of writing, and have a lot of new songs and ideas. I am very excited about the next record, which I think will contain quite a bit of poetry as well as songs. I think it's going to be very interesting work. . . . I think the next work will . . . be even more open with more poetry and experimentation. I'm really looking forward to that."

Although the album would indeed be recorded with the same lineup that cut *Peace and Noise*, their work could not begin until late the following year. Although Patti performed only thirty-four shows in 1999, she continued to make a concerted effort, it seemed, to be everywhere she could, as often as possible. Appearances included another European tour, highlighted by a triumphant spot at England's annual Glastonbury Festival, her first outdoor event in the UK since the Reading Festival in 1978; her first-ever appearances in Israel; and a headlining role at the Sixth International Istanbul Jazz Festival in Turkey.

Her schedule for 1998–1999 was as stuffed as any she could have kept in the 1970s. Patti had discovered, like Dylan before her (and David Bowie at around the same time), that although it's possible to sit back and rest on your artistic laurels, as a true artist you need to be out among your people. The way to make a difference is not to dictate causes to them from on high but to connect with their lives, so that your art can either address or offer respite from the problems that concern them. Again like Dylan, she had become the only performing artist of her generation who both acknowledged and represented the needs of her audience, as opposed to simply speaking for them.

Her political concerns also gained focus as she looked toward her children's futures and pondered the issues that would affect them as they grew older. And she drew inspiration from the past as well, as her father, Grant Smith, passed away on August 27, 1999, just a month after his eighty-third birthday.

Gung Ho, her promised next album, would arrive with a sleeve photograph taken from an old picture of her father, young and proud in his military uniform. He had enlisted in the US Army on May 12, 1941, seven full months before the United States joined World War II, and now his experiences would become one of the influences on her latest writings. As she crafted the new album's content, Patti would ponder the things that her father had fought for—and the things that, as he fought, he had *hoped* for.

A world in which freedom meant truly to be free, not just the puppet of one more violent regime.

It was the age of blame. In 1998, President Bill Clinton came under attack for his relationship with White House intern Monica Lewinsky, in a sequence of events that swiftly swirled from rumor and innuendo to direct questions about Clinton's ability to continue governing the country. For the first time since President Nixon masterminded the Watergate break-ins, a sitting American president faced trial, but not, as in Nixon's case, for any criminal behavior. Clinton faced judgment over his so-called moral standards, a conflict that quickly moved out of the governmental realm to become a straight fight between right- and left-wing politicians over the standards of American life itself.

Patti was swift to respond, not to any perceived wrongdoing on Clinton's part, but to the utterly disproportionate response that his behavior
provoked. Speaking for a *Rolling Stone* feature called "The Clinton Conversations," in which an array of cultural figures were asked to comment
upon the ongoing circus, she sighed, "The Clinton thing is so insidious;
what they're unraveling—you could take any human being, start prob-
ing, and find their little private can of worms. We are becoming our own
Big Brother by allowing all this to happen. If we are going to say it's all
right to take away the privacy of the person who has the highest seat in
the land, how can the rest of us possibly be protected?"

But there was more to her concerns than that. The past decade
had seen American politics, if not Western politics as a whole, devolve
from a conflict of political ideologies into a battle between conflicting
moralities. For years, abortion had been the leading battleground; more
recently, the ability of gays to serve in the military had come to the fore.
Soon, the concept of gay marriage would be exercising the minds of the
nation and dividing once again down political party lines.

"When I look at the crucifixion of Clinton, I look at the crucifixion
of my generation," Patti continued. "They are finally nailing us for introducing new ideas about sexual mores, sexual freedom, personal freedom:
'OK, you wanted sexual freedom, we're gonna give it to you—to the
point where it is going to saturate and sicken the whole planet.'"

Patti's private fury over the state of the world elbowed aside the
personal pains that had preoccupied her for the past five years. Where
she had once used her guaranteed audience to spotlight the issues that
she and her husband held dear, such as the continued plight of Tibet, she
now began to speak equally passionately about more overtly political
matters.

Gung Ho, the warlike title of which would seem more and more apt
as time passed, is the album that confirmed her growing interest in politics. What's more, it did so without any of the embarrassing grandstand-
ing that normally accompanies an artist's attempt to take a political stand.

Patti had watched, doubtless as aghast as many other people, as a host
of well-meaning pop stars and other public figures stepped forth during
the 1980s and 1990s to deliver their personal solutions to any number

of worldly problems, few of which were able to look beyond the view from the penthouse suite. The thirteen songs that made up *Gung Ho*, on the other hand, allowed the listener to make up his or her own mind on whatever issue Patti was putting over, and the ensuing openness permitted the album to become her most musically and lyrically satisfying since *Easter*.

The year ended with Patti onstage at the Bowery Ballroom once again, ringing in the new century onstage with sister Kimberly, Tom Verlaine, and keyboard player Grant Hart. Much of the new album was already in place in the repertoire; no fewer than seven of the unheard record's tracks were in the set, all already flexing their muscles in readiness for the album's March 2000 launch.

The following evening, Patti was at St. Mark's for a brief reading. February brought her now-annual appearance at the Free Tibet benefit, and yet another Bowery Ballroom gig, an Internet broadcast previewing *Gung Ho* to the world. But she was also settling into the routine that would mark her course for the next decade: touring when she wanted to, recording when she felt like it, and speaking out when she needed to.

Reviews of her most political record to date were kind. "It's a fuller, more exhilarating effort than ['Gone Again'] or 'Peace and Noise,'" declared Seth Mnookin of Salon.com. "Smith sings, screams, moans, groans and roars about Mother Teresa, Ho Chi Minh, slavery, Gen. George Custer, Salome, war, redemption and honor . . . [and] veers from anthems to open-ended jams to downright funky ditties."

Jon Pareles picked up the thread in *Rolling Stone*. "With *Gung Ho*, she's back to life, taking on the whole world. She belts manifestoes, plunges headlong into love, offers benedictions and hurls herself into history and myth. She casts herself as Salome in the slinky 'Lo and Beholden,' as the accusatory ghosts of African-American slaves in the tolling 'Strange Messengers,' as General Custer's lonesome wife in the neo-Appalachian 'Libbie's Song.'"

True, producer Gil Norton's work may have been just a little too locked within the sonic pastures that had sounded scintillating when he first unveiled them with the Pixies a decade earlier. True, too, that the full *Gung Ho* experience may last a few songs longer than it needed to.

But there was another Grammy nomination lurking within the album's first single, "Glitter in Their Eyes"; sister Kimberly, son Jackson, Tom Verlaine, Grant Hart, and Michael Stipe all offered audible contributions; and if the album scarcely bothered the US chart, nodding in and out of the lower reaches of the Top 200, then that scarcely bothered Patti.

Again, she wasn't competing for a place within whichever hierarchy ruled the industry this week. She was simply allowing her voice to be heard in the places where she felt it was most needed.

17

SANDAYU THE SEPARATE

I N 2000, THE United States faced a presidential election, and
the upcoming tussle between George "Dubya" Bush, the mass-
executioner governor of Texas and the son of outgoing president
Clinton's predecessor, and Al Gore, Clinton's uncannily uninspiring
vice president, was guaranteed to fill nobody beyond their own address
books with joy.

The result was a contest that aroused so much of the country to
demand an alternative that when consumer advocate Ralph Nader put
himself forward as a third option in the traditional two-horse race, a
surprising number of people who might otherwise have considered
themselves Democratic or Republican Party loyalists cast aside their
allegiances to fight alongside him.

Patti, however, had been a long-standing supporter of Nader's Green
Party. She would joke with Deyva Arthur of the party's quarterly newspaper that her involvement probably dated back to when she "met somebody on the street, and they signed me up." But she also acknowledged,
"I'm really an independent person. I go where there is good, no matter
where it comes from. Also I do a lot of work in Europe where the Green
Party is really strong, like in Germany." She threw herself wholeheartedly into Nader's campaign. "Ralph Nader's activism, in every sense of
the word, is what attracts me. I gravitate toward people and ideology that
is earth- and people-friendly."

She donated "People Have the Power" as a Nader campaign anthem, and the new album's "New Party" too. She added *The Wizard of Oz's* "Over the Rainbow" to her repertoire as further tribute to the hopes she believed Nader embodied. She spoke at his rallies, and as the November election day drew closer, she toured alongside the Nader campaign, performing at rallies in New York City, San Francisco, and Washington, D.C.

"I'm not an entertainer so to say," she insisted. "I don't really care about my career. I just want to do good work, and incorporating Ralph's teachings in all our performances is part of doing good work."

Nader lost, inevitably, and with him fell the Democrats, their traditional support eroded just enough by the Green Party's high-profile campaign to allow Bush to capture a slim majority of votes in the nation's baffling electoral college system—and become the first president over a century to ascend to power despite the fact that a plurality of voters preferred his opponent. People clearly did not have the power after all.

Patti's live schedule through the first years of the new millennium remained packed. She dropped in and out of the highest-visibility venues as she saw fit, but was just as likely to wash up at a benefit, a reading, or simply an impromptu gathering as she was to book a two-night stand at a regular theater. Festival dates and opera house engagements were interspersed with small club appearances, and in March 2000 she even returned to the Waldorf-Astoria to induct the man who signed her to Arista records, Clive Davis, into the Rock and Roll Hall of Fame.

June 2001 opened with Patti playing three nights at the Village Underground in New York City and closed with her triumphing over the Roskilde Festival in Denmark. The following month, she moved from the Ocean club in London to the Fuji Rock Festival in Japan.

And on October 3, with New York City still reeling from the terrorist attacks that brought down the World Trade Center three weeks previous, she was among the throng who turned out at St. Mark's for the reading unequivocally titled New Poems to End Greed, Imperialism, Opportunism and Terrorism: Poets Respond to the September 11th Attacks and Ensuing Events. Alongside Ed Sanders, Edwin Torres, Cecilia Vicuña, Jackson Mac Low, Anselm Berrigan, Todd Colby, and many others, Patti added her shock, rage, and sorrow to the city's outpouring of grief.

Patti spoke further on the subject in a poem published in *Interview* magazine the following month. "Twin Death" was set over six days in September, beginning that first morning when she *awoke to the sound of a passenger plane singing its end. awoke to the sensation of spirits—a purgatory of souls ascending the billowing smoke and ash filling the sky at the base of my street.* The poem passed through the stages of vigilance (*awoke to the sound of f-15's and helicopters circling above*), anger (*awoke to the cries of "usa! usa!"*) and sorrow (*it is a morning for mourning*) and finally onto readjustment (*for the first time since the attack, I enter a subway*). Now she prayed that the government could make that same adjustment.

But she knew that it wouldn't.

Patti shared in America's revulsion over the attacks, and those feelings would never leave her. But they would be pushed to the back of her consciousness by her opposition to the events that followed. Over the course of the next year, the Western war machine swiftly assaulted Afghanistan—where the Taliban government had at least supported the terrorists' aims—and then just as quickly diverted its attention toward Iraq, a country that had nothing whatsoever to do with September 11 but with whom the United States nonetheless had unfinished business. Like many other Americans, Patti questioned the evidence President Bush and his British ally Tony Blair were touting to justify a preemptive strike, and squirmed uneasily at the aggressive actions that were being perpetrated in their names.

On September 11, 2002, the first anniversary of the attacks, Patti appeared at a WBAI New York event titled Patriots for Peace and Global Justice. The following day, she was alongside Louis J. Posner, founder of the electoral reform movement Voter March, protesting the slide to war with Iraq outside the United Nations Headquarters in New York City, while Bush was inside delivering his side of the story to the General Assembly. And on October 26, she was at an antiwar rally in D.C., leading 150,000 people through an impassioned "People Have the Power," a song that was rapidly establishing for itself as potent a place in the new peace movement as "Give Peace a Chance" had occupied at the height of the Vietnam War.

Of course, not everyone opposed the war in Iraq; Patti knew that her political activism would alienate some fans. But it would empower them too, to see beyond the media's insistence that we need to turn to our leaders, in whatever field we perceive them, for the answers we're searching for. Indeed, by setting herself up in opposition to what she was aware many of her fans deeply believed, she was delivering the lesson that she herself had learned when she stood by Jim Morrison's gravesite all those years ago, when she realized that there was no room for heroes in the world that she was entering.

You could listen to what they said and take inspiration from their actions. But ultimately, the final decision was yours to make, and only a fool would blindly follow others.

Within this understanding lies the truth behind the public persona that Patti Smith brought to the first decade of the twenty-first century, a decade during which her own private life receded even further from the spotlight than ever before. She was living *not* the life of an artist, for that implies struggle and disappointment, nor that of a bohemian, for that brings with it its own heavyweight baggage. But somewhere in between those poles, a woman worked in a field that simply hadn't existed before she created it, one in which she could say or do or dress as she wished, knowing that an audience was already out there for her, and that it cared.

It cared when she released *Land (1975–2002)*, a two-disc retrospective that included a dazzling selection of classics and rarities, as well as a newly recorded and highly remarkable cover of Prince's "When Doves Cry." It cared just as much when the Andy Warhol Museum in Pittsburgh staged Strange Messenger, an exhibition of Patti's drawings, silk screens, and photographs, in September 2002. Quite simply, she was a part of America's artistic landscape, as established an insider as it is possible for an outsider to be.

Patti finally left the Arista label, and on October 20, 2002—Arthur Rimbaud's birthday—she signed on with Columbia Records. Two years later, Columbia would release *Trampin'*, Patti Smith's last album of the decade to contain any original songs.

The band for this new project remained the same: Lenny Kaye, Jay Dee Daugherty, Oliver Ray, and Tony Shanahan. Patti and the band produced the album themselves.

Daughter Jesse played piano on the title track, recorded live at the Looking Glass Studios, the house that Philip Glass built. "Trampin'" was a traditional gospel piece that Patti had been singing to herself for a couple of years, ever since she first heard it on an old LP by Marian Anderson, a key figure in the struggle for black artists to win recognition in pre–civil rights America. So liked it so much, she told *Uncut*, that "I asked my daughter if she would learn it on piano. . . . I'm very proud of her, I think she did a beautiful job."

That same mood carried over to the remainder of the album. Patti had now lost both of her parents; three years after her father's death, her mother Beverly passed away on September 19, 2002, at the Underwood-Memorial Hospital in Gloucester County, New Jersey. But if their presence hung over *Trampin'*, it was lightly, gently; "Mother Rose" remembered her mother, but it was gratitude not grief that flavored it, she said. Likewise, she mused, tracks such as "Trespasses" or "Cash" were not about sorrow but "the result of seeing things in life." Seeing things and knowing that there was not much that could be done to change them.

It was not, overall, a strong record. It was, however, well intentioned. "Peaceable Kingdom," her vision for a post–September 11 world that had already been trampled by politics and war, was her most overt reference to the causes that had devoured the last few years—and, perhaps, her weakest. It was, grumbled Rob Horning of *PopMatters.com*, "about as inconspicuous as anything you'd hear on a Sarah McLachlan record; it seems written to be NPR bumper music." "Stride of the Mind," Horning continued, was just "a straightforward rocker."

But then *Trampin'* exploded, across the nine-minute call to arms of "Gandhi" and then through a cut that made even that look brief: the seething, twelve-minutes-plus "Radio Baghdad." The latter song opened with the sound of children playing before slicing angrily into the warzone reality of their playground, with a frenzy that was as jammed as it was cohesive, structured improvisation forged in the same furnace of imagination from which "Radio Ethiopia" was cast, but shaped by rage and despair as well. More than anything else on the album, "Radio Baghdad" reminded us why Patti still made records.

Trampin' did not change the world. Neither did her loud opposition to Bush's reelection campaign in 2004, or her appearances alongside Ralph Nader when he toured in opposition to the Iraq war later that year. And America did not accede to her impassioned demands that it indict Bush "for befouling our country's name," cried live to the nation via Sirius Satellite Radio on New Year's Eve 2005.

But she did not expect them to. Once—thirty years before, for instance—people seemed willing to have their minds changed, if the power of an argument was great enough. Less so today. Not at all so today. Patti acknowledged that sometimes modern activism could feel futile. "We were betrayed," she later sighed to *Time Out London*, "by the media, our government, even the Democratic Party. Now I find it very difficult to be in my country."

Even so, she was hopeful. She would rail against the government because it needed to be railed against. And because, as she told writer Nick Blakey, "If you keep poking someone, they're eventually going to bleed."

Despite her recent political activity, however, and despite a celebrated career that spanned three decades, it was still her first album, *Horses*, by which she would forever be judged and remembered. It was a touchstone that she was now about to revisit as she took over the organization of the 2005 Meltdown festival, the two-week-long celebration of arts, dance, and music hosted by London's South Bank Centre (which comprises the neighboring Royal Festival and Queen Elizabeth Halls).

In the twelve years since Meltdown's inception, it had developed into one of the most eagerly awaited spectacles of the artistic calendar—in no small part because the flavor of each year's event was decided not by the so-called experts that traditionally helm such festivals but by a specially invited curator. Among the notables to have operated past Meltdowns were Elvis Costello, Laurie Anderson, Nick Cave, John Peel, Scott Walker, Robert Wyatt, and David Bowie. Each one strove to present a program that not only reflected his or her personal tastes but also reached beyond his or her traditional fan base to embrace some often shocking extremes. Now it was Patti's chance.

Patti admitted to Tim Cooper of the *Times* that she was initially uncertain whether or not to accept the offer; she wasn't certain whether she could even create *one* "interesting evening, not to mention two weeks of events." She turned for advice to Morrissey, himself a past curator, and "he was very encouraging. He told me to just barrel on through because the Meltdown people shepherd you along. And it's been true."

"This will be the most social experience of my life," she told the *Guardian*'s Ed Vulliamy. "I don't interact with a lot of people; I don't know a lot of famous people. I work very simply. I spend my time with my children and my work. . . . I tend to be insular and opinionated. But for this, I want to, and will, work alongside people. I'll perform myself, but if anyone else needs a bit of backing vocal, clarinet, or a shirt ironed, I'll be there."

The guest list that she presented to London would encompass some of the most dramatic and dramatically flavored performers of the age. The event would be bookended by two performances drawn from Patti's love of William Blake: Songs of Innocence, dedicated to the innocence of childhood, and Songs of Experience, dedicated to Jimi Hendrix. Blake would not be the sole poet incarnated for Meltdown; one night would be devoted to William Burroughs, another to Bertolt Brecht.

Patti would even perform, for the first time in its entirety, *The Coral Sea*.

More than a decade had elapsed since the volume's publication, but as she confessed to Spencer Tricker of *PopMatters.com*, "I had tried to read it publicly, but could never sustain reading the entire piece." Appearing at the New York Public Library on May 28, 1996, she had seemed tearful even before she commenced to read.

In 2005, however, she found a collaborator with whom she could ease the entire piece into a complete performance. Kevin Shields was the English guitarist who had led the ultravisionary band My Bloody Valentine to short-lived but lasting glory at the end of the 1980s; Patti had missed seeing or even hearing the band when it was in its pomp, but she caught up with their music later and immediately fell in love with it. And now her collaboration with Shields "gave me an all-encompassing landscape in which I could explore the emotions that drove me to write it."

Patti and Shields premiered *The Coral Sea* to the world at Melt-down on June 22, 2005. "We didn't rehearse," Patti confessed afterward to Mark Paytress of the *Guardian*. "We simply talked about our expectations and improvised."

This time around, reviews were unanimous in their enthusiasm. *Observer* critic Molloy Woodcraft adored the performance. "Shields, surrounded by effects pedals, rings great sheets of sound from expensive-looking electric guitars beneath and, occasionally, above . . . Smith's declamations as we move around an imaginary ship. It becomes quite mesmerizing at times, Shield's characteristic bending notes making you feel like the room is moving out of shape. The pair finish up side by side on the sofa as the sound dies away, heads down, lank hair over their eyes, Smith grinning madly. When they depart hand in hand, they look for all the world like mother and son."

They would repeat the performance the following year, and release a CD of both shows in 2008. The liner notes would encapsulate Patti's feelings about the events: "I believe we produced together a fitting memorial to Robert, who was, when I was young, my bloody valentine."

Around their first performance, meanwhile, the rest of Meltdown unfolded. John Cale was there; so were the reformed Television. Yoko Ono, Marc Almond, Tori Amos, and Sparks numbered among a cast list drawn from the furthest extremes of the music scene, reflecting Patti's personal vision of who and what an artist should be. The Brecht evening, in particular, offered wild variety, as she called a dozen or more different acts to take the stage and sing a song or two. Another night, titled Peaceable Kingdom for the *Trampin'* track, dwelt on Patti's role as peace activist.

"This may be the most self-referential Meltdown there's been," Glenn Max, producer of contemporary culture at the South Bank Centre, told the *Guardian*'s Faisal al Yafai. "Even though there are big ideas here . . . there's a lot of her in this show. There's a real political view to this."

But there was also nostalgia. Nobody, least of all Patti, had forgotten that 2005 marked the thirtieth anniversary of the release of *Horses*. In 1975, critical opinion as to its merits had been sharply divided. But how thoroughly the positive opinion had won out over the negative would be revealed by the reception for *Horses*' rebirth at Meltdown.

Tickets for the night, June 25, 2005, sold out immediately, while good seats for the other nights were still readily available from the box office. "I was overwhelmed," Patti admitted to journalist Simon Reynolds of the *Observer*. "To tell the truth, it brought tears to my eyes. *Horses* pretty much broke as a record in England. I always think of us as a semi-English band because we were so maverick in America and then we went to London and played that first date . . . and the response gave me my first sense that 'wow, we're really doing something.'"

As for *why* she was recreating the album, beyond the notion that a recording of the show would make a neat addition to the upcoming thirtieth anniversary reissue of *Horses* itself, "I wanted to do it while I'm still physically able to execute it with full heart and voice. I had nicer hair back then, but my voice is actually stronger now!"

Following in the footsteps of David Bowie, the Cure, and Sparks, all of whom had taken to recreating entire classic albums in concert in recent years, Patti would open the show with *Horses* side 1, track 1, "Gloria"; close it with side 2, track 8, "Elegie"; and then follow the most recent CD reissue by encoring with the bonus track, the live "My Generation" that had appeared on the B-side of "Gloria."

The band was as close to the original as death and politics would permit—Sohl and Kral were both sadly missed. But Tom Verlaine expanded his original contribution to the record by remaining unobtrusively onstage throughout the performance, and Red Hot Chili Pepper Flea bounced enthusiastically around on bass.

"Improvising randomly," Tim Cooper would enthuse in the *Independent*, "injecting her songs with love, tenderness, passion and fury, Smith's restless spirit of invention and sheer passion for her art ensured this was more, far more, than mere nostalgia. It was, as it always was, sheer transcendence." "Gloria" opened, as defiant as it ever was. "Elegie" closed, and as elegiac as it sounded, it was as somber and beautiful as any song could be. As it ended, and she sang the final line, Patti glanced to the side of the stage, sadly, remembering the friends "who can't be with us today."

"This was rock as exploration, adventure, freedom, transcendence," swore Andrew Perry in the *Daily Telegraph*. "Hearing it so thrillingly brought to life, one wondered why young rock bands today refuse to uphold rock's questing ideals, happy merely to copy old post punk records."

But most dramatic of all was Pete Clark's review in the *Evening Standard*. "It was as if a punk tear had opened up in the space/time continuum: Patti Smith stepped through it, arriving on stage in black jacket, white shirt, black tie and skinny, ripped jeans, and it was 1975 all over again." Except if time really had been torn open and turned inside out, it was not 1975 that Patti Smith was reincarnating that night at the Royal Festival Hall. It was 1976. May 1976, and she was on her way to London, to oversee the birth of British punk rock.

18

BABELOGUE

JUST WEEKS AFTER Meltdown, Patti was in France, where the Ministry of Culture bestowed on her the government's highest honor given to an artist or writer, naming her a Commandeur dans l'Ordre des Arts et des Lettres. Back home, however, her own government continued to disappoint her.

By 2006, the wars in both Iraq and Afghanistan had settled into sub-Vietnam campaigns of attrition and repression, and she continued to speak out against the administration's misdeeds—which included some of the most flagrant abuses of process that any modern democracy had ever openly admitted to.

"I spent all morning yesterday writing a song about Guantanamo Bay," she told the *Guardian*'s Mark Paytress in September 2006. "Without Chains" was inspired by the story of Murat Kurnaz, a Turkish national living in Germany who was arrested in Pakistan in late 2001 and held at Guantanamo for the next four years. "He is the same age as my son, Jackson," she elaborated in an interview with Louise Jury of the *Independent*. "When I read the story, I realized how I would feel as a mother if my son had been taken away at the age of twenty, put into chains, without any hope of leaving, without any direct charge."

She'd been affected, too, by the story of a Lebanese village that had been hit by an Israeli air strike that July, killing dozens of civilians. She dedicated the song "Qana" to their memory. This kind of anger, she told the *Guardian*, "isn't any different than the outrage I once felt about Vietnam or civil rights. My blood is still burning."

Yet if the fires of past convictions still burned strongly within her, so too did the knowledge that time changes everything, an inexorable process that reached a claw into her own history with the news that CBGB was closing. And shortly after 1 A.M. on October 16, 2006, Patti Smith would sing the final notes of her final song, "Elegie," to conclude a three-and-a-half-hour show marking the end of music at the club that had nurtured her to fame thirty years before.

A victim of the city's skyrocketing rents and the rapacious landlords who uphold them, CBGB had first run into trouble more than a year earlier, when the Bowery Residents' Committee billed owner Hilly Kristal for $91,000 in back rent, based on a rent increase that Kristal himself declared he had never even received. In early August 2005, it was announced that CBGB would close its doors for the final time on September 1—but the race was on to gain a reprieve. A series of nightly benefit shows at the venue was organized, while Steven Van Zandt, of Bruce Springsteen's E Street Band, began arranging a rally and concert (headlined by Blondie's Debbie Harry and Chris Stein) in Washington Square Park.

Kristal himself had remained defiant. "We are doing whatever we can to stay here which includes encouraging people who are in a position to do something about it," he told the BBC. New York City mayor Michael Bloomberg decried the loss of one of the city's best-loved institutions and offered to mediate in the dispute. "It's part of our culture," he said. "[CBGB] bring[s] a lot of business here. I don't think they belong anyplace else other than New York City." Kristal replied, "I just hope that he can back up what he said. I pray that he will."

Ultimately, the best concession that could be won was a final fourteen months of occupancy, and so Kristal began planning to go out in style.

The last weeks of the club's existence were a nonstop festival of remembrance. The acoustic Debbie Harry/Chris Stein act and the Dictators celebrated CBGB's 1970s prime. The hardcore combo Bad Brains stepped up to replay the 1980s. Avail and the Bouncing Souls remembered the venue's role in breaking the alternative acts of the 1990s and beyond. But the final night was turned over to Patti, for a set that promised to be far more than a simple remembrance service.

"It was an honor to be the last group," she told *Rolling Stone*'s David Fricke, "and I really thought about what that meant, what kind of responsibility that was. I thought about all the people that played there and that we lost—about Hilly and the whole history. I just wanted to do a night like any other night, sort of like the nights at the beginning but without being nostalgic."

She recalled her last appearance at CBGB, in 1997, and before that, in August 1979, warming up for that final Patti Smith Group tour of Europe. She remembered, too, the earliest days at the club, the nights in 1974–1975 when CBGB was the womb that nurtured a city's worth of talent. But most of all she recalled the club's role in bringing her back from the half-dead in 1977, as she recuperated from her accident but still needed to play. To live.

Perusing her repertoire almost three decades later, she looked for material that she felt related specifically to CBGB: "We Three," for instance, written with (and about) Tom Verlaine: *Every Sunday I would go / Down to the bar / Where he played guitar.* She sought out songs that had long since fallen from her usual stage repertoire but were an intrinsic component of her own CBGB experience. "The Hunter Gets Captured by the Game" was the first song she ever performed on that stage. The Velvets' "Pale Blue Eyes"—"we did that too. And I wanted to build up to the last piece of the first set, which was 'Birdland.' That was a song that started as a poem, and through several months at CBGB, went from one place to another, morphed and grew. To me, 'Birdland' is the quintessential CBGB song."

But there were so many others, and she cast the net wider, forgiving or forgetting even the past conflicts that had once separated her from the rest of the CBGB regulars. Blondie's cover of the old reggae classic "The Tide Is High." The Dead Boys' "Sonic Reducer." A string of joyous Ramones numbers. Television's "Marquee Moon" and "Little Johnny Jewel," with Richard Lloyd sitting in on lead guitar.

And finally, "Elegie," with Patti reciting a list of the musicians who had passed away since they last played at CBGB: Richard Sohl, Fred Smith, Stiv Bators, Joey Ramone, Dee Dee Ramone, Johnny Ramone. Less than a year later, Hilly Kristal himself would be added to that roll call; the grand old man of New York City punk died of complications of lung cancer on August 28, 2007. Two years later, Jim Carroll would pass away. And, in between, John Varvatos, the high-end men's fashion designer, opened a retail store on the site of CBGB.

New York City was changing all the time. As the Dead Boys' Cheetah Chrome put it to Jennifer Fermino of the *New York Post*, "all of Manhattan has lost its soul to money lords." But some alterations still took your breath away.

And some foes could never be vanquished. But they could be confronted. Eleven years had passed since Patti welcomed the Velvet Underground into the Rock and Roll Hall of Fame; eleven years since she condemned it as a crass commercial venture. Now it was Patti's turn to be recognized. And while she admitted to Jessica Robertson of Spinner. com that "I've never been pro-institution in terms of rock 'n' roll," still she understood that it was an honor to be selected, and she accepted it with grace and gratitude.

She certainly couldn't complain about the company she would be keeping. Bob Dylan had been inducted in 1988, the Stones in 1989, Jimi Hendrix in 1992, Jim Morrison and the Doors in 1993. The Velvets were in and so was Bruce Springsteen. Maybe, if she thought about it, she could bristle over the fact that the Ramones and the Talking Heads made it in before she did—five years before, in fact. Blondie had been honored the previous year.

But the MC5 and the Stooges were still waiting, and Television too, although 2007's inductees also included Grandmaster Flash and Van Halen, together with "my good friend Michael Stipe and REM," she told Spinner.com, and the Ronettes, the early sixties girl group whom "I always loved. . . . I think it's a really diverse year. I'm very happy."

She confessed, however, to one small element of sadness. It was not the first time she'd been nominated for the Hall of Fame—almost a decade has passed since her name was first put forward—and she regretted that "my parents, who really looked forward to this, have both passed away since my first nomination." She added, "I'll have to accept in their spirit."

Theirs and so many others'. There was certainly some controversy when it became apparent that Patti alone was being inducted, without the sidemen who had blazed alongside her: Oliver Ray, Tony Shanahan,

Jay Dee Daugherty, Ivan Kral, Richard Sohl—not even Lenny Kaye, who had played with her for more than thirty years.

Patti knew who ought to be there, though, and so they were. "Rock 'n' roll is collaborative," she told Spinner.com. "You don't do anything by yourself."

So it was strange that neither her guest list nor the event's own included the name Ivan Kral. The guitarist was forced to purchase his own ticket for the event, not only for the privilege of watching somebody else play the guitar lines he'd created but also to hear Patti include in her acceptance speech a sad reference to "the *late* Richard Sohl and Ivan Kral." Generously, he put it down to a slip of the speechwriting pen.

There was no room, either, for Oliver Ray, her near-constant companion for more than a decade. With neither fanfare nor publicity, for that is how Patti now operated, he slipped out of both her life and her band; she performed now with the unadorned trio that had accompanied her for much of the past decade: Lenny Kaye, Tony Shanahan, and Jay Dee Daugherty.

Patti was inducted by Rage Against the Machine front man Zack de la Rocha, but she also received the praise of a fellow inductee, Van Halen's Sammy Hagar. "I'm really happy about Patti Smith . . . who really had such a short, intense career," he told Joel Selvin of the *San Francisco Chronicle*. "She did it so cool. She really deserves it for being such a rebel and being a girl at that time. . . . I think it's cool that they honor those kinds of people. Some awards shows don't. They go with the most commercial. Half the people don't know who Patti Smith is, but I think it's awesome. She was a true artist, a Neil Young kind of artist, where, shit, man, you do it my way or forget it. I like that."

Patti's set kicked off with the Rolling Stones' "Gimme Shelter." "Because the Night" followed, and then came a song that the Internet message boards had only dreamed she might perform, and that she prefaced with the story of her mother doing the vacuuming to it: "Rock n Roll Nigger."

"My mom was the main person in the world who wanted to see me in the Rock and Roll Hall of Fame," she'd told Nick Blakey. "Before my mom died, literally the day before she died, [she asked] if I ever made it, please sing a certain song for her." That was the one.

Patti was back onstage again with REM to perform the Stooges' "I Wanna Be Your Dog"—a little too politely, with Stipe looking and sounding like a high-class waiter. It was a little disorienting, too, when it looked as though Patti was going to don her spectacles to sing the chorus. But it was vicariously thrilling regardless, and it climaxed with guitarist Peter Buck slinging a monitor off the stage and almost crushing a few onlookers' feet.

And then it was into the ceremonial finale: Patti led the traditional all-star band through a pulsating "People Have the Power," with Keith Richards and Stephen Stills dueling guitars behind her, and Sammy Hagar, Eddie Vedder, Michael Stipe, and Ronnie Spector sharing her vocals.

But it was her Hall of Fame performance of "Gimme Shelter" that had provided the first public indication of Patti's forthcoming new album, a dozen-strong collection of cover songs titled *Twelve*.

She had talked of making such a record for years. Even at the height of the original Patti Smith Group, she had kicked back and relaxed into the idea of recording an album of her favorite songs. She still possessed one of the early track listings, too, scrawled on the endpaper of her copy of Jean Genet's *The Thief's Journal* sometime in 1978. Every time the live set bristled with another cover performance, it appeared that the idea's day was dawning, and by the late 1970s, the Patti Smith Group's repertoire had regularly thrilled or astonished audiences with its dips into a shared cultural jukebox.

"I always wanted to do a covers album," she told Jessica Robertson, "but I didn't really feel I had the range to do the kind of album I wanted to do. I didn't know enough about singing. But now it seemed like the right time. As the project evolved, a lot of the songs on the list I made in the beginning didn't make the final cut, and a lot of songs that I didn't plan on doing wound up being the ones I chose."

There were surprises. She remembered performing Neil Young's "Helpless" at one of Young's own benefit concerts as a highlight of her mid-1990s resurgence, and strove now to recapture that moment. She drew inspiration from the random songs she heard while sitting in a New York City cafe with the radio on one day. Stevie Wonder's "Pastime Paradise," for example, and Tears for Fears' "Everybody Wants to Rule the World." Hearing the latter for the first time in years, she recalled, "I never in a million years thought I'd do a Tears for Fears cover," she told Nick Blakey, "but I was buying coffee and thinking about how fucked up the world is, and then it came on and I heard *Everybody wants to rule the world* and I was like 'yeah.' That simple line, in one reference, says it all."

Jimi Hendrix's "Are You Experienced?" had been on her wish list since the 1970s, but she had backed away because she didn't feel experienced enough. Now she could handle it, booking into the Electric Lady to record it live.

The Beatles' "Within You Without You" and Jefferson Airplane's "White Rabbit" took her back to her youth, to that first summer in New York City. "Gimme Shelter" was an invocation of imminent rape and murder that presaged the end of the 1960s; it was recorded with Tom Verlaine and the Chili Peppers' Flea joining the Kaye/Shanahan/Daugherty unit, red hot after cutting the Airplane song. Bob Dylan's "Changing of the Guards" catapulted her forward a decade, to her first summer away from the city: *Street Legal* was the first Bob Dylan album she listened to after she moved to Detroit, and the tangled tale that constitutes its opening track made her weep with its intensity and vision.

Paul Simon's "The Boy in the Bubble" cast her mind back to the *Dream of Life* sessions, when husband Fred and son Jackson had spun Simon's *Graceland* around the house and gotten caught up in the silliness of "You Can Call Me Al." Three years after Patti tackled "The Boy in the Bubble," Peter Gabriel would add his own unique vision to the same tune, which seems odd because it really wasn't that great a song to begin with. But Patti made it all right, and that was good enough.

The Doors' "Soul Kitchen" came to her in a dream; the Allman Brothers' "Midnight Rider" was just a song she wanted to sing.

"But Nirvana was the most emotional experience," she told Robertson. She had originally intended to cover Kurt Cobain's "Heart-Shaped Box," the band's most recent hit at the time of the songwriter's death in 1994. But then she heard "Smells Like Teen Spirit," Nirvana's breakthrough hit, on a Los Angeles car radio, added banjo and fiddle to guitar and upright bass, and had at it.

And so *Twelve* came together as smoothly as an oldies radio show—not the greatest album Patti Smith has ever made, but a great one for driving to, or singing along or just remembering with. She even celebrated the fact that there wasn't a single obscure oldie in sight, not one left-field inclusion to prove how esoteric her ears usually were. Her own records were obscure enough, she told Nick Blakey. "This is not a record for me; this is a record for the people. . . . Something [for them] to think about and enjoy."

And to remind them of what she had always believed and how she had always lived her career. That an artist is nothing if she cannot renew, revisit, and entirely revise her own work—or someone else's.

There have been missteps; there have been misdirections. There have even been moments when you read her sounding off about something in yet another interview and wish that she would just shut up for a moment. But through it all, Patti has remained true to herself and true to her beliefs, which means she has remained true to the people who believe in her.

Today, Patti is in her sixties, but she shows no sign of slowing down. She still calls New York City home and is a familiar sight on the streets of Greenwich Village, marching down Spring Street on her way out or perched in her favorite corner of Da Silvano Italian restaurant, just a few blocks from the Café Wha? and the Bitter End, the citadels of the Greenwich Village that once haunted her youthful dreams, and still a landmark for today's young aspirants.

Her children are grown and living their own lives. Her guitarist son, Jackson, familiar to his mother's fans from his occasional appearances alongside her, is the leader of his own band, Back in Spades, and is himself now married. He wed White Stripes drummer Meg White in May 2009 in Nashville (in White's ex-husband Jack White's back yard!); the couple now live in Detroit. Daughter Jesse, too, is a musician, an accomplished pianist who has also performed alongside her mother, and opened a number of shows for her, as well.

Patti, meanwhile, works not because she has to but because she can. She toured through 2008, and took Rock'n'Rimbaud to the Melbourne International Arts festival. That same year, she played five sets in one night at l'Église Saint-Germain-des-Prés, the Parisian church with a Picasso in its garden that she had been too shy to enter forty years before.

The following year, she returned to Meltdown, a guest of curator Ornette Coleman, and remembered William Blake at the Morgan Library & Museum in New York City.

She remembered Jim Carroll too, struck down by a heart attack as he sat at his desk on September 11, 2009. She attended his memorial at St. Mark's several months later, taking the stage with Lenny Kaye to perform, of course, "People Who Died."

And, in January 2010, she offered at last her definitive account of the life of Robert Mapplethorpe. Not merely a memorial in poetry or impressionistic prose, and destined for a National Book Award, *Just Kids* was the story Patti had witnessed firsthand, as she and Mapplethorpe grew and grew up together—the story she had promised him she would write. The process had taken her a lot longer than she expected it to, not because it was difficult, but because life had gone on around her writing, pulling her away time and time again. When it came to telling the story, however, the words flowed easily. "I had so much material to work from," she told OregonLive.com's Jeff Baker. She had maintained voluminously detailed journals, and as she browsed through them, every entry would bring another snippet: The days when she would cut Mapplethorpe's hair, or chop her own into a style like Keith Richards's. The day they lunched with William Burroughs, or the one when they met Janis Joplin.

"Met Salvador Dalí. He called me a gothic crow."

"Robert took me to the Factory to see *Trash*."

Even after the couple parted and their lives shot off on very different trajectories, they had kept in constant contact through long letters that documented their lives and their work for each other. Patti had pored over them all, and she was now rewarded as *Just Kids* received nothing but fulsome praise.

"Smith's prose," declared reviewer Amy Hanson, "is striking, acerbic and thought provoking. How could it be anything else? This book, a history and eulogy and an offering is as lyrical as anything she has ever done. It's a broad stroke that captures the very essence of what New York City was during this illustrious heyday, but more importantly, *Just Kids* is an honest and intimate portrait of a man who would very quickly

become one of America's eminent photographers, told from a perspective that only memoir can offer."

She retold her own story as well, only this time on film. *Patti Smith:
Dream of Life* was filmmaker Steven Sebring's remarkable documentary
of a life without barriers, autobiography seen through the haze of privacy—a movie, said Patti, that made her cry.

Eleven years in the creation (and deservedly nominated for a 2010
Emmy), *Patti Smith: Dream of Life* was just that, a dream of a life. Sebring first
met Patti when he photographed her for a *Spin* magazine feature in 1995;
she had requested him on Michael Stipe's recommendation, and as they
waited for the shoot to begin, they retired to a nearby coffee shop to talk.

He photographed her, and when she looked at the proofs she realized
that he had captured her as she saw herself, as an artist but also as a mother
and a widow. And he had done so without any artifice. He was not a fan.
"Steven didn't know anything about me when we met," Patti recalled to
writer Tony Sclafani. "He hadn't listened to my music. He didn't know
anything about my history." So when Sebring mooted the notion of film-
ing her over the next few years, she was immediately tempted.

More than a decade later, he put away his camera. "I find it a very
human portrait," Patti said. "It's very present tense, which is the only reason I agreed to do it. I wanted it to be a very present-tense experience.
It's not shackled by too much history or a lot of talking heads. It's life,
you know—I'm not dead! And I like the fact that even though there's
obvious time passing—my children grow within the film, I lose my parents within the film—it's still all shot in present tense."

And she still lives in the present tense, even when time does slip past
too quickly.

Patti's 2005 volume *Auguries of Innocence*, her first collection of all-
new poetic work in a decade, ends with a piece called "The Writer's
Song." Its final words may be the epitaph that awaits Patti Smith at the
end of her life. It reminds us that *it is better to write / then die*. For . . .

> . . . *be we king*
> *or be we bum*
> *the reed still whistles*
> *the heart still hums.*

APPENDIX

PATTI SMITH ON RECORD

BOOKS AND ANTHOLOGIES

Seventh Heaven (1972)
TELEGRAPH BOOKS, BOSTON
Paperback, 47 pp.; publication included fifty signed and numbered first editions: "Seventh Heaven" • "Sally" • "Jeanne Darc" • "Renee Falconetti" • "A Fire of Unknown Origin" • "Edie Sedgwick" • "Crystal" • "Marianne Faithfull" • "Girl Trouble" • "Cocaine" • "Judith" • "Fantasy" • "Marilyn Miller" • "Mary Jane" • "Amelia Earhart I" • "Amelia Earheart II" • "Linda" • "Death by Water" • "Celine" • "Dog Dream" • "Female" • "Longing"

kodak (1972)
MIDDLE EARTH PRESS, PHILADELPHIA
Paperback, 17 pp.; edition of one hundred copies printed by the Middle Earth Bookstore, numbered and signed by the author: untitled ("As close as the killer . . .") • "k.o.d.a.k." • "Star Fever" • untitled ("Renee Falconetti") • untitled ("Georgia O'Keeffe") • "Radando Beach" • "Conch" • untitled ("Prayer") • "Balance"

Early Morning Dream (1972)
PUBLISHER UNKNOWN
Chapbook, 8 pp.; edition of one hundred copies: "Early Morning Dream"

Witt (1973)

Gotham Book Mart, New York

Hardcover and paperback, 45 pp.; edition of one hundred hardcovers signed and numbered: "Notice" • "Witt" • "October 20" • "Dragnet" • "Dream of Rimbaud" • "To Remember Debbie Denise" • "Sonnet" • "Mock Death" • "What Makes Ruda Ivory" • "Rape" • "Georgia O'Keefe" [*sic*] • "Mustang" • "Conch" • "Soul Jive" • "Picasso Laughing" • "Gibralto" • "Precious Little" • "Notice 2" • "Judith Revisited (Fragments)" • "Balance" • "Prayer" • "Translators"

Angel City, Curse of the Starving Class & Other Plays, by Sam Shepard (1976)

Urizen Books, New York

245 pp.: includes *Cowboy Mouth*, which Patti cowrote with Shepard, and a five-page poem by Patti, "Sam Shepard: 9 Random Years [7 + 2]"

The Night, by Patti Smith and Tom Verlaine (1976)

Aloes Books, London

Paperback, 14 pp.: contains twenty-two numbered poems, the odd-numbered ones written by Patti and the even-numbered ones written by Verlaine

A Useless Death (1977)

Gotham Book Mart, New York

Chapbook, 3 pp.; edition of three hundred numbered and signed copies, and twenty-six lettered and signed copies: "A Useless Death"

Ha! Ha! Houdini! (1977)

Gotham Book Mart, New York

Chapbook, 8 pp.; edition of 126 copies signed and numbered (1–100) or lettered (a–z): "Ha! Ha! Houdini"

Patti Smith (1977)

Warner Bros. Publications, New York

Paperback, 104 pp.: collected notes and lyrics to most of the songs from *Horses* and *Radio Ethiopia*, plus poetic entries

Patti Smith—Gallerie Veith Turske (1977)

GALERIE VEITH TURSKE, COLOGNE, WEST GERMANY

Paperback, 44 pp.: gallery catalog from an October 1977 exhibition of Patti's drawings and paintings; includes some poems, lyrics, magazine articles, and other works

Babel (1978)

G. P. PUTNAM'S SONS, NEW YORK

Hardcover and paperback, 202 pp.: "Notice" • "Italy (the Round)" • "The Tapper Extracts" • "Grant" • "Street of the Guides" • "Rimbaud Dead" • "Sohl" • "Neo Boy" • "Dog Dream" • "Mirza" • "The Stream" • "Dream of Rimbaud" • "Doctor Love" • "Munich" • "High on Rebellion" • "Ain't It Strange" • "Egypt" • "Rape" • "Space Monkey" • "Suite" • "Notice 2" • "Judith" • "Georgia O'Keefe" [*sic*] • "A Fire of Unknown Origin" • "Edie Sedgwick" • "Judith Revisited (Fragments)" • "Marianne Faithfull" • "Sister Morphine" • "Bread" • "Sterling Forest" • "Grass" • "Vandal" • "The Amazing Tale of Skunkdog" • "Konya the Shepherd" • "Sandayu the Separate" • "Conté" • "Saba the Bird" • "Thermos" • "Enculé" • "The Sheep Lady from Algiers" • "Penicillin" • "Robert Bresson" • "Carnival! Carnival!" • "k.o.d.a.k." • "Mad Juana" • "The Salvation of Rock" • "Corps de Plane" • "Jeanne Darc" • "Jenny" • "Health Lantern" • "Hymn" • "The Ninth Hole" • "Thread" • "A Fleet of Deer" • "Easter" • "Chain Gang" • "Babel" • "Pinwheels" • "Comic Warrior" • "Babelogue" • "Combe" • "Babel Field" • "Zug Island"

Woolgathering (1992)

HANUMAN BOOKS, NEW YORK

Paperback, 80 pp.: "A Bidding" • "The Woolgatherers" • "Barndance" • "Cowboy Truths" • "Indian Rubies" • "Drawing" • "Art in Heaven" • "Flying" • "A Farewell"

Early Work, 1970–1979 (1994)

W. W. NORTON, NEW YORK

Hardcover and paperback, 177 pp; limited-edition hardcover in slipcase, 150 signed and numbered copies: "Prayer" • "Ballad of a Bad Boy" • "Oath" • "Anna of the Harbor" • "The Sheep Lady from Algiers" • "Work Song" • "Notebook" • "Conversation with the Kid" • "The Ballad of Hagen Waker" • "Seventh Heaven" • "Amelia Earhart" • "k.o.d.a.k." • "Dog Dream" • "Jeanne d'Arc" • "A Fire of Unknown Origin" • "Death by Water" • "The Amazing Tale of Skunkdog" • "Notice" • "Witt" • "Piss Factory" • "Balance" • "Dream of Rimbaud" • "Notice 2" • "Judith Revisited" • "Georgia O'Keeffe" • "Picasso Laughing" • "Rape" • "Gibralto" • "Ha! Ha! Houdini!" • "Schinden" • "16 February" • "Jet Flakes" • "Translators" • "Easter" • "Neo Boy" • "Sohl" • "Land" • "Suite" • "Grant" • "December" • "Doctor Love" • "AFTER/WORDS" • "ps/alm 23 revisited" • "Rimbaud Dead" • "Thermos" • "The Ballad of Isabelle Eberhardt" • "Corps de Plane" • "Babelfield" • "Babelogue" • "High on Rebellion" • "The Salvation of Rock" • "Hymn" • "Munich" • "Health Lantern" • "Penicillin" • "Robert Bresson" • "Burning Roses" • "Thread" • "A Fleet of Deer" • "Scream of the Butterfly" • "Y" • "Combe" • "Wave" • "Florence" • "Wing" • "Italy" • "True Music"

Living with the Animals, edited by Gary Indiana (1994)
FABER & FABER, BOSTON
Hardcover and paperback, 250 pp.: anthology that includes an expanded prose version of "Mirza"

The Coral Sea (1996)
W. W. NORTON, NEW YORK
Hardcover, 72 pp.: "The Passenger M" • "The Throw" • "Light Play" • "Rank and File" • "Music (a Woman)" • "Staff of Life" • "After Thoughts" • "An Auctioned Heart" • "A Bed of Roses" • "Monkeyshines" • "The Herculean Moth" • "The Solomon Islands" • "The Pedestal" • "Crux" • "Magua" • "Imago"

Patti Smith Complete: Lyrics, Reflections & Notes for the Future (1998)
DOUBLEDAY, NEW YORK
Hardcover, 272 pp.: "Piss Factory" • "Format" • "Vera Gemini"; plus song lyrics from LPs and notes, photos, art, etc.

Strange Messenger: The Work of Patti Smith (2002)
ANDY WARHOL MUSEUM, PITTSBURGH
Paperback, 80 pp.: collection of art and drawings

Auguries of Innocence (2005)

Ecco, New York

Paperback, 63 pp.: "The Lovecrafter" • "Worthy the Lamb Slain for Us" • "Sleep of the Dodo" • "The Long Road" • "A Pythagorean Traveler" • "Desert Chorus" • "Written by a Lake" • "The Oracle" • "The Setting and the Stone" • "The Mast Is Down" • "The Blue Doll" • "Eve of All Saints" • "She Lay in the Stream Dreaming of August Sander" • "Fourteen" • "Birds of Iraq" • "Marigold" • "Tara" • "To His Daughter" • "The Pride Moves Slowly" • "The Leaves Are Late Falling" • "Wilderness" • "The Geometry Blinked Ruin Unimaginable" • "Fenomenico" • "Three Windows" • "Our Jargon Muffles the Drum" • "Death of a Tramp" • "Mummer Love" • "The Writer's Song"

Just Kids (2010)

Ecco, New York

Hardcover, 304 pp.: memoir

SELECTED ARTICLES AND REVIEWS

Review of *Runt*, by Todd Rundgren

Rolling Stone, August 19, 1971

"Jag-arr of the Jungle"

Creem, January 1973

"Learning to Stand Naked"

Rock Scene, October 1974

"Flying Saucers Rock 'n' Roll"

Crawdaddy, June 1975

"Jukebox Cruci-Fix"

Creem, June 1975

"You Can't Say 'Fuck' in Radio Free America"

Yipster Times, March–April 1977

SINGLES

Omits promotional stereo/mono, radio edit/album version, and single-track releases.

"Hey Joe (Version)"/"Piss Factory" (1974)
MER RECORDS, 601
No picture sleeve

"Gloria"/"My Generation" (1976)
ARISTA RECORDS, AS 0171 (US)
"My Generation" recorded live in Cleveland on January 26, 1976

"Pissing in a River"/"Ask the Angels" (1976)
ARISTA/EMI ELECTROLA, 1 C 062-98 283 (GERMANY)

"Ask the Angels"/"Time Is on My Side" (1977)
ARISTA/PATHÉ MARCONI/EMI, 2C 006-98.529 (FRANCE)
"Time Is on My Side" recorded live in Paris on October 21, 1976

"Hey Joe"/"Radio Ethiopia" (1977)
ARISTA/PATHÉ MARCONI/EMI, 2C 052-60.133 z (FRANCE)
"Radio Ethiopia" recorded live at CBGB on June 5, 1977

"Hey Joe (Version)"/"Piss Factory" (1977)
SIRE RECORDS, SRE 1009 (US)
Reissue of Mer 601

"Because the Night"/"God Speed" (1978)
ARISTA RECORDS, AS 0318 (US)

Set Free **(1978)**
ARISTA RECORDS, ARIST 12197 (UK)
EP: "Privilege" • "Ask the Angels" • "25th Floor" • "Babelfield"
"25th Floor" recorded live in Paris on Easter Sunday, March 26, 1978; "Babelfield"
recorded live in London on February 28, 1978

"Frederick"/"Frederick" (Live) (1979)
ARISTA RECORDS, AS 0427
Live version recorded in New York on May 23, 1979

"So You Want to Be (a Rock 'n' Roll Star)"/"5-4-3-2-1"/"A Fire of Unknown Origin" (1979)
ARISTA RECORDS, AS 0453 PROMO (US)
"5-4-3-2-1" recorded live in New York City on May 23, 1979

"Frederick"/"Fire of Unknown Origin" (1979)
ARISTA RECORDS, ARIST 264 (UK)

"Dancing Barefoot"/"5-4-3-2-1" (1979)
ARISTA RECORDS, ARIST 281 (UK)

Because the Night (1983)
ARISTA RECORDS, ARIST 12 513 (UK)
EP: "Because the Night" • "Redondo Beach" • "Dancing Barefoot" • "Free Money"

"People Have the Power"/"Wild Leaves" (1988)
ARISTA RECORDS, AS1 9689 (US)

People Have the Power (1988)
ARISTA RECORDS, AD1 9688 (US)
EP: "People Have the Power" • "Where Duty Calls" • "Wild Leaves"

"Looking for You (I Was)"/"Up There Down There" (1988)
ARISTA RECORDS, AS 9762 (US)

Summer Cannibals (1996)
ARISTA RECORDS, 38931-2 (GERMANY)
EP: "Summer Cannibals" • "Come Back Little Sheba" • "Come On in My Kitchen" • "People Have the Power"

Summer Cannibals, **Part 1 (1996)**
ARISTA RECORDS, 74321-40168-2 (UK)
EP: "Summer Cannibals" • "Come Back Little Sheba" • "Gone Again" • "People Have the Power"
"Gone Again" recorded live for Later . . . with Jools Holland *in London*

Summer Cannibals, **Part 2 (1996)**
ARISTA RECORDS, 74321-40299-2 (UK)
EP: "Summer Cannibals" • "People Have the Power" • "Beneath the Southern Cross" • "Come On in My Kitchen"
Spoken-word version of "People Have the Power" recorded live for Later . . . with Jools Holland *in London*

"Higher Learning"/"Higher Learning (Contemplation)" (2002)
ARISTA RECORDS, ARPCD 5088
"Higher Learning (Contemplation)" recorded live in Switzerland in 2001

"Perfect Day"/"Here I Dreamt I Was an Architect" (2007)
COLUMBIA RECORDS, CS7 708959
Promotional vinyl given free with initial release of *Twelve*

ALBUMS

Horses **(1975)**
ARISTA RECORDS, AL 4066 (US)
"Gloria" • "Redondo Beach" • "Birdland" • "Free Money" • "Kimberly" • "Break It Up" • "Land" • "Elegie"

Radio Ethiopia **(1976)**
ARISTA RECORDS, AB 4097 (US)
"Ask the Angels" • "Ain't It Strange" • "Poppies" • "Pissing in a River" • "Pumping (My Heart)" • "Distant Fingers" • "Radio Ethiopia" • "Abyssinia"

Easter **(1978)**
ARISTA RECORDS, AB 4171 (US)

"Till Victory" • "Space Monkey" • "Because the Night" • "Ghost Dance" • "Babelogue" • "Rock n Roll Nigger" • "Privilege (Set Me Free)" • "We Three" • "25th Floor" • "High on Rebellion" • "Easter"

Wave (1979)
ARISTA RECORDS, AB 4221 (US)
"Frederick" • "Dancing Barefoot" • "So You Want to Be (a Rock 'n' Roll Star)" • "Hymn" • "Revenge" • "Citizen Ship" • "Seven Ways of Going" • "Broken Flag" • "Wave"

Dream of Life (1988)
ARISTA RECORDS, AL 8453 (US)
"People Have the Power" • "Going Under" • "Up There Down There" • "Paths That Cross" • "Dream of Life" • "Where Duty Calls" • "Looking for You (I Was)" • "The Jackson Song"

Gone Again (1996)
ARISTA RECORDS, 18747 (US)
"Gone Again" • "Beneath the Southern Cross" • "About a Boy" • "My Madrigal" • "Summer Cannibals" • "Dead to the World" • "Wing" • "Ravens" • "Wicked Messenger" • "Fireflies" • "Farewell Reel"

The Patti Smith Masters (1996)
ARISTA RECORDS, 18933 (US)
Digitally remastered CD versions of Patti's first five albums, complete with original liner notes and bonus tracks as follows: *Horses*, "My Generation" (live) • *Radio Ethiopia*, "Chiklets" • *Easter*, "Godspeed" • *Wave*, "Fire of Unknown Origin" and "54321"/"Wave" (live) • *Dream of Life*, "As the Night Goes By" and "Wild Leaves"; also includes a sixth disc of selected songs: "Gloria" • "Redondo Beach" • "Ask the Angels" • "Because the Night" • "Babelogue" • "Rock n Roll Nigger" • "Dancing Barefoot" • "People Have the Power" • "Paths That Cross" • "Gone Again" • "Summer Cannibals"

Peace and Noise (1997)
ARISTA RECORDS, 18986 (US)
"Waiting Underground" • "Whirl Away" • "1959" • "Spell" • "Don't Say Noth-

ing" • "Dead City" • "Blue Poles" • "Death Singing" • "Memento Mori" • "Last Call"

Gung Ho (2000)

ARISTA RECORDS, 14618 (US)

"One Voice" • "Lo and Beholden" • "Boy Cried Wolf" • "Persuasion" • "Gone Pie" • "China Bird" • "Glitter in Their Eyes" • "Strange Messengers" • "Grateful" • "Upright Come" • "New Party" • "Libbie's Song" • "Gung Ho"

Land (1975–2002) (2002)

ARISTA RECORDS, 14708

Two-CD retrospective: "Dancing Barefoot" • "Babelogue" • "Rock n Roll Nigger" • "Gloria" • "Pissing in a River" • "Free Money" • "People Have the Power" • "Because the Night" • "Frederick" • "Summer Cannibals" • "Ghost Dance" • "Ain't It Strange" • "1959" • "Beneath the Southern Cross" • "Glitter in Their Eyes" • "Paths That Cross" • "When Doves Cry" (new recording) • "Piss Factory" • "Redondo Beach" (demo, 1975) • "Distant Fingers (demo, 1975) • "25th Floor" (live in Eugene, Oregon, 1978) • "Come Back Little Sheba" • "Wander I Go" • "Dead City" (live in Denmark, 2001) • "Spell" (live in Portland, 2001) • "Wing" (live in Paris, 2001) • "Boy Cried Wolf" (live in Paris, 2001) • "Birdland" (live in Los Angeles, 2001) • "Higher Learning" (new recording, 2001) • "Notes to the Future" (live at St. Mark's, New York City, 2002)

Trampin' (2004)

COLUMBIA RECORDS, CK 90330

"Jubilee" • "Mother Rose" • "Stride of the Mind" • "Cartwheels" • "Gandhi" • "Trespasses" • "My Blakean Year" • "Cash" • "Peaceable Kingdom" • "Radio Baghdad" • "Trampin'"

Horses: Legacy Edition (2005)

ARISTA/COLUMBIA/LEGACY, 71198

Two-CD collection containing the original LP and bonus track, and the same track list recorded live at the Meltdown Festival, Royal Festival Hall, London, on June 25, 2005: "Gloria" • "Redondo Beach" • "Birdland" • "Free Money" • "Kimberly" • "Break It Up" • "Land" • "Elegie" • "My Generation"

Twelve (2007)

COLUMBIA RECORDS, 87251 (US)

"Are You Experienced?" • "Everybody Wants to Rule the World" • "Helpless"
• "Gimme Shelter" • "Within You Without You" • "White Rabbit" • "Changing of the Guard" • "The Boy in the Bubble" • "Soul Kitchen" • "Smells Like
Teen Spirit" • "Midnight Rider" • "Pastime Paradise" • "Everybody Hurts" (bonus
track)

SELECTED COMPILATIONS AND SOUNDTRACKS

Until the End of the World: Music from the Motion Picture Soundtrack (1991)

WARNER BROS. RECORDS, 2–26707

Includes "It Takes Time"

Arista Alternative? You're Shittin' Me! (1993)

ARISTA RECORDS, ASCD-2644

Promo CD includes "Piss Factory," recorded live at SummerStage, Central Park,
New York, in 1993

No Alternative (1993)

ARISTA RECORDS, 18737

Promo CD includes "Memorial Song," recorded live at SummerStage, Central
Park, New York, in 1993

Natural Born Killers: A Soundtrack for an Oliver Stone Film (1994)

NOTHING/INTERSCOPE, 92460

Includes "Rock n Roll Nigger," remixed by Flood for 140db

Ain't Nuthin' but a She Thing (1995)

LONDON RECORDS, 828674

Includes "Don't Smoke in Bed"

Dead Man Walking: Music from and Inspired by the Motion Picture (1995)

SONY MUSIC, 76660

Includes "Walkin' Blind"

Kerouac: Kicks Joy Darkness (1997)
RYKODISC, RCD 10329
Includes "The Last Hotel" (with Lenny Kaye and Thurston Moore)

Hashisheen: The End of Law (1999)
SUB ROSA, SR 154
Includes "Morning High" (with Lizzy Mercier Descloux)

SPOKEN-WORD RECORDINGS

The Whole Thing Started with Rock & Roll Now It's Out of Control, by **Ray Manzarek** (1974)
MERCURY RECORDS, SRM-1-1014
Patti reads an excerpt from Jim Morrison's poem "The New Creatures" on the song "I Wake Up Screaming"

Galerie Veith Turske Reading (1978)
S PRESS TONBANDVERLAG
Live reading at from an October 1977 exhibition of Patti's work at Galerie Veith Turske, Cologne, West Germany

Big Ego (1978)
GIORNO POETRY SYSTEMS, GPS 012–013
Includes "The Histories of the Universe"

The Nova Convention (1979)
GIORNO POETRY SYSTEMS, GPS 014–015, 016–017
Includes "Poem for Jim Morrison" and "Bumblebee"

Sugar, Alcohol, & Meat: The Dial-A-Poem Poets (1980)
GIORNO POETRY SYSTEMS, GPS 018–019
Includes "Parade"

You're a Hook: The 15th Anniversary of Dial-A-Poem (1983)
GIORNO POETRY SYSTEMS, GPS 030
Includes "7 Ways of Going" and "Fire of Unknown Origin"

Lenny Kaye Connection: I've Got a Right (1984)
GIORNO POETRY SYSTEMS, GPS 032
Features Patti Smith

Cash Cow: The Best of Giorno Poetry Systems (1993)
GIORNO POETRY SYSTEMS, GPS 044
Includes "The Histories of the Universe"

In Paradisu, by Les Nouvelles Polyphonies Corses (1996)
MERCURY/PHILLIPS, 532453-2
Patti recites a spoken introduction to "Dies Irae"

The Coral Sea (2008)
PASK, 001
Recorded live at Queen Elizabeth Hall, London, on June 22, 2005, and September 12, 2006

MISCELLANEOUS

Tyranny and Mutation, by Blue Öyster Cult (1973)
COLUMBIA RECORDS, KC 32017
Patti cowrote "Baby Ice Dog"

All American Boy, by Rick Derringer (1973)
BLUE SKY RECORDS, 32481
Patti wrote the lyrics for "Hold"

Secret Treaties, by Blue Öyster Cult (1974)
COLUMBIA RECORDS, KC 32858
Patti cowrote "Career of Evil"

Agents of Fortune, by Blue Öyster Cult (1976)
COLUMBIA RECORDS, CK 34164
Patti wrote the lyrics for "Debbie Denise" and "The Revenge of Vera Gemini"; she also performed backing vocals

If I Weren't So Romantic I'd Shoot You, **by Rick Derringer (1978)**
BLUE SKY RECORDS, 35075
Patti wrote the lyrics for "Sleepless"

Nostalgia, **by Ivan Kral (1996)**
BMG ARIOLA CR/SR, 74321-28525-2 (CZECH REPUBLIC)
Patti cowrote "Perfect Moon" (lyrics are from "December" in *Early Work*)

Look Up, **by Bob Neuwirth (1996)**
WATERMELON RECORDS, 1050
Patti cowrote and sings "Just Like You"

New Adventures in Hi-Fi, **by REM (1996)**
WARNER BROS. RECORDS, 46436
Patti cowrote "E-Bow the Letter"

Fuck the Living Fuck the Dead, **by Nick Tosches (2004)**
DSA, 54082
Includes "Wild Leaves," featuring Patti and Oliver Ray

SELECTED BOOTLEGS

Digital storage, the Internet, and other modern technologies have rendered the old notion of the bootleg redundant today; it seems that no sooner does an artist come off stage than somebody is uploading the show to a website or blog, posting footage on YouTube, and so on. Any attempt to document the wealth of unauthorized Patti Smith recordings to have appeared in recent years would ultimately turn into little more than a list of all the shows Patti has played since that time. The following, therefore, notes only Patti's bootleg releases prior to 1980.

Patti Smith and Television
CBGB, NEW YORK, APRIL 1975
Set 1: "We're Gonna Have a Real Good Time Together" • "Redondo Beach" • "Birdland" • "Space Monkey" • "Distant Fingers" • "Gloria"; set 2: "Space Monkey" • "Distant Fingers" • "Gloria"; set 3: "The Hunter Gets Captured by the Game" • "A Little Travelogue" • piano instrumental • "Free Money" • "Piss Factory" • "Snowball" • "Land" • "A Lullaby Poem"; plus Television sets

Free Music Store 1975
WBAI–FM, NEW YORK, MAY 28, 1975
"Space Monkey" • "Snowball" • "Distant Fingers" • "Break It Up" • "The Hunter Gets Captured by the Game" • "Birdland" • "Gloria" • "Scheherazade" • "Down the Aisle of Love"

Live at Bottom Line
BOTTOM LINE, NEW YORK, DECEMBER 1975
"We're Gonna Have a Real Good Time Together" • "Privilege (Set Me Free)" • "Space Monkey" • "Redondo Beach" • "Free Money" • "Pale Blue Eyes"/"Louie Louie" • "Mafia" • "Birdland" • "Land" • "Gloria" • "Time Is on My Side" • "My Generation"

Teenage Perversity & Ships in the Night
ROXY THEATRE, LOS ANGELES, JANUARY 30, 1976
"We're Gonna Have a Real Good Time Together" • "Privilege (Set Me Free)" • "Ain't It Strange" • "Kimberly" • "Redondo Beach" • "Pale Blue Eyes"/"Louie Louie" • "Pumping (My Heart)" • "Birdland" • "Gloria" • "My Generation"
Also released as Canine Teardrop, Patti Smith, *and* Teenage Perversity and Ships in the Night

Turn It Up
UNSPECIFIED PERFORMANCE WITH JOHN CALE, C. 1976
"We're Gonna Have a Real Good Time Together" • "G. Verdi" • "I Keep a Close Watch" • "Ain't It Strange" • "Free Money" • "Pale Blue Eyes" • "Louie Louie" • "Birdland" • "Gloria" • "My Generation"
Also released as Hard Nipples

Superbunny
UNSPECIFIED PERFORMANCE, C. 1976
"We're Gonna Have a Real Good Time Together" • "Privilege (Set Me Free)" • "Ain't It Strange" • "Kimberly" • "Free Money" • "Redondo Beach" • "Pale Blue Eyes"/"Louie Louie" • "The Hunter Gets Captured by the Game" • "Land"

Live in London
CHALK FARM ROUNDHOUSE, LONDON, MAY 16–17, 1976
"We're Gonna Have a Real Good Time Together" • "Kimberly" • "Ain't It Strange" • "Privilege (Set Me Free)" • "Pumping (My Heart)" • "Free Money"

• "Pissing in a River" • "Ain't It Strange" (reprise)/"Gloria" • "Time Is on My Side"

I Never Talked to Bob Dylan
KONSERTHUSET, STOCKHOLM, SWEDEN, OCTOBER 3, 1976

"We're Gonna Have a Real Good Time Together" • "Redondo Beach" • "Free Money" • "Pale Blue Eyes" • "Ask the Angels" • "Ain't It Strange" • "Time Is on My Side" • "Radio Ethiopia"/"Gloria" • "Land"

You Light Up My Life '78
SANTA MONICA CIVIC CENTER, MAY 12, 1978

"The Kids Are Alright" • "Be My Baby" • "Time Is on My Side" • "You Light Up My Life" • "My Generation" • "Rock n Roll Nigger" • "Till Victory" • "Space Monkey" • "25th Floor" • "Because the Night"

"White Christmas"/"No Jestering"
EUGENE, OREGON, MAY 1978

Paris 78
UNSPECIFIED PERFORMANCE, PARIS, 1978

"Ask the Angels" • "25th Floor" • "High on Rebellion" • "Till Victory" • "Privilege (Set Me Free)" • "Because the Night" • "Gloria" • "Ask the Angels" (reprise) • "Free Money" • "Work Song" • "Keith Richards Blues" • "Work Song" (reprise)
"Ask the Angels" (reprise) and "Free Money" recorded December 7, 1976, and "Work Song" and "Keith Richards Blues" recorded April 19, 1977, all for the Mike Douglas Show; *"Work Song" (reprise) recorded in 1978 for NBC's* Today

Live Undercover
GRUGAHALLE, ESSEN, WEST GERMANY, APRIL 22, 1979

"So You Want to Be (a Rock 'n' Roll Star)" • "Star Spangled Banner"/"Rock n Roll Nigger" • "Privilege (Set Me Free)" • "Dancing Barefoot" • "Redondo Beach" • "25th Floor"/"High on Rebellion" • "Revenge" • "Pumping (My Heart)" • "Seven Ways of Going" • "Because the Night" • "Frederick" • "Jailhouse Rock" • "Gloria" • "My Generation"

To the Ones She Loves

TOWER THEATER, UPPER DARBY, PENNSYLVANIA, MAY 13, 1979

"Privilege (Set Me Free)" • "Till Victory" • "So You Want to Be (a Rock 'n' Roll Star)" • "Citizen Ship" • "Redondo Beach" • "Poppies" • "Tomorrow" • "Jailhouse Rock" • "25th Floor" • "5-4-3-2-1" • "Be My Baby" • "Dancing Barefoot" • "Because the Night" • "Frederick" • "Kimberly" • "Jesus Loves Me" • "Gloria" • "Pumping (My Heart)" • "My Generation"

Live at CBGB's

CBGB, NEW YORK, 1979

Untitled poem/"Land"/"Rock n Roll Nigger" • "Redondo Beach" • "Fire of Unknown Origin" • "Kimberly" • "Dancing Barefoot" • "Space Monkey" • "Privilege (Set Me Free)" • "25th Floor" • "Cold Turkey" • "For Your Love" • "Revenge" • "Frederick" • "Seven Ways of Going" • "Poppies" • "All Along the Watchtower" • "Spider and Fly 1985" • "So You Want to Be (a Rock 'n' Roll Star)" • "5-4-3-2-1" • "Twist and Shout" • "My Generation"

Roots

VARIOUS STUDIO SESSIONS, 1974–1979

"Hey Joe (Version)" (Mer single) • "We're Gonna Have a Real Good Time Together" • "Pale Blue Eyes" • "Louie Louie" • "Time Is on My Side" (live at Konserthuset, Stockholm, Sweden, October 3, 1976) • "Gloria" (live in Paris, March 26, 1978) • "So You Want to Be (a Rock 'n' Roll Star)" • "Privilege (Set Me Free)" • "5-4-3-2-1" (live at Grugahalle, Essen, West Germany, April 22, 1979) • "Jailhouse Rock" • "You Really Got Me" (live at the Place, Eugene, Oregon, May 4, 1978) • "Be My Baby" • "Tomorrow" (live at Tower Theater, Upper Darby, Pennsylvania, May 13, 1979) • "Cold Turkey" • "For Your Love" • "All Along the Watchtower" (live at CBGB, New York, 1979) • "It's So Hard" • "You Light Up My Life" • "The Kids Are Alright" (Santa Monica Civic Center, May 12, 1978) • "No Jestering" (live at the Place) • "White Christmas" • "My Generation" (live at the Place)

BIBLIOGRAPHY

In addition to those publications by Patti Smith noted in the appendix.

INTERVIEWS, REVIEWS, AND OTHER ARTICLES

Addicted to Noise. Interview with Wayne Kramer. February 1995. Quoted in
"Fred 'Sonic' Smith," by C. Ross. A Patti Smith Babelogue, n.d., www
.oceanstar.com/patti/bio/fred.htm.

Als, Hilton. "Their Friendship, Their Masterpiece." *The New Yorker*, June 19,
1995.

Amorosi, A. D. "Seventh Heaven." *Philadelphia City Paper*, November 23–30,
1995.

Ann Arbor Observer. "Second Chance to Be Transformed into a More Subdued
Music Scene." N.d., c. April 1984.

Antonia, Nina. Interview with Wayne Kramer. *Record Collector*, September 1996.

Apter, Jeff. "Patti Smith: Return of the Thin White Duchess." NYROCK.com,
November 1997, www.nyrock.com/features/1997/patti_smith.asp.

Arthur, Deyva. "Patti Smith Reaffirms That People Have the Power." *Green Pages*
9, no. 2 (Summer 2005).

Baker, Jeff. Interview with Patti Smith. OregonLive.com, January 31, 2010,
www.oregonlive.com/books/index.ssf/2010/01/post_12.html.

Baker, Robb. Off Off and Away. *After Dark*, September 1974.

Bangs, Lester. Review of *Easter*, by the Patti Smith Group. *Phonograph Record
Magazine*, May 1978.

BBC News. "Final Push to Save CBGB Rock Club." August 31, 2005, http://news.bbc.co.uk/2/hi/entertainment/4201760.stm.

Berman, Bruce. "The Queen of Acid Punk Rock." *Acid Rock*, November 1977.

Blakey, Nick. "Patti Smith 2007: Alive, Well, and . . . Not Looking That Different Than She Did on the Cover of Easter." *YOUR Flesh*, March 19, 2007, http://yourfleshmag.com/music/patti-smith-2007-alive-well-and...not-looking-that-different-than-she-did-on-the-cover-of-easter/.

The Blank Generation official website. Accessed May 16, 2011. www.theblankgeneration.com.

Bohn, Chris. "Patti Smith: A Dream That's Over." *Melody Maker*, September 15, 1979.

————. Review of *Easter*, by the Patti Smith Group. *Melody Maker*, 1978.

Bollen, Christopher. "Patti Smith and Robert Mapplethorpe." *Interview*, January 20, 2010.

Bracewell, Michael. "Woman as Warrior." *Guardian Weekend*, June 22, 1996.

Brazier, Chris. "The Resurrection of Patti Smith." *Melody Maker*, March 18, 1978.

————. Review of the Patti Smith Group, Rainbow Theatre, London. *Melody Maker*, April 8, 1978.

Burchill, Julie. Account of Patti Smith press conference, London, October 1976. Quoted in *Patti Smith: An Unauthorized Biography*, by Victor Bockris and Roberta Bayley. New York: Simon & Schuster, 1999.

Burroughs, William. "When Patti Rocked." *Spin*, April 1988.

Cassata, Mary Anne. "Patti Smith: A Rock Visionary's New Dream." *Music Paper*, October 1988.

Charlesworth, Chris. Interview with Patti Smith. *Melody Maker*, n.d. Quoted in *Patti Smith: An Unauthorized Biography*, by Victor Bockris and Roberta Bayley. New York: Simon & Schuster, 1999.

————. Profile of Patti Smith. *Melody Maker*, n.d., c. 1974. Quoted in *Patti Smith: An Unauthorized Biography*, by Victor Bockris and Roberta Bayley. New York: Simon & Schuster, 1999.

Christgau, Robert. "Patti Smith Pisses in a Vanguard." *Village Voice*, n.d., c. 1977. Reprinted in *Grown Up All Wrong: 75 Great Rock and Pop Artists from Vaudeville to Techno*, by Robert Christgau. Cambridge, MA: Harvard University Press, 1998.

————. Review of *Wave*, by the Patti Smith Group. *Village Voice*, July 2, 1979.

Clark, Pete. "A Timeless Punk Classic." *Evening Standard*, June 27, 2005.

Cohen, Mitchell. Review of Patti Smith, Avery Fisher Hall, New York. *Phonograph Record*, May 1976.

Cohen, Scott. "How a Little Girl Took Over a Tough Gang: The Hard-Rock Poets." *Oui*, July 1976.

———. "Patti Smith: Can You Hear Me Ethiopia." *Circus*, December 14, 1976.

Cooper, Tim. "The Revenge of the Misfit." *Times*, June 10, 2005.

———. Review of *Horses*, by Patti Smith, Meltdown festival, Royal Festival Hall, London. *Independent*, June 27, 2005.

Davis, Clive. "Tales of Mother Rock." *Vanity Fair*, February 2010.

Detweiler, Margit. "20 Questions: Patti Smith." *Philadelphia City Paper*, September 25–October 2, 1997.

Edmonds, Ben. "The Rebel: Patti Smith." *Mojo*, August 1996.

Fermino, Jennifer. "Hobo Goes Haute." *New York Post*, March 25, 2008.

Foehr, Stephen. "Death and the Rebirth of Patti Smith." *Shambhala Sun*, July 1996.

Fricke, David. "Exclusive Q&A: The Final Word from Patti Smith on CBGB." *Rolling Stone*, October 17, 2006.

———. "Patti Smith on Blake and Bush." *Rolling Stone*, May 5, 2004.

Frith, Simon. Review of *Wave*, by the Patti Smith Group. *Melody Maker*, May 5, 1979.

Ginsberg, Allen. Interview with "a Philadelphia journalist," 1973. Quoted in *Patti Smith: An Unauthorized Biography*, by Victor Bockris and Roberta Bayley. New York: Simon & Schuster, 1999.

Gold, Mick. "Patti in Excelsis Deo." *Street Life*, May 29, 1976.

Goldman, Vivien. "Patti Cracks Noggin, Raps On Regardless." *Sounds*, February 5, 1977.

———. "Patti Smith: The Field Marshall on Portobello Road." *Sounds*, November 1976.

Green, Penny. Interview with Patti Smith. *Interview*, October 1973.

Grimes, William. "Jim Carroll, Poet and Punk Rocker Who Wrote 'The Basketball Diaries,' Dies at 60." *New York Times*, September 14, 2009.

Gross, Amy. "Introducing Rock 'n' Roll's Lady Raunch." *Mademoiselle*, September 1975.

Gross, Michael. "Patti Smith: Misplaced Joan of Arc." *Blast*, August 1976.

Gross, Terry. Interview with Patti Smith. *Fresh Air*, National Public Radio, June 24, 1996.

Hanson, Amy. "Just Kids, Patti Smith's Extraordinary Memoir of Robert
    Mapplethorpe." *Wilmington Literature Examiner*, January 21, 2010.

Harron, Mary. Interview with Johnny Rotten. *Punk*, n.d. Quoted in *Patti Smith:
    An Unauthorized Biography*, by Victor Bockris and Roberta Bayley. New York:
    Simon & Schuster, 1999.

Hasted, Nick. Review of Patti Smith, ULU, London. *Independent*, March 19, 2004.

Henderson, Everett. "Jacking Off with Jackie." *Gay*, June 15, 1970.

Hiss, Tony, and David McClelland. "Gonna Be So Big, Gonna Be a Star, Watch
    Me Now!" *New York Times Magazine*, December 21, 1975.

Holden, Stephen. "Patti Smith in the Parlor, Still Raw and Rock 'n' Roll." *New
    York Times*, March 3, 2008.

———. Review of Patti Smith, the Other End, New York City. *Rolling Stone*,
    August 14, 1975.

Horning, Rob. Review of *Trampin'*, by Patti Smith. *PopMatters.com*, May 27,
    2004, www.popmatters.com/music/reviews/s/smithpatti-trampin.shtml.

Ingham, Jonh. "Patti Smith Is Innocent, OK?" *Sounds*, May 29, 1976.

———. "Patti Smith: Once Is Not Enough (Ungh! Choke! Etc)." *Sounds*,
    October 30, 1976.

Jahr, Cliff. "Patti." *New York Times Magazine*, December 26, 1975.

Jefferson, Margo. "Touch of the Poet." *Newsweek*, December 29, 1975.

Jinman, Richard. "High Priestess with a Prayer for Living." *Australian*, January
    21, 1997.

Jones, Allan. "Meet the Press." *Melody Maker*, October 30, 1976.

Jury, Louise. "Patti Smith Rails Against Israel and US." *Independent*, September 9,
    2006.

Kevles, Barbara. Interview with Anne Sexton. *Paris Review* 52 (Summer 1971).

Lake, Steve. "The Big Match." *Melody Maker*, May 22, 1976.

Lim, Gerrie. "Patti Smith: The Power and the Glory, the Resurrection and the
    Life." *Big O*, July 1995.

Marcus, Griel. "*Horses*: Patti Smith Exposes Herself." *Village Voice*, November 24,
    1975.

Marsh, Dave. "Her Horses Got Wings, They Can Fly." *Rolling Stone*, January 1,
    1976.

———. Review of *Radio Ethiopia*, by the Patti Smith Group. *Rolling Stone*,
    January 13, 1977.

Martin, Gavin. "Patti Smith: Patti Noises Off." *Vox*, January 1998.

Masterson, Andrew. Interview with Patti Smith. *Age*, January 1997.

McDonnell, Evelyn. "Because the Night." *Village Voice*, August 1, 1995.

Melody Maker. Review of *Horses*, by Patti Smith. N.d. Quoted in *Patti Smith: An Unauthorized Biography*, by Victor Bockris and Roberta Bayley. New York: Simon & Schuster, 1999.

Meltzer, Richard. Review of *Radio Ethiopia*, by the Patti Smith Group. *Creem*, January 1977.

Miles, Barry. Interview with Patti Smith, March 18, 1977. In *Wanted Man: In Search of Bob Dylan*, edited by John Bauldie. New York: Citadel Underground, 1990.

———. "Patti Smith: At Last, the Lower Manhattan Show." *New Musical Express*, May 22, 1976.

———. "Patti Smith: Roll Over, Rimbaud (Tell Marc Bolan the News)." *New Musical Express*, August 6, 1977.

Mnookin, Seth. Review of *Gung Ho*, by Patti Smith. Sharps & Flats. *Salon.com*, March 23, 2000, www.salon.com/entertainment/music/review /2000/03/23/smith_mitchell.

Moore, Thurston. Interview with Patti Smith. *Bomb*, Winter 1996.

Morley, Paul. "Patti Smith: A Woman's Place." *New Musical Express*, April 1, 1978.

Murray, Charles Shaar. "Down in the Scuzz with the Heavy Cult Figures." *New Musical Express*, June 7, 1975.

———. Interview with Hilly Kristal. *New Musical Express*, March 4, 1978.

———. "New York: The Sound of '75." *New Musical Express*, November 8, 1975.

———. "Patti Smith: Welcome to the Monkey House." *New Musical Express*, October 23, 1976.

———. Review of *Horses*, by Patti Smith. *New Musical Express*, November 22, 1975.

———. Review of *Radio Ethiopia*, by the Patti Smith Group. *New Musical Express*, October 23, 1976.

Needs, Kris. "Lenny Kaye: New York Nuggets." *ZigZag*, May 1977.

———. "20 Minutes with Lenny Kaye . . . ." *ZigZag*, December 1979.

O'Brien, Lucy. "How We Met: John Cale and Patti Smith." *Independent on Sunday*, August 25, 1996.

O'Hagan, Sean. "Patti Smith: Making Waves." *Observer*, June 15, 2003.

Pareles, Jon. "Having Coffee with Patti Smith: Return of the Godmother of Punk." *New York Times*, June 19, 1996.

———. Review of *Gung Ho*, by Patti Smith. *Rolling Stone*, March 30, 2000.

Partridge, Marianne. Review of *Radio Ethiopia*, by the Patti Smith Group. *Melody Maker*, October 23, 1976.

The Patti Smith Fan Club Journal. Various editions, 1977–1979.

The Patti Smith Setlists. Last modified May 15, 2011. http://setlists .pattismithlogbook.info.

Paytress, Mark. "The Lady's for Returning." *Guardian*, September 9, 2006.

Penman, Ian. Review of *Babel*, by the Patti Smith Group. *New Musical Express*, November 11, 1978.

Pennybacker, Ramsay. "Patti Smith Hears Her Muse." *Philadelphia Weekly*, November 22, 1995.

Perry, Andrew. "Patti Brings Her Horses Thundering Back." *Daily Telegraph*, June 28, 2005.

Peter I. "Tapper Zukie: Natty Going on a Holiday." Reggae Vibes, n.d., www .reggae-vibes.com/concert/tapperzukie/tapperzukie.htm.

Rambali, Paul. "Patti Smith: Breaking the Shackles of Original Sin." *New Musical Express*, September 16, 1978.

———. Review of *Easter*, by the Patti Smith Group. *New Musical Express*, March 4, 1978.

Ratliff, Ben. Review of *Peace and Noise*, by Patti Smith. *New York Times*, October 5, 1997.

Reid, Graham. Interview with Patti Smith. *New Zealand Herald*, August 21, 1998.

Reynolds, Simon. "'Even as a Child, I Felt Like an Alien'" *Observer*, May 22, 2005.

Robertson, Jessica. "Patti Smith Q&A." Spinner.com, n.d, accessed February 10, 2011, http://spinner.aol.com/rockhall/patti-smith-2007-inductee/interview (article no longer available).

Robertson, Sandy. "Patti Smith: Behind the Wall of Sleep." *Sounds*, March 25, 1978.

———. Review of *Easter*, by the Patti Smith Group. *Sounds*, March 4, 1978.

Robinson, Lisa. "Back from the Edge." *Elle*, May 1996.

———. Interview with Patti Smith. *Interview*, May 1988.

———. "Patti Smith: Decoding Ethiopia." *Hit Parader*, June 1977.

———. "Patti Smith Talks About Radio Ethiopia." *Hit Parader Yearbook*, Summer–Fall 1977.

———. "Patti Smith: The High Priestess of Rock and Roll." *Hit Parader*, January 1976.

———. "Patti Smith's Intuitive Mania." *Hit Parader*, March 1978.

———. Review of Patti Smith, Arista convention, City Center, New York City, September 18, 1975. Quoted in *Horses*, by Philip Shaw. New York: Continuum, 2008.

Rocktropolis. Online chat with Patti Smith. November 20, 1997. Transcribed at A Patti Smith Babelogue, www.oceanstar.com/patti/intervus/9711cha1 .htm.

Rockwell, John. "Patti Smith Plans Album with Eyes on Stardom." *New York Times*, March 28, 1975.

———. "Patti Smith: Shaman in the Land of a Thousand Dances." *Rolling Stone*, February 12, 1976.

———. "Patti Smith's First Album 'Listens' Well," The Pop Life. *New York Times*, November 7, 1975.

———. The Pop Life. *New York Times*, October 15, 1976.

Rolling Stone. "The Clinton Conversation." November 12, 1998.

Rose, Cynthia. Inteview with Ivan Kral. *Viz*, 1980.

Rothenberg, Jerome. "The History/Pre-history of the Poetry Project." *Project Papers* 1, no. 2 (1987).

Russo, Vito. "Relived Glory: Reno Sweeney's Legendary Alumni Stage Reunion for AIDS." *Advocate*, c. 1988. Quoted in "Lewis M. Friedman," by Nurit Tilles. The Estate Project for Artists with Aids, n.d., www.artistswithaids.org /artforms/music/catalogue/friedman.html.

Salewicz, Chris. "The Runaways: And I Wonder . . . I Wah Wah Wah Wah Wonder . . . ." *New Musical Express*, July 24, 1976.

Schwartz, Andy. "A Wave Hello, a Kiss Goodbye." *New York Rocker*, June/July 1979.

Sclafani, Tony. Interview with Patti Smith. *Perfect Sound Forever*, April 2009, www.furious.com/perfect/pattismith.html.

Selvin, Joel. "Post–Van Halen, Hagar's Been Riding High on His Own Tequila. Now Comes Rock Enshrinement." *San Francisco Chronicle*, March 7, 2007.

Shapiro, Susin. "Patti Smith: Somewhere, over the Rimbaud." *Crawdaddy*, December 1975.

Simels, Steve. Interview with Patti Smith. *Stereo Review*, August 1978.

Snow, Mat. "Punk in New York: Blitzkreig Bop." *New Musical Express*, February 15, 1986.

Snowden, Don. "Patti Smith: At the Roxy Theatre." *Pasadena Guardian*, Fall 1975.

Strauss, Neil. "Patti Smith, Surrounded by Ghosts, Still Rocks." *New York Times*, June 24, 1996.

————. "Poet, Singer, Mother: Patti Smith Is Back." *New York Times*, December 12, 1995.

Sullivan, Jim. Interview with Patti Smith. *Boston Globe*, December 2, 1997.

Thorpe, Vanessa. "Punk Rock Icon to Run Meltdown." *Observer*, March 20, 2005.

Time Out London. Interview with Patti Smith. May 16, 2007.

Tobler, John. "15 Minutes with Patti Smith." *ZigZag*, October 1978.

————. "High on Rebellion: Patti Smith Speaks, Part 2." *ZigZag*, June 1978.

————. "Horse Latitudes: The Possession of Patti Smith." *ZigZag*, April 1978.

Tosches, Nick. "Patti Smith: A Baby Wolf with Neon Bones." *Penthouse*, April 1976.

————. "Patti Smith: Straight, No Chaser." *Creem*, September 1978.

————. Review of *Easter*, by the Patti Smith Group. *Creem*, June 1978.

Tricker, Spencer. "Patti Smith & Kevin Shields: The Coral Sea." *PopMatters.com*, July 10, 2008, www.popmatters.com/pm/review/patti-smith-kevin-shields-the-coral-sea/.

Uncut. Interview with Patti Smith. November 5, 2004.

Village Voice. Review of Patti Smith, Kenny's Castaways, New York, c. May 1973. Quoted in *Patti Smith: An Unauthorized Biography*, by Victor Bockris and Roberta Bayley. New York: Simon & Schuster, 1999.

Vogue. "People Are Talking About . . . Youthquakers." August 1965.

Vulliamy, Ed. "Some Give a Song. Some Give a Life . . . ." *Guardian*, June 3, 2005.

Wasserman, John. "Open Letter to Lily Tomlin." *San Francisco Chronicle*, February 13, 1976.

Weinter, Robert L. On the Town. *After Dark*, March 1976.

Wolcott, James. "Tarantula Meets Mustang: Dylan Calls on Patti Smith." *Village Voice*, July 7, 1975.

Woodcraft, Molloy. "Patti Has the Power." *Observer*, June 26, 2005.

Yafai, Faisal al. "Patti Smith to Head Meltdown, with a Tribute to Brecht and Rock for All Ages." *Guardian*, April 29, 2005.

Young, Charles M. "Visions of Patti." *Rolling Stone*, July 27, 1978.

BOOKS

Angell, Callie. *Andy Warhol Screen Tests: The Films of Andy Warhol Catalogue Raisonné*. New York: H. N. Abrams, 2006.

Auslander, Philip. *Performing Glam Rock: Gender and Theatricality in Popular Music*. Ann Arbor, MI: University of Michigan Press, 2006.

Bangs, Lester. *Psychotic Reactions and Carburetor Dung*. London: Heinemann, 1988.

Bockris, Victor, and Roberta Bayley. *Patti Smith: An Unauthorized Biography*. New York: Simon & Schuster, 1999.

Cale, John, and Victor Bockris. *What's Welsh for Zen: The Autobiography of John Cale*. New York: Bloomsbury, 1999.

Cohn, Nik. *Awopbopaloobop Alopbamboom*. London: Weidenfeld & Nicolson, 1969.

Downing, David. *Future Rock*. St. Albans, England: Panther, 1976.

Farren, Mick. *The Black Leather Jacket*. London: Plexus, 1985.

Frame, Pete. *Rock Family Trees*. Various editions. London: Omnibus, 1979, 1983, 1999.

Green, Jonathon. *Days in the Life: Voices from the English Underground, 1961–1971*. London: Heinemann, 1989.

Griffin, Sid. *Shelter from the Storm: Bob Dylan's Rolling Thunder Years*. London: Jawbone Press, 2010.

Guinness World Records. *British Hit Albums*. 15th ed. London: Guinness, 2002.

———. *British Hit Singles*. 15th ed. London: Guinness, 2002.

Hamilton, James. *You Should Have Heard Just What I Seen*. New York: Ecstatic Peace Library, 2010.

Johnstone, Nick. *Patti Smith: A Biography*. London: Omnibus, 1997.

Linn, Judy. *Patti Smith 1969–1976*. New York: Abrams Image, 2011.

Marshall, Bertie. *Berlin Bromley*. London: SAF, 2006.

Matheu, Robert, and Brian J. Bowe, eds. *Creem: America's Only Rock 'n' Roll Magazine*. New York: Collins, 2007.

McNeil, Legs, and Gillian McCain. *Please Kill Me: The Uncensored Oral History of Punk*. New York: Grove Press 2006.

Melly, George. *Revolt into Style: The Pop Arts in Britain*. London: Penguin, 1970.

Morrisroe, Patricia. *Mapplethorpe*. New York: Da Capo Press, 1997.

Murray, Charles Shaar. *Shots from the Hip*. London: Penguin, 1991.

Paytress, Mark. *Break It Up: Patti Smith's* Horses *and the Remaking of Rock 'n' Roll*. London: Portrait, 2010.

Reade, Lindsay. *Mr Manchester and the Factory Girl: The Story of Tony and Lindsay Wilson*. London: Plexus, 2010.

Reed, Lou. *Between Thought & Expression: Selected Lyrics of Lou Reed*. New York: Hyperion, 1991.

Rock, Mick. *Blood and Glitter*. London: Vision On, 2001.

Rolling Stone. *Rolling Stone Cover to Cover: The First 40 Years*. New York: Bondi Digital Publishing, 2007.

Sewall-Ruskin, Yvonne. *High on Rebellion: Inside the Underground at Max's Kansas City*. New York: Thunder's Mouth, 1998.

Shaw, Philip. *Horses*. New York: Continuum, 2008.

Sinclair, John. *Guitar Army: Street Writing/Prison Writings*. New York: Douglas Book Corp., 1972.

Stein, Jean, and George Plimpton, ed. *Edie: An American Biography*. New York: Knopf, 1982.

Thompson, Dave. *London's Burning: True Adventures on the Front Lines of Punk, 1976–1977*. Chicago: Chicago Review Press, 2009.

————. *Your Pretty Face Is Going to Hell: The Dangerous Glitter of David Bowie, Lou Reed, and Iggy Pop*. New York: Backbeat, 2009.

Tobler, John, and Stuart Grundy. *The Record Producers*. London: BBC Books, 1982.

Vanilla, Cherry. *Lick Me: How I Became Cherry Vanilla*. Chicago: Chicago Review Press, 2010.

Warhol, Andy, and Pat Hackett. *Popism: The Warhol '60s*. Orlando: Harcourt, 1980.

Watson, Steven. *Factory Made: Warhol and the Sixties*. New York: Pantheon, 2003.

Whitburn, Joel. *Top Pop Albums, 1955–2001*. Menomonee Falls, WI: Record Research, 2002.

————. *Top Pop Singles, 1955–1996*. Menomonee Falls, WI: Record Research, 1997.

Witts, Richard. *Nico: The Life & Lies of an Icon*. London: Virgin, 1993.

Young, James. *Nico: The End*. New York: Overlook, 1993.

Zanetta, Tony, and Henry Edwards. *Stardust: The Life and Times of David Bowie*. London: Michael Joseph, 1986.

INDEX

"A Time for Us," 56
"About a Boy," 206, 214
Abyssinia. *See* Ethiopia
accident and recovery, 159–165
Adventure (Television), 185
Aerosmith, 94, 136
Afghanistan war, 198–199, 237, 245
Aftermath (Rolling Stones), 25
Agents of Fortune (Blue Öyster Cult), 79
Aïda (Verdi), 2
Aimée, Anouk, 13
"Ain't It Strange," 126, 133, 136, 137, 144, 151, 153, 159–160, 162
Ain't Nuthin' but a She Thing, 207
Alcott, Louisa May, 4
Alice Cooper, 136
Alice in Wonderland (Carroll), 5, 28
Alk, Howard, 112
"All Along the Watchtower," 186
"All the Hipsters Go to the Movies," 97
Allen, Woody, 197
Allman Brothers, 48
Almond, Marc, 242
"Amelia Earhart," 66
"American Prayer," 139
Amos, Tori, 242
Andersen, Eric, 113
Anderson, Laurie, 173, 240
Anderson, Marian, 239
Andy Warhol's Pork, 69
"Angel," 131
"Anita Pallenberg in a South American Bar," 77
"Annie Had a Baby," 80
Another Side of Bob Dylan (Dylan), 20
Apocalypse Now (Coppola), 227

Arcade, Penny, 50
"Are You Experienced?" 251
Arista, 108–109, 121–122, 128–129, 168, 172, 177, 208, 212, 238. *See also* Davis, Clive
"Around and Around," 20
art, visual, 10–11, 15
art exhibitions, 170, 238
Asheton, Kathy, 137
Asheton, Scott, 137
"Ask the Angels," 136, 137, 151, 155, 159
Association, the, 28
Auden, W. H., 78
Auguries of Innocence (P. Smith), 254
"Autobiography," 64
Avail, 246
Ayler, Albert, 143

"Babel," 138
Babel (P. Smith), 162, 166, 167, 172, 178, 188
"Babelfield," 142, 162, 172, 177, 209
"Babelogue," 168
"Baby Ice Dog," 105
Back Bog Beast Bait (Shepard), 61
Back in Spades, 252
Bad Brains, 246
Baez, Joan, 13, 20, 48, 112, 113
"Ballad of a Bad Boy," 59–60, 64, 80, 153, 210
"Ballad of Hagen Waker, The," 97
Ballard, Hank, 80
"Banana Boat Song," 8
Bangs, Lester, 174
Bard, Stanley, 44
Basketball Diaries, The (Carroll), 51–52
Bators, Stiv, 107–108, 126, 247
Bay City Rollers, 108

BBC, 63–64
Beach Boys, 120–121
Bearsville Studios, 181
Beatles, the, 25, 28, 35, 41
"Because the Night," 169–170, 172, 173–174, 176, 180, 197, 209, 216, 249
Beck, 210
Bee Gees, 117, 174
Belafonte, Harry, 8
"Beneath the Southern Cross," 213, 216
benefit concerts, 187, 193, 206, 208, 229
Berrigan, Anselm, 236
Bertolucci, 197
Betrock, Alan, 103
Better Books, 67
Big Brother and the Holding Company, 37
Big Ego (Giorno Poetry Systems), 173
"Birdland," 110, 121, 126, 247
Blackburn, Paul, 34
Blair, Tony, 237
Blake, William, 31, 241, 253
Blank Generation (Kral and Poe), 105
Blonde on Blonde (Dylan), 217
Blondie, 80, 103, 108, 144, 165, 166, 174, 185, 247, 248
Bloomberg, Michael, 246
"Blowin' in the Wind," 217
Blue, David, 113
Blue Bitch (Shepard), 76
Blue Öyster Cult, 62–63, 74, 79, 104, 145, 159
Bockris, Victor, 65, 67–68
Bohn, Chris, 187
Bolan, Marc, 59
Boney M., 174
Born to Run (Springsteen), 166
Bottom Line, 153
Bouncing Souls, 246
Bowie, David, 81, 103, 136, 240
"Boy from New York City," 174
"Boy I'm Going to Marry, The," 127, 187
"Boy in the Bubble, The," 251
Brancusi, 129
Brazier, Chris, 174
"Break It Up," 110, 121
Brecht, Bertolt, 58, 241, 242
Brentano's (bookstore), 30
Bringing It All Back Home (Dylan), 58
Brody, Bruce, 153, 180
"Broken Flag," 184
Brown, Andreas, 78
Buck, Peter, 250
Buckley, Jeff, 210, 213, 225
Buckley, Tim, 35, 213
Buddhism, 9–10
"Buffalo Ballet," 135
Bull, Sandy, 97

"Bumblebee," 142, 173
Burchill, Julie, 150
Burdon, Eric, 104
Burnett, T-Bone, 112
Burroughs, William, 49, 67, 86–87, 163, 173, 184, 241, 253
Bush, George W., 235–236, 237, 240
Byrds, the, 182
Byrne, David, 135
Byron, Lord, 19

Calder, John, 67
Calder and Boyars, 67
Cale, John, 29, 117–122, 127, 135, 153, 163, 180, 212, 218, 242
Callas, Maria, 2
Carroll, Jim, 51–52, 57, 62, 69–70, 87, 126, 226, 248, 253
Carroll, Rosemary, 211
"Cash," 239
Cassidy, Shaun, 102
Cave, Nick, 240
CBGB, 86–88, 101, 104–105, 106–107, 109, 144, 164–165, 170, 180, 228, 246–248
censorship, 128–129, 154
Chalk Farm Roundhouse, 133
Chamberlain, Cathy, 77
"Changing of the Guards," 251
Chapin, Harry, 154
Chelsea Girls (Warhol), 44
Chelsea Hotel, 43–44, 47–49, 63–64
"Chelsea Hotel #2," 44
"Chelsea Morning," 44
"Chestnut Mare," 113
"Chiklets," 136
Childers, Leee Black, 50, 69
Christgau, Robert, 156, 186
Christian, John, 50
Christianity, 175–176
Christy, June, 2
Chrome, Cheetah, 248
"Citizen Ship," 182
"City Slang," 193
civil rights movement, 11–12
Clapton, Eric, 64, 117
Clark, Pete, 244
Clark, Tom, 226
Clash, the, 152
Clinton, Bill, 230–231
Cobain, Kurt, 206–207, 251
Cochran, Eddie, 227
Cohen, Leonard, 44
Cohn, Nik, 185
Colby, Todd, 236
"Cold Turkey," 186
Coleman, Ornette, 253

college, 14–15
Coltrane, John, 14, 35, 42
Columbia Records, 238
"Come as You Are," 206
Commander Cody and His Lost Planet Airmen, 113
Connor, Chris, 2
Cool Cats, the, 3
Cooper, Tim, 243
Cooper Union, 33
Coppola, Francis Ford, 227
Coral Sea, The (P. Smith), 222, 241–242
Costello, Elvis, 240
County, Wayne, 49–50, 69, 75, 81, 87, 105
Cowboy Mouth (Shepard and P. Smith), 60–62, 96
"Cowboy Truths," 204
Crabtree, Lee, 63
Craven, Hal, 70
Crawford, Brother JC, 129
"Crazy Like a Fox," 56
Creem (magazine), 64, 66, 105, 142, 218
Crenshaw, Marshall, 226
Crisp, Quentin, 76
Cromwell, Link, 56. See also Kaye, Lenny
Cros, Charles, 39
"Cry Me a River," 80
Currie, Cherie, 125
Curtis, Jackie, 49–51, 76, 173
Curtis-Hixon Hall, accident at, 159–161
Cypress Hill, 211

Dalai Lama, 9, 203
Daley, Sandy, 45–46, 55
Dalí, Salvador, 19, 253
"Dance of the Seven Veils," 180
"Dancing Barefoot," 182, 209, 216
"Dark Eyes," 217
Darkness on the Edge of Town (Springsteen), 166, 176
Darling, Candy, 49
Darts, 174
dating, 11–12, 13–14
Daugherty, Jay Dee
    Cale and, 180
    comeback and, 210, 212–213
    Dream of Life and, 197
    "Gimme Shelter" and, 251
    joining band, 110
    Kral and, 103
    "Little Johnny Jewel" and, 96
    on P. Smith's fall, 160
    "Pumping (My Heart)" and, 137
    Rock and Roll Hall of Fame and, 248–249
    touring and, 187, 215
    Trampin' and, 238
    writing credits and, 168

Davis, Clive, 108–109, 119, 121, 123, 172, 194, 236. See also Arista
Davis, Michael, 129
Davis, Miles, 14
de la Rocha, Zack, 249
Dead Boys, the, 107–108
Dead Man Walking soundtrack, 210
"Dead to the World," 214
Dean, Tommy, 106
"Death by Water," 66
Death in Venice (film), 85
Deerfrance, 119
"Denis," 174
Derringer, Rick, 63
Desire (Dylan), 114
Detroit, move to, 171, 189, 191
Detroit Energy Asylum, 208–209, 212
Detroit Symphony Orchestra, 187, 193
"Devil Has a Hangnail, The," 59
Di Carlo, Jamie, 69
Dictators, the, 246
"Distant Fingers," 110, 136
DNV (Richard Sohl), 85–86, 110
"Doctor Love," 46
"Doctor Robert," 25
"Dog Dream," 77, 206, 209
"Don't Hang Me Up, Jesse James," 59
Dont Look Back (documentary), 47
"Don't Smoke in Bed," 207–208, 209
Doors, the, 28, 37, 42, 72, 81, 248. See also Morrison, Jim
Douglas, Jack, 136, 140–141
Dowd, Tom, 117
Dream of Life (P. Smith), 197–200, 207, 214, 251
dreams, remembering, 3–4
drugs, use of, 138
Dylan, Bob
    Brecht and, 58
    comparison to, 230
    Ginsburg and, 58
    Grossman and, 55
    guitar and, 56
    H. Smith and, 48
    influence of, 19–20, 21, 120
    innovation and, 42
    at Max's, 95
    Neuwirth and, 46–47
    religion and, 175
    Rock and Roll Hall of Fame and, 248
    Rolling Thunder Revue and, 111–115
    touring with, 215–217

E Street Band, 166, 246
Earhart, Amelia, 66
Early Work, 1970–1979 (P. Smith), 211
"Easter," 162, 164, 165, 166

Easter (P. Smith), 165–170, 172, 173, 175, 181,
    202, 222
Easy Rider soundtrack, 53
"E-Bow the Letter," 229
"Edie Sedgwick," 162
education, 11, 14–15
Electric Lady, 92, 212, 251
"Elegie," 121, 122, 243, 246, 247
Elliott, Ramblin' Jack, 112, 114
Emerson, Lake & Palmer, 124
Empire Burlesque (Dylan), 217
"End, The," 227
Eno, Brian, 95, 136
Eric Emerson and the Magic Tramps, 94
Ethiopia (Abyssinia), 138
"Even the Cowgirls Get the Blues," 180
"Everybody Wants to Rule the World," 250–251
Ezrin, Bob, 136

Faces, 48
Factory, the, 32–33, 34, 44, 253. *See also* Warhol,
    Andy
Faithfull, Marianne, 43, 66
Falconetti, Renee, 66
Fancy, 98
Fanny, 83
FAO Schwarz, 36
"Farewell Reel," 209, 214, 224
Fear (Cale), 118
Fellini, Federico, 13
"Female," 25
"Femme Fatale," 50
Femme Fatale (Curtis), 50–51
Ficca, Billy, 87
Fields, Danny, 45, 57, 85
Fillmore West, 98
"Fire of Unknown Origin, A," 59, 77
"Fireflies," 209, 213
"5-4-3-2-1," 186
Flame, 166
Flea, 243, 251
Fleischer, Walt, 72
Fliegler, Ritchie, 180
"Florence," 204
"Footnote to Howl" (Ginsburg), 228
"For Bob Neuwirth," 64
"For Sam Shepard," 64
"For Your Love," 186
Forced Entries (Carroll), 52
Fowley, Kim, 125
Foxe, Cyrinda, 50
Franju, Georges, 74
Frank, Anne, 12
"Frederick," 182
"Free Money," 4, 121, 132, 151, 155, 159
Freedom in Exile (Dalai Lama), 203

Friedman, Ed, 49
Friedman, Jane, 74–75, 84, 92, 118, 125, 163
Friedman, Lewis, 76

G. P. Putnam's Sons, 162
Gabriel, Peter, 251
Gadbois, Hearn, 200
"Gandhi," 239
Gardner, Ava, 13, 83
Genesis, 96
Genet, Jean, 202
"Georgia O'Keefe," 79, 162
"Get Off of My Cloud," 41
"Ghost Dance," 167, 202, 209, 210, 216
"Gimme Shelter," 249, 250, 251
"Gimme Some Lovin'," 164
Ginsberg, Allen
    death of, 225, 226
    first reading of, 67
    Gotham Book Mart and, 78
    influence of, 178
    Jewel House reading and, 203–204
    meeting, 49
    P. Smith's performance and, 57, 75–76
    recordings of, 58
    Rolling Thunder Revue and, 112, 114
    tribute to, 229
Giorno, John, 57, 173
"Give Peace a Chance," 237
Glass, Philip, 173, 239
Glaudini, Robert, 61
"Glitter in Their Eyes," 233
"Gloria," 93, 103, 110, 128, 130, 133, 152, 175,
    189, 219, 223, 243
Godard, Jean-Luc, 41, 197
Godfather, The, soundtrack, 56
"Godspeed," 137, 166, 170
Goldsmith, Lynn, 170
"Gone Again," 213, 223
Gone Again (P. Smith), 213–214, 222–223, 225–226
Goo Goo, 87
Goodbye and Hello (T. Buckley), 213
"Goodnight Irene," 114
Gore, Al, 235
Gorey, Edward, 78
Gotham Book Mart, 78
Graceland (Simon), 251
Graham, Bill, 37, 98
Grandmaster Flash, 248
Green Party, 235–236
Grossman, Albert, 55
Guantanamo Bay, 245
Guitar, Johnny, 61
guitar-smashing, 152, 156
Gung Ho (P. Smith), 230, 231–233
Gunhill Road, 76

"Ha! Ha! Houdini," 162
Hagar, Sammy, 249, 250
Hamill, Janet, 36, 37, 138
Hamilton, James, 48
Hanson, Amy, 253–254
Hanson, Ed, 182
Hardin, Tim, 35
Harris, Emmylou, 114
Harris, Shayne, 102
Harry, Debbie, 80, 103, 108, 126, 185, 246
Hart, Grant, 232, 233
health issues, 6–7, 159–165
Hearst, Patty, 90–91
"Heart of Glass," 107
"Heart-Shaped Box," 251
Heartbreakers, the, 95
Helen of Troy (Cale), 127
Hell, Richard, 80, 87–89, 95, 126, 163, 165, 185, 196
"Helpless," 250
Hendrix, Jimi
    death of, 42, 71–72
    "Elegie" and, 121, 122
    guitar and, 140
    "Hey Joe" and, 91
    Kaye compared to, 111
    Meltdown and, 241
    Old Grey Whistle Test and, 131
    Rock and Roll Hall of Fame and, 248
    studio of, 92, 212
    Twelve and, 251
Hendryx, Nona, 76
Hepburn, Audrey, 202
Her Kind, 58
"Hey Joe," 91–93, 131–132, 163, 209, 212
High Action Boys, 226
"High on Rebellion," 140, 167, 168
"Histories of the Universe, The," 173
Hit Factory, 29
Hoffman, Abbie, 81
Hofsiss, Jack, 70
Holden, Stephen, 108, 110, 208
Hole, 210
Holy Modal Rounders, 53, 62
Holzman, Jac, 82
Horning, Rob, 239
Horovitz, Michael, 67
"Horse Latitudes," 99, 146
"Horses," 146
Horses (P. Smith), 121–125, 135–136, 212, 223, 225–226, 240, 242–243
Hubbard, Eliot, 76
Hungerthon, 154
"Hunter Gets Captured by the Game, The," 94, 110, 247
"Hymn," 193

"I Get a Kick Out of You," 83
"I Wanna Be Your Boyfriend," 164
"I Wanna Be Your Dog," 250
Illuminations (Rimbaud), 17, 24, 117
"(I'm Always Touched by Your) Presence, Dear," 174
"I'm So Bored with the USA," 152
"I'm So Lonesome I Could Cry," 226
"I'm Waiting for the Man," 135, 164
Imagine (Lennon), 136
Imaginos (Pearlman), 62
Independence Day (P. Smith and Verlaine, unpublished), 162
Ingham, Jonh, 132
Ingrassia, Tony, 51, 69
Iovine, Jimmy, 166–167, 168–169, 177, 197
Iraq war, 237–238, 240, 245
Island (Ingrassia), 69–70
"It Takes Time," 200
Italy, concerts in, 188–189
"Italy (the Round)," 188
"It's So Hard," 186
"I've Been Working on the Railroad," 114
Izambard, Georges, 18

Jackson, Jesse, 198
Jackson, Luscious, 207
"Jackson Song, The," 209
Jagger, Mick, 20–21, 25, 41
"Jailhouse Rock," 186
Jane's Addiction, 210
jazz, 2, 14
Jefferson Airplane, 28
Jeffreys, Garland, 94
Jehovah's Witnesses, 9, 85
Jericho, 3
"Jesus Loves Me," 2
Jett, Joan, 126
Jewel House reading, 203, 205
Jewish culture, 15
Joan of Arc, 66
Joel, Billy, 94
Johansson, David, 76
"Jolene," 153
Jones, Brian, 21, 40–42, 69, 172
Jones, Paul, 126
Joplin, Janis, 34, 37, 42, 44, 47, 55, 71–72, 253
"Jukebox Cruci-Fix," 105
Just Kids (Smith), 253–254

Kaye, Lenny
    auditions and, 103
    background of, 56–57
    benefit concerts and, 206
    Bull and, 97
    Carroll memorial and, 253

comeback and, 210, 212–213, 223
in concert, 227
debut performance and, 57–60
Easter and, 167–168
"Gimme Shelter" and, 251
Hell and, 88
"Hey Joe" and, 92
Horses and, 137
Kerouac celebration and, 215
Mer and, 93, 163
"My Generation" and, 127
Nuggets and, 82
P. Smith's recovery and, 164
performance and, 153
pianist and, 84–85
reunion with, 76, 77
Rock and Roll Hall of Fame and, 248–249
Rock'n'Rimbaud and, 80–81
Shangri-Las and, 144
Television and, 89
touring and, 186, 215
Trampin' and, 238
waiting for, 111
Wave and, 183
Keats, John, 19
"Keith Richards Blues," 164
Kennedy, Jackie, 213
Kennedy, Margaret, 32
Kennedy, Patrick, 32
Kenner, Chris, 94
Kenny's Castaways, 77
Kent, Nick, 67
Kerouac, Jack, 215, 227, 229
Kick Out the Jams (MC5), 130
"Kids Are Alright, The" 186
"Kimberly," 10, 121, 132, 137, 151, 164
Kinks, 109
Klein, Allen, 102
"k.o.d.a.k.," 162
kodak (P. Smith), 74, 79
"Konya the Shepherd," 111
Kral, Ivan
 audition of, 103–104
 background of, 101–103
 Blondie and, 108
 Cale and, 180–181
 collaboration with, 137
 comeback and, 212
 credit and, 168
 Daugherty and, 110
 Dowd and, 117
 New Year's show and, 156
 Old Grey Whistle Test and, 131
 P. Smith's recovery and, 164
 performance and, 174
 "Pissing in a River" and, 137

Rock and Roll Hall of Fame and, 248–249
 Runaways and, 125
 Sparks and, 155
 touring and, 132, 152
 Wave and, 182–183
Král, Karel, 101–102
Kramer, Wayne, 129, 130, 192, 193
Kristal, Hilly, 87, 101, 246, 247–248
Kristofferson, Kris, 47
Kurasawa, Akira, 197
Kurnaz, Murat, 245
Kusik, Larry, 56

La dolce vita (Fellini), 13
L.A. Woman (the Doors), 98
Ladies and Gentlemen, the Rolling Stones (concert
 film), 88
"Land"
 Bull and, 97
 County and, 105
 development of, 94, 98–99
 Kral and, 103
 "Memento Mori" and, 227
 performance of, 121, 126, 131–132, 133, 146,
  152, 153, 159, 209, 210
 review of, 106
Land (1975–2002) (P. Smith), 238
"Land of 1000 Dances," 94
Lanier, Allen, 63, 74, 79, 110, 121, 137
"Last Call," 226
Late Show with David Letterman, The, 223
Later . . . with Jools Holland, 223
Lee, Eric, 84
Lennon, John, 25, 41, 74, 136, 168, 198, 206
Lennox, Annie, 207
Lenya, Lotte, 58
"*Les etrennes des orphelines*," 18
Lewinsky, Monica, 230
"Libbie's Song," 232
Life of Lady Godiva, The (Ridiculous Theatrical
 Company), 49–50
"Light My Fire," 28, 99
"Like a Rolling Stone," 20
Linn, Judy, 66
"Little Johnny Jewel," 96, 247
Little Richard, 7–8, 9
Little Women (Alcott), 4
Live 1969 (Velvet Underground), 109
Living at the Movies (Carroll), 52
Lloyd, Richard, 89, 96, 247
"Lo and Beholden," 232
Lofgren, Nils, 87
Lollapalooza, 210–211
London, Julie, 80
London performance, 67–68
Longfellow, 102

Looking Glass Studios, the, 239
Lorca, Federico García, 19
"Louie Louie," 126, 151
Love, Courtney, 210
Love, Darlene, 127
"Love of the Common People," 223
Ludlam, Charles, 49
Luger, 81, 102

Mac Low, Jackson, 236
"Mack the Knife," 58, 202
Mad Dog Blues (Shepard), 56, 62
Madame Butterfly (Puccini), 8
Mael, Russell, 85
"Mafia," 126
Magic, Butchie, 14
Makonnen, Ras, 18, 138
Malanga, Gerard, 44, 57–58, 65, 67, 68
"Mama, You've Been on My Mind," 217
Man Ah Warrior (Zukie), 151, 163
"Man Who Couldn't Afford to Orgy, The," 119
Manfred Mann, 126
Manhattan Transfer, 76
Manilow, Barry, 108–109, 121
Manitoba, Handsome Dick, 226
Manzarek, Ray, 71
Mapplethorpe (Morrisroe), 221–222
Mapplethorpe, Robert
   biography of, 221–222
   Carroll and, 51–52
   CBGB and, 87
   at Chelsea Hotel, 44–46
   correspondence with, 42
   death of, 200, 202
   the Doors and, 72
   early relationship with, 30–37
   first performance and, 57
   Horses and, 22, 92, 122–123
   Just Kids and, 253–254
   "Land" and, 210
   on Max's, 94
   memories of, 212, 213
   photos of, 67–68
   reunion with, 43
   separation from, 74
   Television and, 89
Marcus, Griel, 123
"Marianne Faithfull," 162
Marley, Bob, 94
"Marquee Moon," 106, 247
Marquee Moon (Television), 88, 165
Marsh, Dave, 141–142
"Mary Jane," 66
Max, Glenn, 242
Max's Kansas City, 34–35, 45, 50, 51, 52, 55, 74,
   81–82, 86, 93–95, 105–106, 179

MC5, 129–130, 191–193, 196, 248
McCain, Gillian, 49
McCarthy, Eugene, 59
McCarthy, Joseph, 5
McCartney, Paul, 41
McDonnell, Evelyn, 209, 211–212
McGrath, Tom, 67
McGuinn, Roger, 112, 113
McLaren, Malcolm, 75, 134
McNeil, Legs, 49
Meibach, Ina, 163
Meinhof, Ulrike, 145
Melody Maker (newspaper), 124–125, 128, 141,
   174
Meltdown, 240–244, 253
Meltzer, Richard, 128, 142
"Memento Mori," 226
Mer (record label), 93, 163
Mercer Arts Center, 74–76, 93, 94
Mercier Descloux, Lizzy "Lyzzy," 154
Metalious, Grace, 12
Michaels, Hilly, 103, 155–156
Michaels, Howard "Howie," 27, 37
Middle Earth Press, 74
Midler, Bette, 112, 113
"Midnight Rider," 251
Mike Douglas Show, 155, 164
Miles, Barry, 133
Miller, Geri, 69
Miller, Thomas, 81
Mishima (Schrader), 197
Mitchell, Joni, 44, 112
Mnookin, Seth, 232
Moby, 211
Modern Lovers, 117
Modigliani, Amedeo, 19
"Money Tree, The," 8
Monk, Thelonious, 14
Monroe, Marilyn, 66
Moogy and the Rhythm Kings, 76
Moore, Thurston, 64, 214–215
More American Graffiti (film), 187
Moreau, Jeanne, 12, 13
Morgan, Scott, 206
Morley, Paul, 175
Morrison, Jim. *See also* Doors, the
   death of, 42, 71–73, 78
   "Land" and, 98–99, 105
   as poet-rocker, 59
   poetry and, 79
   Rock and Roll Hall of Fame and, 248
   similarity to, 81
   spirit of, 70, 146–147
   tribute to, 206
Morrison, Sterling, 218
Morrison, Van, 42, 93

Morrisroe, Patricia, 221–222
Morrissey, 241
"Mother Rose," 239
"Mother's Little Helper," 25
Mottram, Eric, 67
MPLA (Zukie), 151–152
"Mr. Wilson," 121
Mumps, 96, 103, 110
"Murdered Boy, The," 59
Murphy, Elliott, 72
Murray, Charles Shaar, 124–125, 144–145, 165
Museum of Art (Philadelphia), 15, 23
My Bloody Valentine, 241
My Favorite Things (Coltrane), 14
"My Generation," 104, 127, 128, 130, 133, 156,
     177, 189, 243
"My Madrigal," 213
Myers, Richard, 81

Nader, Ralph, 235–236, 240
"Nature Boy," 14
Nazz, 55
"Neo Boy," 133–134
Neon Boys, 87
Nerval, Gerard de, 60–61
Neuwirth, Bobby, 46–47, 52, 55, 57, 59, 97, 112,
     114
Never Ending Tour, 216, 217
New Musical Express, 124, 128, 131, 145, 165,
     175, 178
"New Party," 236
New York Dolls, 75, 76, 81, 87, 88, 94, 136
Nico, 33, 44, 45, 50, 117, 119, 145–146, 218
"Nigger Book," 126
Night, The (P. Smith and Verlaine), 162
"1959," 227–228
Nirvana, 251
Nixon, Richard, 230
Norton, Gil, 232
"Not Fade Away," 153, 216
"Notice," 162
Nuggets, 82
#18 (Mahagonny) (H. Smith), 48
Nureyev, Rudolf, 202
Nylon, Judy, 119, 180

"Oath," 59, 93, 175
Ocean Club, 135
Ochs, Phil, 81
O'Connor, Billy, 103
O'Connor, Sinead, 207
O'Keeffe, Georgia, 74, 79
O-Lan, 62
Old Grey Whistle Test (TV series), 131, 173
"On a Plain," 206
On the Road (Kerouac), 227

Ondine, 44
100 Club Punk Festival, 149
One Plus One (Godard), 41
"One Too Many Mornings," 113
Ono, Yoko, 74, 168, 242
operas, 2
Orange Festival, 135
Ork, Terry, 57, 88, 89, 95
"Orphans' New Year Gifts, The," 18
Ostrowe, Andi, 156, 162, 206
Other End, the, 110–111
"Out on the Street," 144
Outrageous Lie, 50
"Over the Rainbow," 236

"Pale Blue Eyes," 126, 247
Paley, Andy, 143–145, 152
Pallenberg, Anita, 66
Pareles, Jon, 232
Paris trip, 39–42
Parker, Charlie, 121
Parker, Graham, 87
Parton, Dolly, 153
Partridge, Marianne, 141
Pasolini, Pier Paolo, 188
"Pastime Paradise," 250
"Paths That Cross," 198, 209, 210
Patti Smith: Dream of Life (Sebring), 254
Patti Smith Masters, The (P. Smith), 208
Paul, Steve, 57, 63
Paulin, Mister, 102
Peace and Noise (P. Smith), 225–229
"Peaceable Kingdom," 239
Pearlman, Sandy, 62
Peel, John, 240
"Penicillin," 162
Penman, Ian, 178
"People Have the Power," 198–199, 201, 209,
     210, 211, 216, 223, 236, 237, 250
"People Who Died," 253
Perry, Andrew, 243–244
Peyton Place (Metalious), 12
Phonograph Record Magazine, 174
Piaf, Edith, 13
pianist, search for, 84–85
Picasso, Pablo, 40
Pickett, Wilson, 94
"Pierrot," 102
"Piss Factory," 13, 91, 93, 142, 206, 209
"Pissing in a River," 133, 137, 142, 164
Pixies, 232
Plant, Robert, 125
Plastic Letters (Blondie), 166
Playhouse of the Ridiculous, 78
Poe, Amos, 105

"Poem for Jim Morrison," 173
poetry
  hybrid form of, 79–80
  Mapplethorpe and, 200–201
  Neuwirth and, 46–47
  publication of, 201
  readings, 187, 202–204, 236, 241
  Rimbaud and, 17–19
  See also specific poetry collections
Poetry Project, the, 34, 66, 173
politics, 230–232, 235–236, 237–238, 240, 242, 245–246
Polk, Brigid, 44
"Poor Circulation," 107
Pop, Iggy, 63, 128, 192
"Poppies," 137, 209
Porco, Mike, 113
Portrait of Dora Maar (Picasso), 40
Posner, Louis J., 237
Pound, Ezra, 68
"Power to the People," 198
"Prayer," 59, 79, 164
pregnancies, 25–26, 194
"Privilege," 126, 132–133, 166, 167, 177, 186
Puccini, Giacomo, 2, 8
"Pumping (My Heart)," 126, 137, 151, 159, 186
punk rock
  CBGB and, 87
  development of, 149–150
  emergence of, 156–157
  See also specific punk artists
Purple Rose of Cairo, The (Allen), 197

"Qana," 245
Quatro, Suzi, 83
Queen Elizabeth, 75

"Radio Baghdad," 239
"Radio Ethiopia," 60, 133, 136, 138, 139–141, 143, 144, 152, 153, 174, 226, 239
Radio Ethiopia (P. Smith), 135–147, 150, 162, 168, 177, 226
Rage Against the Machine, 249
Rag'n Roll Revue, 77
Ramone, Dee Dee, 87, 247
Ramone, Joey, 76, 107, 185, 247
Ramone, Johnny, 107, 247
Ramones, 103, 107, 159, 165, 171, 185, 247, 248
Ran (Kurasawa), 197
"Rape," 77–78, 79, 80
Rasmussen, Gary, 206
Rastafarianism, 138
Ratcliff, Ben, 228
Rather Ripped Records, 97–98
"Ravens," 214

Ray, Oliver, 205, 209–210, 213, 216, 227, 229, 238, 248–249
Raymond, Marge, 166
Reade, Lindsay, 124
reading, influence of, 4–5, 13, 37
Record Plant studios, 136, 140
Red Hot Chili Peppers, 243, 251
Redding, Otis, 131
"Redondo Beach," 77, 107, 110, 120, 121, 132, 151, 159
Reed, Lou, 33, 44, 50, 96, 109, 120, 135, 136, 164, 218
Reeves, Martha, 121
Relf, Keith, 133
religion
  Buddhism, 9–10
  during childhood, 8–9
  Christianity, 175–176
  Jehovah's Witnesses, 9, 85
  Rastafarianism, 138
REM, 214, 229, 248, 250
"Renee Falconetti," 66, 74
Reno Sweeney, 76, 83, 130
Resto, Luis, 212, 213
retirement
  album work during, 194–195
  announcement of, 189
  lead-up to, 183–185
  silence during, 194, 196
"Revenge," 182, 184
Revolver (Beatles), 25
Richard, Cliff, 152
Richards, Keith, 21, 25, 41, 250
Richman, Jonathan, 98
Ridiculous Theatrical Company, 49, 57, 78
Rimbaud, Jean Nicolas Arthur, 17–18, 24, 35, 39, 73, 80, 117–118, 138–139, 178
Robert Having His Nipple Pierced (Daley), 46, 67
Robinson, Lisa, 57, 83, 122
Rock (magazine), 64
Rock and Roll Hall of Fame, 217–219, 236, 248–250
"Rock n Roll Nigger," 135, 152, 153, 166, 168–169, 173, 187, 216, 249
Rock'n'Rimbaud, 80, 97, 252
Rockwell, John, 81–82, 123
Rolling Stone (magazine), 62, 123, 141, 177–178, 223, 232
Rolling Stones, the, 20–21, 25, 35, 41, 43, 70, 110, 134, 149–150, 177, 248
Rolling Thunder Revue, 111–114
Romeo and Juliet soundtrack, 56
Ronettes, 248
Ronson, Mick, 103, 112, 114, 155
"Rosalita," 153
Rothenberg, Jerome, 34

Rotten, Johnny, 134
Ruby and the Rednecks, 76
Runaways, 125–126
Rundgren, Todd, 55, 62, 181–183
Runt (Rundgren), 62
Ruskin, Mickey, 34, 95, 106, 135

"Sad-Eyed Lady of the Lowlands," 60
"Saint in Any Form, A," 59
Salewicz, Chris, 126
"Sally," 127
Salt-N-Pepa, 207
Sánchez, Fernando, 76
Sanders, Ed, 236
"Satisfaction," 41
Saturday Night Live, 130
Saturday Night Special (TV series), 223
Saville, Peter, 124
Saze, 102
scarlet fever, 6
Schrader, Paul, 197
Scott-Heron, Gil, 121
Scribner's, 36–37
Sebring, Steven, 254
Second Chance, 170–171, 185–186
Sedaka, Neil, 8
Sedgwick, Edie, 21–23, 45, 46, 49, 50, 66
Seger, Bob, 159
Selassie, Haile, 18, 138
September 11, 236–237
"Seven Ways of Going," 126, 182
"Seventh Heaven," 66, 126
Seventh Heaven (P. Smith), 66
Sex Pistols, 134, 149, 156, 179
Sexton, Anne, 58–59
sexual awakening, 12–13
Sgt. Pepper (Beatles), 28
Shanahan, Tony, 210, 212, 215, 238, 248–249, 251
Shangri-Las, 143–144
"She Walked Home," 213
Shelley, Percy Bysshe, 19
Shepard, Sam
    "Ballad of a Bad Boy" and, 210
    Blue Bitch and, 76
    career of, 52–53
    Cowboy Mouth and, 60–62, 96
    first performance and, 57
    introduction to, 55–56
    Rolling Thunder Revue and, 112, 113
    visit with, in London, 68
Shields, Kevin, 241–242
Simon, Paul, 251
Simone, Nina, 208
Sinatra, Frank, 83
Sinclair, John, 129, 130, 191–192
"Sister Morphine," 43
Sitwell, Edith, 78
Slow Dazzle (Cale), 121

"Smells Like Teen Spirit," 251
Smith, Beverly Williams, 1, 3–4, 5, 9, 239, 249
Smith, Fred (of Television), 103
Smith, Fred "Sonic"
    benefit concerts and, 187, 206
    career of, 191–193
    credit to, 139
    death of, 202
    Dream of Life and, 197, 199
    "Elegie" and, 247
    Graceland and, 251
    marriage to, 193, 195–196
    MC5 and, 129–130
    new songs from, 213
    Peace and Noise and, 225
    "People Have the Power" and, 198
    "Pissing in a River" and, 137
    plans for P. Smith's career, 205–206
    relationship with, 166, 176
    retirement and, 189
    Second Chance and, 171
    Verlaine and, 163
    work with, 200
Smith, Grant H., 1, 5, 20, 42, 230
Smith, Harry, 48
Smith, Jack, 78
Smith, Jackson Frederick, 194, 208, 223, 233, 251, 252
Smith, Jesse Paris, 194, 208, 239, 252
Smith, Kimberly Ann, 10, 206, 210, 232, 233
Smith, Linda, 1, 3, 4, 6, 39–40, 66, 70, 77, 198
Smith, Sigrid, 137
Smith, Todd, 2, 4, 6, 179–180, 202, 204
"Smoke on the Water," 223
Snow, Phoebe, 76
"Snowball," 126
Snowden, Don, 125
So It Goes, 124
"So You Want to Be (a Rock 'n' Roll Star)," 182, 186
Soft White Underbelly, 62
"Sohl," 85, 206
Sohl, Richard Arthur (DNV)
    audition of, 85–86
    on auditions, 103
    on Blondie, 108
    Bull and, 97
    death of, 201, 205
    in Detroit, 193
    Dream of Life and, 197
    "Elegie" and, 247
    exhaustion and, 143
    "Hey Joe" and, 92
    on Kral, 104
    on Max's, 94–95
    P. Smith on, 110
    Rock and Roll Hall of Fame and, 248–249

Television and, 89
on tour, 127, 187
Wave and, 181, 183
Solanas, Valerie, 49
Some Girls (Rolling Stones), 177
"Somethin' Else," 227
Songs of Experience (Blake), 31, 241
Songs of Innocence (Blake), 31, 241
"Sonic Reducer," 247
Sonic Youth, 210, 214
Sonic's Rendezvous Band, 130, 137, 171, 192, 193
"Soul Kitchen," 251
South Bank Show, The, 173
Soutine, Chaim, 19
"Space Monkey," 106–107, 126, 166
Sparks, 85, 155–156, 242
"Speak Low," 83
"Speak Softly Love," 56
Speck, Richard, 77–78
Spector, Ronnie, 250
"Spell," 228
Spin interview, 184–185
Springsteen, Bruce, 87, 94, 105, 153, 166, 169, 170, 176, 248
Spungen, Nancy, 180
St. Mark's Church, 33–34, 56, 62, 68, 70, 103, 104, 173, 202, 226, 232, 236, 253
"Stairway to Heaven," 8
Stalk-Forrest Group, 62
"Star Spangled Banner," 186
Stein, Chris, 80–81, 87, 103, 246
Stein, Jean, 21–22
Stein, Seymour, 163
Steinman, Jim, 76
Stern, Theresa, 88
Stewart, Rod, 48, 131
Stilettos, the, 80, 81, 103
Stills, Stephen, 250
Stipe, Michael, 214, 216, 226, 229, 233, 248, 250, 254
Stoner, Rob, 114
Stooges, the, 29, 117, 248
"Strange Messengers," 232
Strauss, Neil, 209, 224–225
Street Hassle (Reed), 109
Street Legal (Dylan), 251
"Stride of the Mind," 239
Striho, Carolyn, 206, 208
Sulton, Kasim, 200
"Summer Cannibals," 213, 223
Summer of Love, 28
"Sweet Surprise," 113
"Sympathy for the Devil," 41

Talking Heads, 165, 185, 248
"Tapper the Extractor," 160
Tears for Fears, 250–251

Teenage Lust, 76, 87
Teenage Perversity & Ships in the Night (P. Smith), 128, 145
Telegraph Books, 65–66, 67
Television
breakup of, 185
at CBGB, 104, 106–107
debut album of, 163, 165
early career of, 87–89, 95–96, 103
Eno and, 136
Meltdown and, 242
Rock and Roll Hall of Fame and, 248
Them, 93
Thomas, Dylan, 78
Thomas, Jon, 102
Thompson, Dennis, 129
Thorpe, Jeremy, 131–132
"Thread," 166
Through the Looking-Glass (Carroll), 5
Thunders, Johnny, 76, 95
Thunderstorms New York Style (Craven), 70
Tibet, 9, 203, 208, 225, 227, 229, 231, 232
"Tide Is High, The," 247
"Till Victory," 167
"Time Is on My Side," 20, 94, 110, 134, 151, 174
"To Remember Debbie Denise," 79
Tomlin, Lily, 128
Tommy (the Who), 156
"Torn Curtain," 107
Torres, Edwin, 236
Tosches, Nick, 79
touring
contemporary, 252
with Dylan, 215–217
Easter and, 173–175, 177
Gone Again and, 224
Horses and, 125–129, 130–134
in Italy, 188–189
Peace and Noise and, 228–230
Radio Ethiopia and, 141, 143–145, 150, 152
schedule, 232
with Sparks, 155–156
Wave and, 184, 186–187
"Trampin'," 239
Trampin' (P. Smith), 238–240, 242
Trash, 253
"Trespasses," 239
Tucker, Maureen, 218
"Tutti Frutti," 7
"Twelfth of Never, The," 204
Twelve (P. Smith), 48, 250–252
"25th Floor," 137, 166, 167, 168, 173, 177
"Twin Death," 237
Tyner, Rob, 129, 192–193, 196
Tyranny and Mutation (Blue Öyster Cult), 104

UFOs, 5
Until the End of the World (Wenders), 200

"Up There Down There," 198
"Useless Death, A," 162

Van Halen, 248, 249
Van Ronk, Dave, 113
Van Zandt, Steven, 246
Vanilla, Cherry, 69, 81
Vanilla Fudge, 35
Varvatos, John, 248
Vedder, Eddie, 250
Velvet Underground, the, 33, 109, 117, 119, 126, 146, 218, 248
Verdi, Giuseppe, 2
Verlaine, Paul, 18
Verlaine, Tom
    as art patron, 126
    "Break It Up" and, 110
    comeback and, 212
    in concert, 232
    "Fireflies" and, 213
    first album and, 121
    "Gimme Shelter" and, 251
    Gung Ho and, 233
    Heartbreakers and, 95–96
    "Hey Joe" and, 92
    Meltdown and, 243
    The Night and, 162
    Ray as replacement for, 227
    recording of, 107
    Television and, 87–89
    touring and, 215
    visits with, 163
    "We Three" and, 247
Vicious, Sid, 179–180
Vicuña, Cecilia, 236
Village Voice, 77, 156, 209, 211
Villon, François, 59
visual art, 10–11, 15

Wagstaff, Samuel J., 198
Wainwright, Loudon, III, 121
"Wait for You, The," 59
Waits, Tom, 113, 131
"Walk Away Renee," 206
Walker, Scott, 240
"Walkin' Blind," 210, 216
"Wander I Go," 210, 213
Wanna Go Out? (Stern), 88
Warhol, Andy, 21–22, 23, 29, 32, 34, 49, 94
Wasserman, John, 128
"Wave," 182–183
Wave (P. Smith), 181–184, 186, 222
"We Three," 167, 174, 247
Weill, Kurt, 58
Weinter, Robert L., 81, 128

Wenders, Wim, 200
"We're Gonna Have a Real Good Time Together," 109, 151, 153
"What's Wrong with Me," 72
"When Doves Cry," 238
"Where Duty Calls," 198
White, Meg, 252
"White Lightning," 59
"White Rabbit," 28, 251
White Stripes, 252
Who, the, 104, 156
"Who Do You Love," 226–228
"Whole Lotta Love," 174
"Wicked Messenger," 214, 216
Wild Boys, The (Burroughs), 163
"Wild Thing," 98
Wilde, Oscar, 131
Wilson, Tony, 124
"Windy," 28
"Wing," 210, 214
Winter, Edgar, 47, 57
Winter, Johnny, 47, 57
"Within You Without You," 251
"Without Chains," 245
Witt (P. Smith), 79, 161
Wizard of Oz, The, 236
WNEW radio, 154
"Woman Is the Nigger of the World," 168
Woodcraft, Molloy, 242
Woodlawn, Holly, 49, 76
Woolgathering (P. Smith), 201, 204
work life, early, 23–24
"Work Song," 127, 164, 231
"Working on the Chain Gang," 164
Woronov, Mary, 51
"Writer's Song, The," 254
Wyatt, Robert, 240
Wylie, Andrew, 65, 67, 68, 88

"Y," 210
Yardbirds, the, 133
Yellow Flowers (Wylie), 88
"Yesterday," 41
Yipster News, 154
"You Can Call Me Al," 251
"You Don't Want to Play with Me Blues," 77
"You Light Up My Life," 187
Young, Chris, 177–178
Young, Neil, 250–251
"You're the River," 59

Zanetta, Tony, 69
Zoo, the, 57
Zukie, Tapper, 151–152, 160, 163, 173